Lessons in Leadership

D0828819

Lessons in Leadership

Fifty Respected Evangelical Leaders
Share Their Wisdom on Ministry

DISCARDED
JENKS LRC
GORDON COLLEGE

Randal Roberts

General Editor

JENKS LIBRARY
GORDON COLLEGE
255 GRAPEVINE RD.
WENHAM. MA 01984

kregel
PUBLICATIONS

Grand Rapids, MI 49501

Lessons in Leadership: Fifty Respected Evangelical Leaders Share Their Wisdom on Ministry

Copyright © 1999 by Randal Roberts

Published by Kregel Publications, a division of Kregel, Inc., P. O. Box 2607, Grand Rapids, MI 49501. Kregel Publications provides trusted, biblical publications for Christian growth and service. Your comments and suggestions are valued.

All rights reserved. No part of this book may be reproduced, stored in a retrieval system, or transmitted in any form or by any means—electronic, mechanical, photocopy, recording, or otherwise—without written permission of the publisher, except for brief quotations in printed reviews.

Scripture quotations marked AV are from the Authorized Version of the Holy Bible (1881). Quotations marked KJV are from the King James Version.

Scripture quotations marked LB are from *The Living Bible,* copyright © 1971 by Tyndale House Publishers, Wheaton, Illinois. Used by permission.

Scripture quotations marked NASB are from the *New American Standard Bible*, © the Lockman Foundation 1960, 1962, 1963, 1968, 1971, 1972, 1973, 1975, 1977.

Scripture quotations marked NIV are from the *Holy Bible*: *New International Version®*. Copyright © 1973, 1978, 1984 by International Bible Society. Used by permission of Zondervan Publishing House. All rights reserved.

Scripture quotations marked NKJV are from *The New King James Version.* Copyright © 1979, 1980, 1982, Thomas Nelson, Inc., Publishers.

Scripture quotations marked NLT are from the *Holy Bible,* New Living Translation, copyright © 1996. Used by permission of Tyndale House Publishers, Inc., Wheaton, Illinois, 60189. All rights reserved.

For more information about Kregel Publications, visit our web site at http://www.kregel.com.

Cover and book design: Nicholas G. Richardson

Library of Congress Cataloging-in-Publication Data
Roberts, Randal.
    Lessons in leadership: fifty respected evangelical leaders share their wisdom on ministry / edited by Randal Roberts.
        p.   cm.
    1. Christian leadership. I. Roberts, Randal.
    BV652.1.I3   1999   253—dc21   98-44654
                                                               CIP
ISBN 0-8254-3630-3

Printed in the United States of America

1 2 3 / 05 04 03 02 01 00 99

Contents

Acknowledgments

No book reflects the solitary efforts of just one individual, much less one comprised of fifty contributors! It is therefore both salutary and customary to acknowledge those who played an especially significant role in making a volume possible. In that spirit I wish to thank:

The fifty men and women who graciously took the time to share both their successes and mistakes so that others might learn what they've learned about leadership.

Dennis Hillman, Stephen Barclift, and their colleagues at Kregel Publications, for their support and valuable assistance.

My mother and father, for sacrificially giving of themselves so that I could be trained for Christian leadership.

And my wife, Susan, who not only is a God-given gift as a lifelong ministry teammate, but who also manifested her genuine servant spirit in typing much of this text to minimize overhead expenses and maximize the blessings others could receive from the book's royalties.

Soli Deo Gloria.

Introduction

Why another book on leadership? Hasn't this topic been more than adequately addressed by both secular and sacred writers over the past three decades? What more could possibly be said without merely rehearsing the familiar?

As a faculty member and administrator at a seminary that exists to prepare evangelical ministry leaders, I am constantly seeking out texts and other resources that might help me contribute to the task of leadership development. As a result, dozens of books on leadership sit on my shelves. But there is one type of book that I have been unable to find, namely, a volume comprised of wisdom acquired "on the job" by a variety of respected evangelical leaders. For while some elements of leadership theory and practice can be learned in a classroom, other dynamics of leadership can best—perhaps only—be learned through "real life" interactions between leaders and those they are seeking to lead. I knew there would be significant interest in what lessons effective Christian leaders have learned in the school of life. But how might that wisdom be compiled and made accessible to others who will succeed them as the next generation of ministry leaders? Pursuing the answer to that question has led to this volume.

I began by developing a list of more than one hundred evangelical ministry leaders who I felt had something distinctive and important to share about leadership effectiveness. I sought to include representatives of the diversity found in contemporary evangelicalism. That meant inviting contributors from both genders and from a variety of geographic, ethnic, and denominational backgrounds. It also meant drawing upon individuals in both congregational and parachurch leadership roles. Some contributors have both national and international reputations; others are known more locally (though I believe they are deserving of expanded influence, and hope that this volume might serve as a foundation to facilitate that if God so desires). I wasn't sure how many of these busy people would catch the vision for what I hope to accomplish, but it seemed an appropriate time to apply the principle of "nothing ventured, nothing gained."

I then sent invitations to this pool of potential contributors, asking them to consider prayerfully submitting a letter of response to the question: "What have you learned about ministry leadership that you wished you had learned earlier?" I asked them to imagine that question being posed by a person who was either preparing for leadership or who had just assumed that role. I suggested a potential response of approximately 1,500 words that could either develop a single topic in some depth or address a variety of topics more briefly.

Furthermore, I suggested that this would be a wonderful opportunity to practice disinterested servant leadership (in other words, to have as our primary motivation the blessing of others rather than personal gain); hence I proposed that all royalties received by the editor and the contributors from the resulting book would be given to Western Seminary's student scholarship program to help future leaders receive foundational ministry training.

Then I waited to see how many would accept the invitation to participate.

To my surprise, over half of those invited expressed a willingness to send a letter. A few of these had to drop out of the process along the way, but we ended up meeting our goal of fifty contributors. Some sent letters that had earlier been sent to a real correspondent asking a similar question (these are noted in the biographical introduction); most composed a fresh letter responding to an imaginary inquirer. The length of responses varied considerably, but that was acceptable as long as each contributor felt the freedom to share what he or she wanted to say.

As editor, I shaped the responses into an essentially similar format, suggested some slight edits to clarify the author's intent where I felt necessary, developed both a title and set of reflection questions for each letter (if these were not submitted by the contributor), arranged the letters in alphabetical order, and wrote this introduction to them. Brief biographies were also written for each contributor, emphasizing past or present leadership roles and any key publications authored. Each contributor, of course, had the right of final approval for the title, edited text, and reflection questions.

The letters that follow all assume that the roles and tasks of leaders can be distinguished from those of their followers. Although emphases and details may vary a bit from author to author, students of leadership generally agree that the essential nature of leadership is found in influence over others, especially over a group. In other words, those in leadership ordinarily serve as catalysts and guides for a group's attitudes and actions. Applying this definition to leadership that is distinctively *Christian,* we find that Christian leaders are human instruments used by God to stimulate and guide a group into greater conformity to His will for them. Thus, due to the leader's Spirit-enabled influence, they become more of what God would have them to become and accomplish more of what He would have them accomplish. Learning how to relate effectively to God, others, and oneself are key prerequisites for effective ministry leadership. The letters that follow offer field-tested wisdom that should help you distinguish between effective attitudes and skills and those that hinder leadership.

A suggested method for profiting from this book would be to review one letter a day, perhaps by imagining that each day's mail brings a letter from a different evangelical mentor (some of the longer letters might best be digested over two or more days). Reflect on each letter's content using the application questions that follow. Following this meditative review and personal application, take the time to extract and record key principles learned. This should be very helpful as you construct a working biblical philosophy of leadership. Be sure to read these letters formatively so that their shaping and mentoring potential is fully realized in your life.

You will quite likely join me in not agreeing fully with everything you read in this volume. But I believe it reflects appropriate humility to avoid concluding immediately from any such disagreement that the author is necessarily wrong. Instead, I urge you to first try to understand why an author espouses a certain position, and then give it a fair hearing as you evaluate to what extent it conforms to the criteria of truthfulness found in God's revelation (both special and general). Should the evidence for that position still not be as compelling to you as it is to the author, then that idea may more safely be bypassed (at least for the present). But by not dismissing it prematurely you will practice critical thinking at its best, for it is through such even-handed mental discipline that one can experience needed growth in both discerning and applying wisdom.

May you, by God's grace and call, follow in the footsteps of these faithful leaders and exert a redemptive influence in the lives of those you touch!

ONE

Learning to Remember Jesus in All Things

James Abrahamson is the pastor of Chapel Hill Bible Church in Chapel Hill, North Carolina. Founded by Jim in 1971, this large congregation ministers in particular to the academic communities of Duke University and the University of North Carolina. He is also the author of *Put Your Best Foot Forward: How to Minister From Your Strength* (Abingdon, 1994). This letter was originally addressed to a young man Jim had been mentoring in ministry and who had just graduated from seminary.

Dear Friend,

Congratulations. I am proud of you and excited as I anticipate what might lie ahead for you in the service of the Lord Jesus. You have been faithful in little things and now you will be entrusted with much. In contemplating what I could leave with you now that you have completed your formal preparation for ministry, I decided to offer some final words of advice.

Some of what I have to say here will likely not be fully appreciated until you have more experience in life and ministry. But I urge you to tuck all this away in your heart, so that when these issues do come up you can respond appropriately.

If I could summarize my advice to you, it would be in these words of Pilate concerning Jesus: "Behold the man." In other words, remember Jesus.

Remember Jesus in things pertaining to you and God.

First, the main thing is to keep the main thing the main thing. Major on majors, minor on minors. You will be surrounded by folks who will be preoccupied with what is appropriate music for worship, what is fundamental to participation in church leadership, what we should emphasize in ministry, what is the "Christian" form of education, etc. As you struggle with such issues, remember that Christ is the main thing. The word of the cross of Christ, the radical love of God expressed through Christ, and the personal love relationship binding God's family together in Christ are always more important than being "successful" in ministry, being correct in arguments, and being liked by others. Being right starts with being clear about what is central, fundamental, and core to the Kingdom of God. It won't be easy to keep the main thing the main thing. There will be no end to the potential distractions. People may withhold financial support from the church for not getting their way on minor issues. Some will even leave a church over trivial matters. What these folks need to see in you is an example of consistent noble priorities. They will not ignore nor forget what you live for.

Remember that Jesus could have done a lot of things—good things, and perhaps even in the eyes of others, needed things—that He didn't do because He had a clear set of priorities. You need a clear set of priorities as well. Asking and answering three questions will help you identify your current priorities: (1) For what do you make sacrifices? (2) What occupies your mind at times of leisure? (3) What motivates the big decisions of your life? Again, the main thing is to keep the main thing the main thing.

Second, develop an attitude of gratitude. Be thankful. God is more concerned about your being thankful than just about anything else. The first and biggest charge brought against humanity by Paul in Romans was man's lack of thankfulness to a self-revealing God. Whenever you see God's hand and presence and fail to recognize and respect God as God, you are guilty of a fundamental sin: ingratitude.

How you tell your story (the story of your life, family, ministry, church, etc.) to yourself and others will be a powerful indication of your thankfulness or bitterness. You have the power to put different spins on all the phenomena of your life. You can (without lying) tell your story so as to make people cry for you out of pity or envy you out of awe. Let others sense your thankful heart when they hear your story.

I believe that thankfulness for all things may even be more important than faith to change things. Note how often Jesus expressed thanksgiving even when His circumstances were difficult. Thankfulness will foster a gracious ministry, a joyful heart, and a life of worship. So be a thankful person.

Third, develop a theology of suffering and pain. Life will not be fair, but God is still there and God still cares. Blessings are not always free, and work is not always fun—but life is still worth it. When entering ministry you may be tempted to entertain the notion that if you are faithful, you will be fruitful, and if you give, it will be given back to you in measure. However, it will not take long for you to realize that in a broken world many such popular expectations will not always materialize. You will see faithful people mistreated. You will see God-fearing families stumble and fall. Innocent friends will suffer, and you also may be numbered with them. You will be tempted to feel that God is not there or that He does not care. You will need faith to trust God in the dark because your eyes may not give you reason to hope.

Your theology of suffering, pain, and death must be consistent with both the realities of your experience and the oft forgotten truths of Scripture. Jesus could embrace the cross without losing hope even though Peter could not. It was only later that Peter's theology of suffering developed and was passed on to us in his first letter. The apostles certainly knew a world of injustice and saw no inconsistency between present pain and the hope that they embraced in Christ. They expected a broken world to respond like a broken world. They were not ashamed of pain and expected that servanthood would involve sacrifice. Don't be cynical like those who cannot see God through the eyes of faith in times of trouble.

Fourth, learn when to care and when not to care. For example, learn not to take the cares of the world on your shoulders. Don't try to take over your boss's job. Let God be God. You will be enticed by those around you to take responsibility for things you can't control. They will want you to make them happy, save their children from mistakes, and create God's kingdom on earth. You might be tempted to try to meet their expectation. Resist the temptation to be God. Only by limiting your sense of responsibility to those things that you can control will you be able to sleep at night and not worry about the many things that can—and often do—go wrong.

At the same time learn to care for people. Put forth an effort to cultivate a caring style of ministry. Love should be natural for the Christian; but it is also learned, so don't take it for granted. Empathize with people's joy and pain, then help them see life in an enlightened way. Help them as well learn how to care and not care. Too often people will care too deeply about their own pain, or about such things as the rights of animals, and not care enough about those things that are of even greater concern to God (e.g., the unity of the church, the eternal welfare of others, honest dealing with others). Remember that Jesus did not heal everyone. It was not because He did not care but rather because He was unwilling to take over His Father's role. He could say "it is finished" when we would be tempted to say "it is overwhelming."

Fifth, take risks of faith. Faith requires risk. Unfortunately risk invites fear, and decisions controlled by your fears can deprive you of both social impact and personal blessing. To be sure, caution is always to be encouraged—but being overly cautious can all too easily hinder your impact for Christ. No place is more exciting and secure than a position of wise faith in a God who is alive and active in the world. Put your career on the line for the Kingdom, along with your fortune and your freedom. Nothing is too great to risk in following Christ.

Jesus lived His life on the edge of great uncertainty from a human perspective. He had little of the world's security. Like Jesus, those who walk by faith and in the light will live with risk. Risk is scary. But "no risk" means "an inactive faith."

In taking risks of faith, remember that "defensive" faith is just as legitimate as "offensive" faith. At times you will be asked to endure and learn from a trial instead of removing it or escaping from it. Some of the greatest challenges might come when you are disillusioned with yourself and others. You therefore need both an offensive faith that will move mountains and a defensive faith that will trust God unto death. Don't downplay the role of a strong faith to endure hardship and failure. Remember that both Judas and Peter denied Christ when tempted. But while both of them despaired as they saw what their sin had done to Jesus, only Peter persevered to see what Jesus would do to his sin. Abide in faith.

The wisdom to know when to be offensive and when to be defensive with your faith will come with my next point.

Sixth, learn to detect God's hand in the mundane fabric of life. God is active in ways that are not always dramatic but nonetheless significant. As you experience and learn about God's agenda for creation, you'll be better able to listen for His voice and look for His hand in the affairs of life. Take care not to put words in His mouth or ascribe to Him things that do not belong to Him, but have an ear to hear what truly comes from Him. Study the Bible to know the sound of His voice and the priorities of His kingdom, and then listen to the subjective leading of His Spirit in your heart. Expect His Spirit to lead you. Don't be afraid of making mistakes as you respond by stepping out in faith. You will learn to hear more clearly through this process of listening and responding.

Jesus lived His life in constant fellowship with His Father. Knowing God's will was not a matter of dramatic revelation to Him as much as it was an intimate relationship in the midst of the mundane events of life.

Finally, always remember that God accepts you without approving of all that you believe or do. Avoid the cult of "grace lite" (which is usually accompanied by "law lite" and "sin lite"). When you doubt God's grace you will be tempted to make the Law manageable and sin tolerable. Don't be afraid of acknowledging your depravity. Things are not as bad in your soul as you think they are; they are much worse! But God's grace is able to cover the greatest sin. So let the holy Law of God convict you deeply—but don't ever base your relationship with God on the verdict of the Law. In other words, don't link the fact of God's acceptance of you in Christ with God's approval of all your beliefs or behaviors. Remember that you walk with a God who "justifies the ungodly" by faith.

Similarly, God's love for you is not increased by your obedience nor is it diminished by your disobedience. The exact same love that the Father has for Jesus, His Son, is also offered to you because you are hidden in Christ.

This leads me a second set of observations about you and ministry.

Remember Jesus in things pertaining to you and ministry.

Again, let me be more specific.

First, if something is worth doing, it's worth doing imperfectly. The perfectionistic impulse can keep you from doing a lot of good things. Much of what you need to do in ministry cannot be done perfectly. You do not have enough time. You do not have enough control. You do not have enough resources. So do your best under the circumstances and keep going. Your sermons can always be better. Your time can always be more wisely spent. Your relationships can always be deeper and more edifying. Your growth can always be faster. Learn to appreciate a less-than-perfect job. I am amazed that in God's timetable the first century was labeled "the fullness of the time." How much more could Jesus have done had He come in our day with all the advancements in technology and travel. But then I am reminded that had He not come when He did, there quite likely would be no modern age of technology and travel.

One of the great challenges you will face is your own failures. Expect to grow in your knowledge of your own depravity. As you grow in your faith do not be surprised if you feel a greater need of grace than when you started. Remember that David killed the giant when he was young in his ministry, but killed an innocent servant while stealing his wife when he was old in his ministry. Don't follow his example, but be careful to learn from it. Something similar can happen to the best of us if we lower our guard.

People (including yourself) will not change as fast or as much as you want, but that doesn't mean that your efforts are in vain.

Remember that God is changing you in ways that you may not expect or want.

You will need to seek forgiveness and offer it often. Don't be slow to forgive or to seek forgiveness. Never forget that God is opposed to the proud but gives grace to the humble.

You will never outgrow your need for grace. Your striving for discipline and victory over every selfish thought, deed, and word is admirable but futile—and may even be blasphemous if it assumes that you can outgrow your need for forgiveness and dependence on the cross of Christ. Too often we start with an inflated idea of how far we have come in our life with God, and He has to back us up and work basic realities into our souls.

Second, aspire to greatness after the manner of Jesus. Jesus' greatness was marked by a life that was self-sacrificing and persistently faithful, even when disregarded by the world and the church. He was honored only after He died. Aspire to be no greater than your master. If you are honored, let it be after you die and for your Christ-likeness.

You are entering a calling and vocation that prescribes a life of self-less service to God in the context of a demanding and desperate world. Don't expect to have an easy time of it. Some people will see your position as one of privilege and honor. Don't be seduced into feeding off their esteem. Be gracious to those who mistreat you, and be a model to others in how to take criticism. Never forget that while you are serving people, people are not your master. Keep a soft heart and a hard mind. To be a servant leader you will need the heart of a child, the brains of a genius, the faith of a saint, and most of all, the hide of a rhinoceros. A servant is identified by how he responds when he is treated like one. Use your life as a visual aid for your teaching.

Third, learn healthy self-critical skills. If you can see your own faults and acknowledge them openly, you will save yourself the social embarrassment of being exposed by another while also gaining the respect of those who need you to lead them. Jesus grew in His wisdom; so must you. Your own life will be the great laboratory for learning about all of life. Don't fear to enter that lab—it's the only way you'll learn.

A fair test of your self-critical skill will be seen in your ability to identify your weaknesses and failures as easily as you can identify your successes and strengths—and then have your observations confirmed by those who know you best.

Don't forget that your credibility is based less on your image of having it all together than by walking in the light—that is to say, living in touch with the reality of who you are, who God is, and what other people are like.

Fourth, love for people covers a lot of stuff. It's trite but true: people don't care how much you know until they know how much you care. Remember that Jesus was not so much a scholar as a lover. His teaching and actions grew out of a deep love for God and people.

We are drawn to those who love us. It is hard to argue with lovers. It is easy to follow those who care for us. If you want to influence others with your insights, first desire to earn a hearing through your investment in them personally.

People will put up with a lot from those who they know love them. Many of your mistakes, failures, weaknesses, and sins will be tolerated (and even overlooked) if you faithfully love.

Fifth, make both R&R and R&D a priority. Rest and relaxation (with reflection) is not a waste of your time. Rest is an important theme in both the Old and New Testaments. There will be tremendous pressure to stay busy for God. You may find, however, that it is more fruitful in the long run to wait on the Lord rather than always be running a race. There is a time and place for both.

Every successful company puts time and resources aside for research and development. It knows that it will not stay in business without R&D. You too will not be spiritually sharp without time to explore and develop your personal life. You should not feel guilty for taking "down time" to read, reflect, meditate, pray, and chase thoughts, ideas, and dreams. In spite of the powerful demands on Jesus, He understood the importance of time alone.

Remember that Martha worried while Mary sat at Jesus' feet. Like Martha, you will feel pressure to be constantly busy serving and worrying. Don't neglect the best place, the place that Mary chose and yet was criticized for occupying. While faith moves mountains, worry creates mountains. A frantic disciple is one who has lost his script and is trying to take everyone else's part in the play. Learn your role, play your part, and sit down so that others can do their thing. There is no good rationale for an obsessive-compulsive ministry style. If you don't take the time to smell the roses and enjoy some intellectual and spiritual R&R, you are probably abusing yourself, others, and your calling.

Sixth, listen well and be slow to speak. People don't want you to solve their problems as often as they want you to listen to their problems and care. Learn to ask good questions and then listen. When you do speak, be sure you have something worth saying; if you don't have a good word, just listen some more. The most important part of communication is listening. You will never be faulted for being a good listener and you will be surprised how many people will be helped, even delivered, as you listen to them.

What strikes me as wondrous in Jesus' interaction with people is

His skill in listening both to His Father and to the hearts of people. This is evident in the sensitivity and power with which He spoke to people's hearts.

As you prepare to speak on Sunday, make it a point to listen during the week. You will probably feel obligated to give people answers to life's questions on a day to day basis as people seek you out for help. It may be wise to spend most of your time asking questions and listening to people talk during the week, and then speak on Sunday out of the context of what you have heard.

Seventh, develop a "world Christian" perspective. Your expectations of life will govern your peace and joy. If you allow your culture to shape your expectations of the kingdom of God then you will be very disappointed.

American culture is not the kingdom. The world was not created in 1776. Don't let popular American culture's notion of happiness through material gain and social power seduce you into thinking that God is a chaplain for the American dream.

Expect the abundant life promised by Jesus to be a lot like the abundant life He and the apostles both experienced and expressed. Is their life-style and experience in this world what you expect for yourself? It will help to listen carefully to those who share your faith but not your culture. They can teach you much about which is which.

Remember, Jesus is the whole world's Messiah. Your experience and culture are just a small part of what He loves, cares for, and uses.

Finally, remember Jesus in things pertaining to you and people.

To be specific, first remember that people will often take out their anger toward God on you and the church. Remember that you represent God to most people. It is not good and it is not fair, but you must take this misconception into account when assessing people's responses to you. You will sometimes receive great respect just because of your position. At other times, your position will make you the target of scorn. When people are angry at God, realize that your relationship with them could also be affected.

Don't always assume that you caused the problem for which you are blamed, or that you can fix it by altering your behavior. This transference of anger may have little or nothing to do with you. And there may be little that you can do to alleviate it. What is needed from you is understanding, security, and patience. Be quick to listen, slow to speak, and slow to get angry.

Remember that Jesus was despised and rejected largely because He did not fulfill people's expectations. He does not fulfill our selfish dreams either.

Second, recognize that people are not always rational. Many things motivate human behavior. Logic is only one of them. Many people use logic only when it suits their cause. More often the real motive behind a person's behavior is fear or anger. Critically examine your own motives, for you too are not above irrational behavior.

You are going to encounter people at their best and at their worst. Usually they will want to impress you with their best behavior, but at times you will see a side of folks that only their most intimate acquaintances know. It is at those times especially that you will find some remarkable lapses in people's logic and reasonableness. People will need to sense God's love and patience through you in such circumstances. Unfortunately, it is at those times that people can be hardest to love.

Many of the decisions that are made in a church touch on the most sacred of people's traditions and insecurities. It is in such vital contexts that their anxieties, bitterness, disappointments, and prejudices will creep out. Be wise, patient, and gracious.

You will make many blunders in planning if you count on people being as rational and objective as you think you are. Try to anticipate people's responses and give lots of time for them to come to their senses. An old hunter's motto goes like this: "Never aggravate a wounded bear." It has application to wounded people as well.

Take many things into account in anticipating human responses to an issue—things like past experiences (especially hurtful experiences), temperament differences, social pressure (fear of rejection), and personal relationships. Seek to understand the context from which people are making decisions.

People tend to respond to superficial impressions and "appearances" more than you would like. You will therefore be tempted to create and maintain an image that works for you and helps you get what you want. Rather than working on an image, work on communicating honestly. Too often an image is a crutch for someone who does not want to invest the time needed to communicate true substance. So work at communicating truth and love rather than just cultivating a perception. By refusing to manipulate people (even though you may be able to), the end result will be a noble one. People made in the image of God deserve to be treated with great respect.

Remember the respect and patience that Jesus displayed to people, many of whom we would have no doubt discarded.

Third, you must address people's fears if you want them to follow your leadership. People need to know that you understand the terror represented by their fears. If you ask someone who is not accustomed to public speaking to make a public announcement, realize that they may be terrified at the prospect of embarrassing themselves, you, and the church.

How would you feel if someone asked you to sing a solo in public? If you are not sure that you could do a credible job, you may be anxious. Now assume that the person asking you to do this has the power to reject you if you do not do a good job. You are in a bind that can produce irrational behavior, like making up excuses that you think will be convincing. On the other hand, if you sense that the person asking you to sing knew how risky this felt to you and went to great lengths to make the experience safe, would you not be willing to at least consider the request?

I am struck by how often Jesus addressed fear (for examples drawn from Matthew alone see 6:25–34; 10:26–31; 14:27; 17:7; 25:25; 28:5–10). He knew that people would not follow Him unless and until their fears were overcome. If you do not help people overcome their fears, their fears will overcome both their faith and their better judgment.

Fourth, you will not be able to impact all people alike. People are wonderfully different. It will take many kinds of gifts, styles, emphases, and temperaments to reach the world. Do your part but realize that you do not have what it takes to reach everyone.

Accept the fact that not everyone will—or even should—like your style or be a part of your ministry. The fact that they leave the sphere of your ministry does not necessarily mean you have failed or that you should change. Cultivate a healthy respect for people and ministries that have different strengths and emphases than yours. We all need one another.

Remember that you are but one part of the body of Christ. The work of Christ will require the input of many more people than just you!

Fifth, your opponents can teach you if you know how to listen to them. Much can be learned in and from the nonbelieving world, but only if you are a critical listener. Jesus saw the image of His Father in all people. He recognized that evil as well as good was present in everyone, even His own disciples. He resisted the popular tendency to trust or distrust anyone fully.

The image of God is hard to repress in people and it will often bear witness to its presence in unexpected ways. For example, the violence, immorality, and lawlessness of many Hollywood films can be too quickly dismissed as only an example of human depravity. A more sensitive assessment may also see a desperate longing for the kingdom of God (justice, fulfillment, peace, and happiness), albeit couched in strange language. What you will discover is that it is not the kingdom that is in disfavor with much of the world, but rather it is the King who is despised and rejected.

Sixth, most of what you learned in seminary may not ever be used directly in ministry, but it is nonetheless a vital part of your preparation. There may be a great temptation to downplay the significance of your education. In some ways you will be disappointed because the world that your professors led you to believe was waiting for you may not exist as you or they imagined it. Moreover, your education will continue on the job—and in some ways it will just begin as you start walking in the trenches of the local church. Never stop being a student of life. The world has much to teach a wise observer.

Jesus learned the Scriptures early in His life, at a time when much of what He learned could not be applied to His experience. But it was this early preparation that equipped Him for three years of unparalleled significance.

Seventh, set and guard your boundaries. Many individuals who go into vocational ministry have a strong desire to please people. While on the surface this impulse seems noble, it can be neurotic. You cannot be the leader people need if you let them manipulate your behavior for fear of their rejection or criticism.

Remember that Jesus disappointed every one of His followers in the short term so that He might provide for their good in the long term. Know when and how to say "no." Be a person of strong principles, clear boundaries, and long perspective.

Remember Jesus,
Jim Abrahamson

Questions for Reflection

1. The author suggests asking and answering three questions to discern your current priorities: (a) For what do you make sacrifices? (b) What occupies your mind at times of leisure? (c) What motivates the big decisions of your life? To what extent do your responses to these questions reflect the priorities of Scripture? If you believe God would have you adjust your priorities, what will you do to begin moving in the right direction?

2. "A servant is identified by how he responds when he is treated like one." How do you respond when people treat you as a servant?

3. Reflect upon your last few significant encounters with other people, especially those in which their words or actions surprised you. What feelings or factors might have influenced those words and actions? How might greater sensitivity to those internal dynamics enhance your future personal interactions?

Learning to Serve, Listen, and Reconcile

Lawrence Ayers is director of EDIFY, a Christian consulting ministry which he founded, and is also active in both teaching and writing. For twenty-seven years he held several teaching and administrative positions within the Portland (Oregon) Public School system, including high school principal and Director of Instruction. He served for nine years as a trustee of Western Seminary (four of those years as board chairman) and later was president of that institution for three years. His letter responds to a request from several seminarians for fatherly advice as they embark upon their ministries.

Dear Friend,

I have pondered, meditated, and prayed for insight regarding your inquiry at the end of our last session. Responding to your request for counsel places me in a role akin to being your sage and parent, and those roles bear great responsibility. So I proceed with humility.

Years ago while serving as student body president at Bob Jones University, I occasionally had informal conversations with Bob Jones, Sr. His conservative worldview, incredible scriptural understanding, and common sense laid the foundation for my future as a Christian leader. He would often say to me and to other students that we could get more common sense from the Bible than from any other literature in the world. He also believed in hard work, and would declare to us, "If you turn back from difficulty you will either go hungry one day or somebody else will have to feed you." Perhaps the greatest piece of common sense I gleaned from Dr. Bob was about success. He told us that success is not about making money or receiving honor; rather success is finding out what God wants us to do and then doing it. He reminded us that doing God's will is also the secret of happiness.

Through the years, involvement with other significant leaders has influenced me professionally and personally. Billy Melvin and I washed each other's feet. Our discussions about church ordinances and evangelism helped me better understand the diversity of beliefs within evangelicalism. Haddon Robinson once told me that a significant part of leadership is to keep in touch with the people you lead. We often discussed men who were either too preoccupied with other things, too far out in front, too aloof, too impersonal, or too self-important so that they lost those whom they were called to serve.

Casual conversations with Joe Aldrich provided me with insight about relational evangelism and praying with other men. My pastor, Stu Weber, introduced me to one of the most difficult concepts I have ever had to deal with in leadership, the "piton" of friendship (so-named because it helps to protect from a dangerous fall). My conversations with other leaders reveal they too struggle with this concept. They desire—and sometimes achieve—an anchor bolt in a relationship with other leaders, but then too often are betrayed. They may possess the piton, but the substance into which the piton was placed was not strong enough to hold a credible relationship. I have finally learned and experienced that there can and must be a "piton" of friendship among Christian leaders, even if it involves considerable risk.

These men and others have influenced my life significantly. For my journey they have built many bridges across deep chasms, they have helped me navigate swift waters, and they have protected me spiritually, mentally, and emotionally. Yet, there are other things that I wish I had learned sooner. I regret that I was not astute enough to ask about things that could have shielded me from—or prepared me for—the many dangers, pitfalls, and trials that accompany living and leading in both the Christian and secular cultures of the 20th century.

In the spirit of Psalm 78:4–7, I want to share with you some of the things I wished I had known and practiced earlier. These are practical, common sense concepts that are intended to build bridges for you and influence your future leadership habits.

First, *I wish someone had urged me to establish for myself a very clearly understood biblical philosophy of leadership and management, and to translate that understanding into personal habits of action.*

Too many of us have allowed secular leadership philosophy to penetrate and dominate our thinking and actions. Secular philosophy commonly seeks to inspire and motivate followers for the best interest of the leader and to manage by getting work done through people. The practical application of this approach is to use power and authority to "lord it over" those who serve the leader. Furthermore, all goals, outcomes, and results are focused on providing more for the leadership. But if your philosophy and actions manifest the world's approach, how can you be expected to accomplish God's work God's way?

In contrast, look at Christ's statement in Matthew 20:32: "What do you want Me to do for you?" (NASB). This same self-giving attitude is expressed in Philippians 2:7. How many times as leaders have we asked this question to those who follow us? We are far too often telling them instead what they are to do for us. And if they do not do it the way we want, then harsh consequences are applied. This question opens meaningful dialogue around mutually perceived needs and expectations. It inspires growth in our followers.

Not only have I provided leadership, but I have also followed a variety of leaders. Most have wanted me to do something for them. However, there was one fellow who seemed to be sensitive to my most critical needs. He helped me regain my true identity during a difficult time. Others had abandoned me. He used his ability to lead and nurture me while maintaining a "piton relationship" that is still strong today. I found that we could lead each other in various ways, although his influence on me was significantly more than my influence on him. I would follow him through joyous experiences and difficult, terrifying times. I know that he would never betray me nor abandon me. He has taught me commitment, teamwork, mentoring, and listening skills.

I encourage each of you to focus your future leadership philosophy on the biblical approach to serving people described here by Lee Brase, a Christian leader on the West Coast of the United States. "Those of us in leadership positions frequently have difficulty with the idea of serving others. We tend to assume that since we have worked our way to the top, we are the ones who should be served. I guess we get to thinking that we have earned that right. I discovered that if you train a man, he will become what you are, but if you serve him, the sky is the limit as to what he can become. When I learned this, it freed me to serve men who have greater capacity than I have."

If only someone had told me to focus on the biblical approach to leadership, I could have served many more leaders and potential leaders who had a greater capacity than I. I have heard it said, "To know and not apply is worse than not knowing." Now I know how to serve as a leader.

Second, *I wish someone had told me that learning to listen well is the key both to true understanding and to trusting relationships among Christian leaders and followers.* Listening well means active listening. We may hear people but we often do not listen to them. Stephen Covey calls it empathic listening. He also says, "Most people do not listen with the intent to understand; they listen with the intent to reply. They're either speaking or preparing to speak. They're filtering everything through their own paradigms, reading their autobiography into other people's lives." Isn't that true? We as leaders are filled with our own rightness and our own autobiography. Covey goes on to say that "empathic listening gets inside another person's frame of reference. You look out through it, you see the world the way they see the world, you understand their paradigm, you understand how they feel." You cannot get this done without really seeking to understand the other person. Listening well takes focus, thought, training, and concentration.

Jesus, in a dialogue with fellow Jews, wanted them to listen. As He expressed in John 8:43, "Why do you not understand My speech? Because you are not able to listen to My word" (NKJV). They were more involved with themselves than finding out who Christ was and seeking to understand Him. Isn't it interesting that we spend much more time listening than we do reading, writing, or speaking, yet few of us have had any purposeful training in listening? This lack of training leaves us wide open for many misconceptions and poor perceptions of who people are, what they are saying to us, and how we respond to them. Proverbs 17:27–28 tells us to speak less and listen more: "He who has knowledge spares his words, and a man of understanding is of a calm spirit. Even a fool is counted wise when he holds his peace; when he shuts his lips, he is considered perceptive" (NKJV). Only when you truly understand someone are you calm in your spirit and able to maintain a wholesome, trusting relationship. You can only understand when you listen well.

Judi Brownell, a teacher of communication, says that we must learn to listen to the meaning behind the words, because over 90 percent of the message is communicated in the tone of voice and various nonverbal behaviors. She also says that the proof of listening well is an appropriate response. The ability to paraphrase, ask clarifying questions, pursue perception checks, and provide constructive feedback are all learned skills that lead to a dynamic reciprocal process and the accurate exchange of meanings.

How many of us are ready to tell others what the will of God is for their lives? I know a Christian leader who will assertively tell you God's will for you after only a two-minute conversation. What is worse, he doesn't listen to what you have to say about it. Rightness for you is reflected through his own righteousness and his own autobiography. He would be a much more effective servant-leader by instead participating in active listening with the intent to understand those he is supposed to serve.

Only within the last ten years have I learned to use the skills of active listening effectively. It has greatly helped my relationship with God as well. My worldview has expanded, my relationship and sensitivity with people have improved, I am a better problem solver, and life is much more meaningful. I am a more effective servant-leader. If only someone had taught me active listening when I was learning to read, write, and speak. It would have had a significant impact on my ability to help people solve problems and resolve conflicts.

Third, *I wish someone had told me to learn the fine art of reconciliation.* To reconcile is to reestablish friendship between people or to resolve a dispute between people. It has been my experience that we don't do this very well. It is tough for us to deal with negative relationships, conflict, and confrontation. Not only is it distasteful, but most of us claim not to know how to bring about reconciliation. We should do it the same way we were reconciled with God. We admit our wrongdoing (sin) to the person we offended (God) and ask for His forgiveness. He forgives us and our relationship with Him is restored. Granted this may be oversimplified, but using these same basic principles can be very helpful in enabling us to become reconciled with each other (especially when our wrongdoing produced the breach).

Ken Sande says that instead of reacting to disputes in a confused, defensive, or angry manner, we can learn to manage conflict confidently and constructively. He has developed a systematic theology for conflict resolution that can easily be applied in everyday life. His approach is based on four key principles:

1. Biblical peacemaking is motivated and directed by a desire to please and honor God (1 Cor. 10:31).
2. Peacemaking requires facing up to our own attitudes, faults, and responsibilities before pointing out what others have done wrong (Matt. 7:5).
3. At times peacemaking also requires constructive confrontation (Matt. 18:15).
4. Peacemaking involves a commitment to restoring damaged relationships and developing agreements that are just and satisfactory to everyone involved (Matt. 5:24).

Conflict resolution and constructive confrontation are God-given responsibilities for every believer. Titus 3:9 tells us to avoid disputes. Colossians 3:16 tells us to teach and admonish each other. Matthew 18:15–17 tells us to go tell our brother his faults, and 2 Corinthians 5:18 says that Christ has given us the ministry of reconciliation. So while we should try to avoid unnecessary conflict, we are still going to face it. We need to be able to do corrective action to fulfill our responsibility of peacemaking.

Recently Emily, a member of my growth group, asked me to help her with a problem in her Christian organization. Her boss, the CEO, was dissatisfied with the behavior of another executive. He had written a ten-page letter to the other executive and asked Emily to talk to her; in other words, the CEO wanted Emily to act in his place. He did not intend to deal personally with the other executive as his discomfort was so strong that he could not face her. Obviously Emily was distraught, uneasy, and concerned that she was about to get caught in the middle of a dispute. She was in a no-win situation.

I advised Emily to focus on the key issues. Identify the CEO's issues expressed in the letter. Then go to the other executive, who had the letter, and identify her issues. Then armed with the identified issues of both executives, Emily was to go back to the CEO and arrange for a meeting involving the two principal parties. During the meeting she was to help the two executives seek agreement on the real issues and then prioritize them. Then she was to have the two executives select the order in which they wanted to resolve each issue. The issues were to be dealt with one at a time, seeking a mutually agreed upon remedy. Three weeks after our first discussion, Emily reported that most of the issues had been resolved. Forgiveness had been expressed by both executives and positive relationships had been restored. She had credibility as a neutral facilitator because she had the initiative to fulfill her God-given responsibility. She was a servant-leader in the area of conflict resolution. She also learned a process in resolving conflict that works for her.

I suggest that all of us have a conflict resolution process that works for us. I now have a biblical process that I have used for the last fifteen years. I just wish that someone had told me earlier that there was a biblical approach and a God-given responsibility for reconciliation among people; if so, I would not be carrying so many battle scars and would not have suffered the guilt, anger, and relational destruction of my early years of Christian leadership.

On the other hand, I may not have had this opportunity to cite so much firsthand knowledge to help you avoid some of the pitfalls and crevasses that linger in your future. In this season of my life I am committed to building bridges and assisting other Christian leaders to improve themselves. Perhaps they in turn will also be bridge builders as expressed in this poem by Will Allen Dromgoole:

An old man going along a highway came at the evening,
    cold and gray,
To a chasm vast and wide and steep, with water rolling
    cold and deep,
The old man crossed in the twilight dim the sullen stream
    had no fears for him;
But he turned when safe on the other side, and built a
    bridge to span the tide.
"Old man," said a fellow pilgrim near, "you are wasting
    your strength with building here.
Your journey will end with the ending day, you never
    again will pass this way.
You've crossed the chasm, deep and wide, why build you
    this bridge at eventide?"
The builder lifted his old gray head, "Good friend, in the
    path I have come," he said,
"There followeth after me today a youth whose feet must
    pass this way.
The chasm that was as nought to me to that fair-haired
    youth may a pitfall be;
He, too, must cross in twilight dim—
Good friend, I am building this bridge for him."

I hope there is a bridge out there with my name on it. May God bless the exciting journey each of you will experience.

Your friend and mentor,
Larry Ayers

Questions for Reflection

1. Are you involved in a close friendship that can provide the accountability and encouragement needed to keep you from falling spiritually? What commitments and actions are needed to help that friendship fulfill that purpose, and how well are you doing with those?

2. In what ways are you using your leadership role to serve others rather than requiring them to serve you? What indicators do you need to watch for that suggest you may be "lording your authority" over others?

3. Do you have a biblically sound procedure for resolving conflict? If not, what will you do to develop one? In what ways might active listening skills help you reconcile conflicts more effectively?

THREE

Learning to Shepherd, Jethro-Style

Tom Baker is senior pastor of Portland Foursquare Church in Portland, Oregon. He assumed that position in 1990, after spending the prior twenty years in various church staff and senior pastoral roles. From 1973–76 he directed the Nicky Cruz Center in Portland, a street outreach and drug rehabilitation center. Tom also serves as superintendent of the Columbia N.E. Division of Foursquare Churches.

Dear Friend,

I saw it coming. I knew he was going to ask me to be the new Youth Pastor. But I didn't want to do it. I'd been there, done that. Later, as I was still settling into the role which I had finally accepted with great reluctance, I remember sharing with the Lord words of protest that went something like this: "I don't think being a youth pastor is even scriptural! Where is it in the Bible? Do you really expect one person to be at the same time an athletic director, competitor, fund-raiser, personable and witty emcee, expert on adolescence and family issues, program planner, and much more?" For me in particular, the transition from a street ministry with addicts and homeless folks who were aware of their desperate need, to entertaining spoiled, middle-class white kids with about as much zeal for the Lord as an uncapped bottle of Pepsi, was going to be a difficult transition indeed!

The answer I got back from the Lord, however, introduced a radically different perspective that is prompting this letter. For I sensed the Lord saying to me, "What did I tell Peter to do when he said that he loved me?" "You told him to feed your sheep," I replied. "But what did I say first?" He continued. "Feed my lambs?" I asked. "Right! Forget about just being a youth pastor and instead focus on feeding my adolescent sheep. Can you do that?" "I think I may be able to handle that, Lord."

Four years later, as I was beginning the assignment of pioneering the Foursquare Church in Yakima, Washington, I was again overwhelmed with the multitudinous aspects of what lay ahead. Going from an institution to the prairie left me floundering regarding where to begin. No secretary, no office, no other job—no way! In spite of these reservations and other unknowns, I did know for certain that He had sent me. By His grace, God led me to Ezekiel 34 and said to my heart, "Memorize this chapter, do right what they did wrong, and you'll do fine." So Ezekiel 34 was added to Jesus' words to Peter in John 21, and my list of "shepherding verses" began to grow. Since then Jacob, Moses, Joshua, David, Solomon, Isaiah, Jeremiah, Micah, Zephaniah, Malachi, the Bethlehem shepherds, Paul, and John have joined Jesus and Ezekiel as my scriptural mentors.

What model of pastoring should be included in a pastor's job description? I basically had three models demonstrated to me before I became "the man" in Yakima. I had previously ministered with Pastor Bob Church (of the First Christian Church in Newport, Oregon), Dr. Greg Romine, and Dr. Allan Hamilton (Greg and Allan were both Foursquare missionaries and pastors). Three very distinct styles! Which of the three, if any, should I try to replicate in Yakima? I remember asking Rev. Mitch Belobaba (at the time a Foursquare missionary to Africa), "What's the best piece of advice you'd give me as a young pastor going out to pioneer a church?" He said, "Be yourself." But at that time I did not find his advice to be very compelling or encouraging. The first sermon I preached in Yakima, I tried sitting on a stool like Pastor Jerry Cook (another man whose ministry I admired) and felt like a duck on a perch. The next Sunday I instead used a pulpit. But deep inside I was wondering, what does the method of presentation have to do with pastoring? Systems and methods are meaningless if we don't know why we're using them.

No matter the method or the man, I'm now convinced there are at least three primary principles of shepherding that are essential to every pastor everywhere, and three ways a flock that enjoys such care will respond. To introduce the principles, let's be reintroduced to Jethro.

Jethro was duly impressed with the size of flock his shepherd son-in-law had amassed since he last saw him on the backside of the desert. I think, however, he was more than a bit concerned that he might be taking his daughter and grandkids back home with him when he saw how Moses was dealing with the needs of his mega-flock! In the advice he offered to Moses I've found what I consider to be the three primary principles of shepherding. Open your Bible to Exodus 18:17–24 and you'll see what I mean.

So what are the three principles? They can be summarized in three simple words: *brought, taught, and sought.*

The first of these is found in verse 19: ". . . be for the people to God-ward, that thou mayest bring the causes unto God" (KJV). Unless we're providing prayer cover for the flock, watching over them, keeping our spirit tuned to what the Spirit is saying to them, being a pastor is going to get real dry real fast.

The second principle is found in verse 20: "And thou shalt teach them ordinances and laws, and shalt show them the way wherein they must walk, and the work that they must do" (KJV). In other words, show and tell. Disciple. Equip the saints to do the work of the ministry. But it's not just telling, it's also modeling. Or as Paul reminded the Ephesian elders in Acts 20:20, "I kept back nothing that was profitable unto you, but have showed you, and have taught you publicly and from house to house" (KJV). That's show and tell, public and private.

The third principle comes from verse 21: "Moreover thou shalt provide out of all the people able men, such as fear God, men of truth, hating covetousness, and place such over them, to be rulers of thousands, and rulers of hundreds, rulers of fifties, and rulers of tens." A shepherd needs help. There's simply no way one man can do it all for everyone, all the time. Moses started out with what I call the "Vending Machine Model" of pastoring. Since a vending machine is stationary, you must come to it. In Moses' case, there was a very long line at the vending machine. People get what they want by just pushing the right button when their turn comes. Now it may be ego-satisfying to be the only vending machine in the house, but that machine is soon going to be depleted and people will start getting frustrated. The Spirit once said to me, "A shepherd must seek and not just be sought." To do this effectively, we must share the pastoring task with elders who meet the qualifications of 1 Timothy and Titus. This not only prevents one person from experiencing otherwise inevitable burnout, but it also better meets the needs of the saints.

Unfortunately, it seems much of the Church in America has adopted the "professional clergy/passive laity" model of ministry. One of the ways I am attempting to shift the flock I pastor from this focus is to teach that we are all called to shepherd. I suggest that there are four classifications of shepherds: staff shepherds (who pastor a congregation), husband shepherds (who pastor their wives), parent shepherds (who pastor their children), and one-to-another shepherds (who pastor other believers in general as need and opportunity arise).

Some of us shepherd on all four levels. But while not all of us have been given the office gift of pastor, all of us are called to be our brother's keeper. Jesus said, "Those that thou gavest me have I kept, and none of them is lost, but the son of perdition: that the scripture might be fulfilled" (John 17:12 KJV). Before we can "keep" or "protect" our flock, we must identify it. (Husband shepherds and parent shepherds should have no trouble with this!) I encourage "one-to-another shepherds" that even a flock of one is validated by Jesus in Matthew 12:11, where he mentions the one with one. (Nathan also used a "one-sheep shepherd" illustration in his rebuke of David over the Uriah debacle). Although formal church membership may seem stuffy or political, it's not a bad place for "staff shepherds" to begin identifying their flock. With all the cross-grazing going on these days, I don't assume that every face that shows up in the "pen" on a given Sunday will necessarily settle down and take our name—but for those who do, I should know their names (John 10:3). When we pioneered the work in Yakima, I was concerned about the number of people who immediately joined us from other churches. Being the new guy in town, I didn't want to get an immediate reputation of being a sheep stealer! My fear was checked by this thought: "My sheep hear My voice, and I know them and they follow Me. My sheep can't be stolen. You be concerned about hearing My voice and teaching My Word and I'll be concerned about who's hearing My voice through you. Those that I have not sent to you will not stay." I've since discovered that the door does indeed swing both ways!

It would take much more space than I have in this letter to discuss all that I've discovered in the passages alluded to previously. It's been rich grazing though, and the triad of brought, taught, and sought does seem to provide a satisfactory format for capturing the Lord's focus for His flock.

So much for three principles of shepherding. Now, what about three ways a flock will respond when it receives such care? A flock that is brought, taught, and sought will respond by *reaching up, reaching in, and reaching out.* Let me briefly elaborate. The congregation will respond by reaching up to the Lord in prayer and worship, reaching in to the Body of Christ by being approachable and accountable, and reaching out to the lost through home and foreign missions. In other words, worship, fellowship, and discipleship will be expressed and enhanced. Praising the Lord, loving one another, and witnessing to the world.

The following verse speaks volumes to me: "The remnant of Israel shall not do iniquity, nor speak lies; neither shall a deceitful tongue be found in their mouth: for they shall feed and lie down, and none shall make them afraid" (Zeph. 3:13 KJV). The remnant may "do lunch" but they don't "do iniquity." Why? They are being fed and able to lie down without fear. I am led to conclude that much iniquity, lying, and deceitful words are present in our flocks because they are hungry, tired, and afraid. One of the reasons sheep scatter is because there is no shepherd. A body at rest is able to worship, fellowship, and multiply. As Jeremiah wrote, "And I will give you pastors according to mine heart, which shall feed you with knowledge and understanding. And it shall come to pass, when ye be multiplied and increased in the land, in those days, saith the LORD" (3:15–16 KJV).

Sheep multiply when they are pastored. It comes naturally. The lack of a shepherd allows "attack sheep" to make life miserable for the rest of the flock, making the healthy "up, in, and out" response non-existent, or at least greatly reduced. Ezekiel expands, "Behold, I, even I, will judge between the fat cattle and the lean cattle. Because ye have thrust with side and with shoulder, and pushed all the diseased with your horns, till ye scattered them abroad. Therefore will I save my flock, and they shall no more be a prey; and I will judge between cattle and cattle" (34:20–22 KJV).

Church discipline is scary but necessary. When a flock is biblically fed it can risk reaching out to the lost, reaching in to one another, and reaching up to the Lord—even in the presence of its enemies (Ps. 23:5).

Perhaps one of the most critical points to remind shepherds of is that we also are sheep. We not only need to bring our flock to the Father in prayer, we need to be brought; we must not only teach, we need to be taught; we must not only seek, we need to be sought!

Finally, being a busy pastor doesn't necessarily mean being a fruitful or even a "biblical" pastor. One of the ways I've used to help evaluate the priority of various church programs, traditions, and opportunities is to run them through a "Shepherding Grid." I simply take the activity in question and ask myself how it helps fulfill the primary shepherding principles of brought, taught, and sought, or how it helps to facilitate the flock responses of reaching up, reaching in, and reaching out. Let's say, for instance, I receive a letter from the "John Jacobs Power Team" offering to come and minister. To run it through the grid, the first question I might ask is, "Will bringing the John Jacobs Power Team to Portland Foursquare help me fulfill my responsibility of bringing the flock to the Father in prayer?" My answer: no. Will having them come help me teach the flock "the way wherein they must walk and the work that they must do" (Exod. 18:20 KJV)? Probably not much. Will they help me touch base with "my" people and be more informed of their needs and provide a way to meet them? Unlikely. Would having them come facilitate the expression of prayer and worship of the flock? That's not their focus. Would it be a way to encourage my church to fellowship with one another and minister the gifts they have received? I don't think so. Would it facilitate them reaching out to the lost? *Bingo*—if indeed, that is how we used the opportunity. On the other hand, if it's just exciting entertainment for bored believers, then it definitely shouldn't be pursued.

What about our ongoing programs and responsibilities—where do they fall on the grid? What percentage of my time am I spending as a shepherd praying for my charges, training them, or intentionally finding out how they are doing? (It's truly amazing how much mileage an unsolicited note, phone call, or visit can yield!) How much of my energy and time am I investing as a sheep in reaching up to the Lord in prayer and worship (not meetings I'm in charge of), reaching in to the body of Christ (probably a lot!), and reaching out to the lost? (Do most pastors even have relationships with unsaved folks other than family?) It's simple, fast, and focusing for me.

By the Father's grace, as I've sought to do right what the shepherds of Ezekiel 34 did wrong, I've done fine. I pray these thoughts will be useful to you as well.

Love,
Tom Baker

Questions for Reflection

1. What is most influential in your approach to ministry: human models that you have seen, or the transcendent principles of Scripture? Are you able to distinguish between the "optionals" of the former and the "essentials" of the latter?

2. How much of your current leadership style reflects what the author calls the "Vending Machine Model"? What do you need to do to delegate and share the load more effectively?

3. Do you agree with the "Shepherding Grid" proposed by the author to assess ministry opportunities and balance? If so, how will you use it in the future? If not, what criteria will you use instead?

FOUR

Learning to Profit from Observation and Advice

T. Allen Bethel is senior pastor of Maranatha Church in Portland, Oregon. Prior to coming to Maranatha, he pastored the Shawmut Community Church in Boston, Massachusetts, from 1984–1994. During this time he also was appointed by then-Governor Michael Dukakis to chair the Parcel 18 Plus Developmental Task Force. T. Allen serves currently as vice-president of the Contextualized Urban Ministry Education/Northwest and as trustee for Bay Ridge Christian College, North Portland Bible College, and the International Institute for Christian Communication.

Dear Friend,

It is essential that you know your ministry calling and its implications (including the promises of God that accompany your calling). This helps in both your visioning and your commitment to stay in ministry. Along with that knowledge I urge you to be faithful to the most strategic plan you will ever have: prayer.

I learned the most about leadership by observation. I encourage you to seek positive leadership role models and to observe them carefully so you can learn from them. It was my privilege in my early twenties to serve in ministry at the Third Street Church of God in Kansas City, Kansas, with Dr. Sethard Beverly, the senior pastor. Dr. Beverly allowed me to watch and learn from him. Often I'd ask him why he did things one way and not another. I remember on one such occasion, when we were discussing some issue on which we disagreed, he finally said to me, "Purchase a notebook. Everything you see me do that you do not agree with, write it down in that book, along with why you do not agree and what you would do differently—and when you become a pastor, do it." I started that book that day, but soon threw it away and instead just watched and learned all I could. I should also speak of George Free Sr., who taught me that you must get the facts first and seek to be a reconciler in a situation. If it were not for him playing that role in my life, I do not know where my life would be today. William Beachum taught me that hard work is a hallmark of a leader as he demonstrated a self-sacrificing lifestyle in giving, leading, and working. In my seventh grade yearbook from Fairwald Elementary School in Columbia, South Carolina, Mrs. Lassiter wrote this familiar quote that has challenged me ever since: "If at first you don't succeed, try, try again." These lessons I have learned from key people in my life, and they have shaped both me and my leadership style.

The pressures and struggles will come! At times, my friend, they seem to come at you from all sides, and sometimes from the most unexpected sources. You can best navigate through these pressures and struggles by staying on the offensive and not losing control of your emotions. My former pastor, Dr. Jordan D. Smith, taught me this principle that I apply to leadership. He would often say to me, "Son, sometimes you have to smile and walk away"; and I admit that it was only after many tough times that I later came to understand the wisdom of his advice. To elaborate upon this principle, Dr. Smith pointed out that while situations demand an answer, they do not always demand an answer immediately—the timing of the response is mine to determine. Time allows one to gather the facts, see the different perspectives, think, reflect, and then make decisions soundly, not based on the emotions or circumstances of the moment.

Perhaps one of the greatest lessons I have learned is from the business world. I learned it from an African-American entrepreneur, Luther Davis White, founder and president of D&H and D&B Tire Company. I was working in his employ one day servicing an automobile. Mr. White came from his office and proceeded to help me while still dressed in his Botany 500 suit. I protested, but his reply has stayed with me now over twenty-five years: "These tires put this suit on me and they can clean it or buy me another one. You must never lose touch with your customers if you are to serve them." The effective leader is one who never loses touch with the people he leads. This I wish I had learned years earlier. My friend, I urge you to maintain sincere involvement in the lives of those whom you lead. That will help you in discerning needs, direction, opposition, and finding solutions drawn from their experiences as well as yours. Dr. J. Horace Germany, President Emeritus of Bay Ridge Christian College, states, "For out of the typical experiences of life come love, understanding, and the solution."

Today there are leaders who think that it all happens because of them, who they are and what they do. These were my sentiments at one time as well. Avoid this age-old pitfall of pride. Never give yourself—or allow others to give you—more credit than you deserve! I was told by one deacon after a powerful moving of the Holy Spirit in a worship service, "Pastor, don't let this go to your head; it is not you, it's the Holy Spirit." I was reminded of that recently as I fussed with the Lord about declining attendance and offerings and wondering what I could do. It was only after humbly going to prayer that God spoke to me from His Word. He spoke from Zechariah chapters 7 and 8, and from Isaiah 43:11–12, reminding me that He is the One who does all—and even if a situation looks difficult for me, does it appear the same way in His eyes? (cf. Zech. 8:6). I released my efforts and once again turned to rely on the provision of God. In response, He is doing "a new thing" within us.

Also, my friend, do not succumb to the competitive spirit that exists among some of our leaders and churches. They boast that their ministry or church is better than the next, and seek to exalt themselves above all others or compete with them. This leads to alienation, isolation, and a life and ministry that are not pleasing to God. If you know your calling and the implications of that call, stay true to the calling, true to God and to yourself—and give God all of the glory. Changes come only as the whole kingdom of God advances! So seek to increase the kingdom totally in your city. That means you must cooperate instead of compete, and rejoice in the success of other ministries rather than begrudge them.

So often in leadership we are tempted to agree just for the sake of peace. Sometimes that is good, but other times it may involve an unwise compromise that weakens our integrity and ability to take a stand on a key issue. I wish someone had taught me the difference. The following story about an incident of church discipline that I had to initiate illustrates the lesson that truth is essential in leadership, and that if you stand on the truth it will vindicate you.

A church officer was charged with a serious offense. The investigation proved the charges to be true, which resulted in the discipline of the officer and her removal from office. The onslaught of problems that followed was great (to say the least!) and our attempts to handle them were not totally successful. The most difficult episode took place one Sunday morning after the service when the removed officer chose that time to confront me and question my integrity in the presence of a guest speaker. You can imagine my embarrassment! Some months later at a congregational meeting, this same person once again confronted me and the church with the accusation, "I have been treated wrongly." I wanted to shout at this person that her life and actions have not been consistent with Christian standards, and that she needed to ask the entire church for forgiveness. Instead, several members made that point for me. Truth had done its job well, and had set me free! In times of trial, when you must face opposition in its multifaceted forms, be sure to stand on the truth for the truth will vindicate you. A commitment to truth is essential for all leaders if they are to manifest the integrity needed in the various circumstances of ministry.

Balance in life is also needed for successful leadership. My father and my father-in-law taught me two principles about balance that I want to share with you. My father, Clarence Bethel Sr., an ordinary blue-collar worker and small farmer, was a committed Christian and church leader. He taught me at a young age this work ethic: "Anything worth doing once is worth doing right the first time." My father-in-law, James P. Davis Sr., an attorney, state legislator, and county commissioner, taught me a complementary principle: "You have to learn not to let all these things upset you." That helped me to see that I have to stay on the offense and not let situations control me. I have taken these two principles and applied them not only to leadership, but to many other areas of life as well and found them helpful. I always seek to stay in control of myself and put my best effort "up front" into everything I do. This not only gives me satisfaction, but reduces the stress as well.

The adage "practice makes perfect" carries a measure of truth; one must be sure, however, to practice the right principles. The effective leader can be taught the right principles but that leader must be willing to practice them. To gain more knowledge, sharpen skills, and build character, I encourage you to consider these five points. First and foremost, stay involved with the people that you are leading or seek to lead. Second, study, read, observe, and model those principles you see in positive leaders around you. Third, surround yourself with the tools of leadership. These tools include books on leadership and successful companies, biographies of leaders, interviews with leaders, seminars, an attentive ear to the Spirit, and study of the Word of God (especially biblical models of leadership). Fourth, do not be afraid to make mistakes. Learn from them, for nothing beats a failure but another try. Fear most the man who has failed or been knocked down but gets up again. Finally, listen to good advice and maintain a humble and teachable spirit.

How does one measure success? I believe that it is measured as you remain true to your calling and vision, stay involved with those you lead, and continue moving forward. Success is sensed as you know you are doing your best as a leader, learning from your mistakes and victories, and applying them to the future. When your confidence rises but your dependence on God is keener, then you are succeeding.

Sincerely,
T. Allen Bethel

Questions for Reflection

1. Do you feel called to leadership? Why or why not? How can a sense of personal calling help a leader persevere through difficulties and disappointments?

2. Do you often find yourself responding prematurely or emotionally to situations (e.g., before you have discovered the facts or in a way that makes a bad situation worse)? If so, what can you do to respond more appropriately in the future?

3. To what extent do you find yourself competing with others rather than cooperating with them or rejoicing in their successes? Do you need to pray for and pursue an attitude change in this area?

Learning the Value and Challenges of Music and Worship

Gordon Borror is pastor of First Baptist Church of Milwaukie, Oregon, and adjunct professor of Music and Worship at Western Seminary in Portland, Oregon. A career churchman and educator, Dr. Borror began formal ministry while still in college, and has continued for over forty years as both a teacher and pastor. He coauthored with Ronald Allen *Worship: Rediscovering the Missing Jewel* and is a frequent contributor to worship periodicals.

Dear Friend,

I began my church music career in 1956 in a small church in Glendale, California. I could not possibly have known then what I am about to suggest, because the local church was very different at that time. A church musician was someone who would direct a choir, and perhaps choose some of the musical activity of the assembly, but was usually not a part of the church staff in any official way. The musician worked directly for the pastor—and as the pastor wished—leaving very little room for creativity or leadership as it is now known. I speak from firsthand experience, as I have held the positions of Choir Director, then Minister of Music, then Pastor of Music Ministries, and Pastor with emphasis in Worship and Music before assuming my present pastoral role.

When I consider what I wish I had known from the beginning of my career, several things come to mind. First, I would have benefited greatly in knowing that the Church exists for *ministry,* and not just as another place for musicians to make music. When you begin it is too easy to become so involved in impressing the people, in proving that you know what you're doing, in teaching notes, in preparing programs (each Christmas and Easter a little better than last year) that *it is easier to "use" people than to grow them.* You miss the point of ministry when you begin to wear people down, to mistreat assisting crews, to make demands on performers that result in discouragement or fatigue, or to place the performance in some way above the people and their progressive spiritual growth. It took me a long time to realize that while performances are important, and high quality and excellence should be the norm, I had failed in my purpose if the people are beaten down when it is over. The process is just as (if not more) important than the product because the process builds people who are eternal. Performances, great or not so great, will be forgotten, but what happens to individuals and their relationship with God and His people remains! The sooner we recognize that the glory of God is the *real* issue, then music ministry will find its appropriate place in the work of worship, discipleship, and outreach!

Second, I wish I had understood *practically* (not just theoretically) that music is one of the most changing phenomena in all the world. Music never has—and never will—sit still right where we like it, nor right where we can best and most comfortably perform it! Musicians must develop many skills while becoming proficient in the field; very few become equally competent in all styles. The individual's most satisfactory performance medium tends to reflect the genre in which he or she has received the principle training. To stretch beyond those limits requires ongoing study, practice, and stylistic adaptability. My observation is that while preachers may develop a fine preaching style and use the same basic style for decades of ministry (perhaps even a lifetime of preaching), that is simply not possible for musicians.

During my years of ministry, musical genres have run the gamut of the gospel song style of the nineteenth-century revivalists, through the "revolution" of John Peterson with his pseudo-pop of the 1950s–60s, into the folk era, and on to multiple pop/rock styles. We are challenged to speak the musical language of the current trend while attempting to keep touch with preceding generations. Music is the place in the church where much of the burden of change is placed, probably bearing an unhealthy majority of the responsibility for keeping the church relational and relevant to each generation.

So much of my life of ministry has been spent defending what we were doing (it is either too contemporary or too traditional, depending upon who is doing the evaluating) that great energy is consumed which robs the time and strength needed for true creativity. Keeping a strong musical and spiritual foundation upon which inevitable change can rest securely is a very large part of what the church musician must do. Working with younger musicians who can influence our thinking regarding musical direction while discipling them about our collective heritage makes a great difference. I had some well-meaning mentors when I was being coached in the 1950s, but they could not have known what I would face throughout the subsequent years of my ministry. I'm sure my coaching in the present is done in a similar vacuum of what may be ahead for church music! In any case, awareness at the beginning of this confusing issue would have either forced me out of the field entirely or at least prepared me somewhat for what was ahead.

The third thing I wish I had understood from the outset is the tremendous influence leadership has on followership. I would have worked more diligently with other staff so that we could better understand and support one another's ministries. For too many years my fellow team members and I went our own ways working hard to establish and maintain our respective ministries. They were good ministries—Music, Education, Adult, Outreach, Youth, Children, Missions—but we did not take time to know where the other ministries were heading. The result was significant (but comparatively unintegrated) ministries in several areas. It took many years for me to discover that the church *will* be in *macrocosm* what the staff is in *microcosm.* I now strive to know the other ministries well enough to support them (sometimes even advising them) so that the local church can truly be one body. When we are not all on the same page, the people tend to become confused and frustrated. It takes time together, prayer together, playing together (emphasis on "together") to learn to think alike and therefore lead the people in!

Finally, I wish I had better understood the power of music to express, teach, unify, give identity and satisfaction—in general to impact people indelibly! Perhaps if I had better recognized the power of the music I was (or wasn't) using, I would have been even more careful and selective about what we sang. Not that I was careless; I knew people were more apt to remember what they sang than any other thing that went on in church (including preaching!). But literally hundreds of people who have been involved with me at one level or another over the years have testified of the life-aligning and changing influence the music had on them! They just couldn't get away from the truth they had sung. We *must* choose music that teaches a powerfully *accurate* view of God. Don't have people sing what is theological error! (Many "poets" write catchy phrases and nice lyrics, but they may be dead wrong regarding biblical truth!) If you're not sure regarding the integrity of what you are about to sing, *don't* sing it without having some respected pastor or theologian check it out for you! I feel very responsible for the flock entrusted to my leadership, and if I allow them to sing what is questionable regarding eternal truth, *their* error is *my* failure.

Music ministry is truly challenging. Don't enter it unless you are definitely called and ready to make the necessary personal sacrifices. Your spouse, family, and ambitions will all be impacted by this calling due to the amount of energy and physical resilience it requires. Because music is an art form, the people with whom you work may be prone to the "star syndrome"—your people skills will be *very* necessary to keep them on task and committed to God at every point. I encourage you to remain optimistic while leading and motivating them. You must also be able to take the inevitable criticism without being crushed and defeated. When it occurs, however, try to listen and evaluate carefully, because proactive change often comes when our critics are heard and proper response is made.

I can honestly say after all my years in music ministry that it has been *most* rewarding. I have no regrets. I am eternally grateful for the people with whom God has allowed me to work and for His rich blessing on my life and the lives of my family. I would try to do some things differently if I could begin again, but I would choose the same field of endeavor. I truly praise God for that fact!

Sincerely,
Gordon Borror

Questions for Reflection

1. How well does your leadership balance emphasis upon the "process" and the "product"? Do people feel used when serving with you? If so, what corrective actions might you take?

2. If you are serving as part of a ministry team, how aware are you of what is happening in the ministry areas of your teammates? What might you do to facilitate a greater level of integration and interdependence so as to facilitate biblical synergy?

3. How much care are you giving to ensuring the theological accuracy of the songs you sing at worship?

SIX

Learning to Distinguish Between Degrees of Certainty

Gerry Breshears is professor of systematic theology at Western Seminary in Portland, Oregon, and chair of that school's Division of Biblical and Theological Studies. He also serves as an elder and member of the preaching team at Grace Community Church in Gresham, Oregon. Gerry is a past president of the Evangelical Theological Society.

Dear Friend,

Leaders know that the main thing is to keep the main thing the main thing. They have a nose for significance, creating a climate of unity around central issues while moderating and directing discussion over secondary issues. They see how seemingly insignificant matters may undercut the central points of the gospel even as they appear so benign, so cultured, so loving. They sense that other issues which appear so fundamental are actually seeds of division planted by the enemy of our souls.

Leaders understand Paul's admonition to "avoid foolish controversies and genealogies and arguments and quarrels about the law, because these are unprofitable and useless" (Titus 3:9 NIV) but also know to "warn a divisive person once, and then warn him a second time. After that, have nothing to do with him" (v. 10). They balance that with his advice to Timothy and us: "Those who oppose him he must gently instruct, in the hope that God will grant them repentance leading them to a knowledge of the truth, and that they will come to their senses and escape from the trap of the devil, who has taken them captive to do his will" (2 Tim. 2:25–26 NIV).

Is there a way to help us choose which battles to fight? Is there a way to differentiate between wolves in sheep's clothing and sheep in wolves' clothing?

If I am vigilant about essentials, I am less likely to fall for the cultural accommodations of Christianity which lead to liberalism or legalism. That also helps me keep secondary issues in perspective and avoid the divisions they create.

I have found it most helpful to distinguish levels of certainty. Then I can differentiate what's essential from that which is merely controversial.

I break this down into four levels: first, things I would "die for." Knowingly deny these and you show that you are outside the realm of evangelicalism and perhaps exclude yourself from the salvation in Christ. Second, things I would "divide for." We are Christians, fellow members of the body of Christ. But we won't be in the same local fellowship. Third, things I would "debate for." We are in the same church, but we will wrestle with these issues, sometimes heatedly. Fourth, things we "decide for." These are issues where differences are little more than personal opinion.

Let me discuss each in turn.

Die for: These are the evangelical essentials, the fundamentals of the faith. Knowingly to deny them would indicate that you are not a Christian.

They include the inspiration and authority of Scripture, the Trinity, one God subsisting in three coeternal persons, the incarnation of the second person of the Trinity in the God-man, Jesus, including His virgin birth, sinless life, substitutionary atonement, bodily resurrection, and personal return. They also cover justification by grace alone through faith in Christ alone, the personal Spirit's indwelling believers constituting the one body of Christ, and the final judgment leading to hell and heaven.

These are the foundations of the faith once delivered to the saints. These things we contend for earnestly (Jude 3). If necessary we would die for the truth of the gospel incorporated in these propositions.

Humility concerning these items can never be a virtue. Calling a person who knowingly denies evangelical essentials a brother or sister in Christ for the sake of "unity" truly denies the unity that is founded on the truth of Jesus Christ.

Divide for: Everyone who genuinely affirms the evangelical essentials is a fellow member of Christ's body, one whom we call brother or sister in Christ. However, there are other important issues that are so foundational to our life with God that we will divide fellowship over them. In ancient times such an issue led to the division between Paul and Barnabas (Acts 15:39). In modern terms, these are the foundations of the denominational differences.

Wesleyans will divide from Reformed over the issue of entire sanctification. Both may divide from Pentecostals over the nature and timing of the baptism of the Holy Spirit. Does God speak only through Scripture or does He speak today through prophetic revelation? Is baptism the sign and seal of membership in the covenant community appropriate for infant children of believers or is it a sign of Spirit baptism and personal faith appropriate only for believers? Should the mission of the church include reshaping society as a major component along with winning the lost and worshiping God? Separate churches will form depending on whether the Sunday morning church service should be liturgical, expositional, or celebrative.

It seems to me that such differences are legitimate so long as the overall unity of the body is affirmed and the dividing points are truly central issues.

They become problematic when the dividing walls are so high that there is little contact between different groups, or when arguments between the groups drain significant energy from our worship of God, building godliness, or proclaiming the gospel.

When we recognize that these are "divide for" and not "die for" issues, we can pray for each other and cooperate in issues of Christian life, worship, and evangelism.

Unfortunately many less important issues cause division and divisive spirits. I see an emerging neofundamentalism that seeks to define issues more narrowly and focus on what we deny more than what we affirm.

Because Jesus calls us to unity, we should pursue evangelical ecumenism, a spiritual unity that still respects the important differences. This kind of ecumenism promotes true understanding between fellow believers instead of caricatures of another group that are intended to point up the differences and errors of that group. It speaks first and primarily of our unity in Christ, and approaches the differences between us as differences between fellow believers.

In recent years we evangelicals have reduced the number of issues in the "divide for" category. The result is that many denominational labels have lost dividing significance. Often this is because there is an attempt to look for unifying points and see the differences within that light. When the power of the Spirit's work and the fullness of the gifts are emphasized, the evidentiary significance of speaking in tongues that used to divide Pentecostals and charismatics is much less significant. When a "whole person" spirituality (including mind, will and emotions, body and spirit) is emphasized, Pentecostals give more attention to careful exposition of the Word and non-Pentecostals expect an emotional response to the exposition of the Word. All can and do affirm the powerful work of the Spirit even as we differ significantly on the specifics.

Debate for: These are the issues we wrestle with inside a church or denomination. The wrestling may be prolonged or painful, but we do it while maintaining regular fellowship, joining together in worship and proclamation. Debated issues may include the leadership roles appropriate for women, the extent of involvement the church should have in compassionate ministries in the community, the balance between elements of a worship service to accomplish the purposes of the gathering of believers, etc. The list here can become quite long as we bring in cultural and traditional elements associated with our particular church.

It seems to me that we must keep "debate fors" from escalating into "divide fors." The best leaders keep the unity of the body at the center of our thinking as Paul admonishes us in Ephesians 4:3. These leaders are also able to keep the focus on the essentials even when the wrestling is strenuous.

I find that when we try to control the debates by silencing the wrestling or smoothing things over with nice words, we actually empower divisive folk. The divisive people continue to promote their wrangling without being called to responsibility by the wisdom of the group.

The ground rules of Acts 15 seem appropriate here. Paul took the divisive people back to their body, Jerusalem, where everyone spoke for themselves before the whole church. They spoke what they believed and to the issue at hand rather than to the errors of the other group and to irrelevant issues. The whole congregation listened and recognized the wisdom of James as he stood for essentials (salvation by faith alone) and proposed compromise on secondary issues (eating blood, etc.).

Leadership is leading the group in wise decision making rather than making decrees and enforcing decisions by weight of authority.

Decide for: these are the *adiaphora* of Romans 14–15, the areas of belief and behavior about which there is no law. This is where acceptance is a virtue and legalism a real danger.

Paul instructs us to stop judging one another over such issues, to stop showing contempt for others just because they differ here. Rather he directs us to accept each other. He urges us, "Let us therefore make every effort to do what leads to peace and to mutual edification" (Rom. 14:19 NIV).

Note well, this attitude applies only in the non-essentials. Difference in essential matters "brought Paul and Barnabas into sharp dispute and debate with them" (Acts 15:2 NIV).

How do you discern the differences between these levels of certainty? In my judgment the discernment revolves around the centrality and clarity that the issue takes in Scripture and the significance of the issue for our faith.

We can illustrate the different levels in our understanding of Christology. The sinlessness of Christ is a "die for." Whether Jesus possessed all the divine attributes or left His incommunicable ones behind when He took on humanity might be a "divide for." Jesus' possession of a sin nature could be a "debate for." Whether Jesus truly struggled internally with Satan's temptation (Matt. 4:1–11) probably would fall into the "decide for" category. How long Jesus' hair was would be even lower—a "who cares?"

Scripture is absolutely clear that Jesus did not sin. Those who affirm that He did in order to establish His full humanity may appear sensitive to human problems, but they exclude themselves from evangelical orthodoxy when they do. Understanding such divine attributes as omnipresence in the incarnate Lord stumps everyone. But those who say He laid them aside, the kenotic Christology, compromise the church's foundational "fully God" affirmation. Because they affirm the full pre-existent deity of the second person of the Trinity, I could accept them as evangelicals but would have great difficulty ministering with them. Scripture does not have direct statements about omnipresence, but the affirmations of His deity are unmistakable. While Hebrews 7:26 leads me to believe that He did not have a sin nature, others see Romans 8:3 indicating that He overcame "sinful flesh." We would wrestle with this difference, but I would not divide over it.

Divisive people are ones who elevate lower level issues. For example, I see groups raising the issue of limited atonement from a "debate for" to a "divide for." Others make the practice of tongues a divide for issue when Paul only rates it a "do not forbid" level of certainty (1 Cor. 14:39).

As we comprehend these levels of certainty and begin to employ them as a community of believers, we can avoid the trap of being unnecessarily divisive on one hand and compromising the faith on the other. I hope my words help you to become a leader who can discern the difference.

Sincerely yours,
Gerry Breshears

Questions for Reflection

1. Think through for yourself what types of issues you personally would put into each of the four categories of certainty described by the author and try to develop a biblically based rationale for why you'd place it in one category rather than another.

2. To what extent might you more effectively cooperate with other believers who might disagree with you on matters other than those worth "dying for"?

3. How might you as a leader help other believers make more prudent judgments in developing levels of certainty and relating to fellow members of the body of Christ?

SEVEN

Learning to Value Servanthood, Submission, and Communication

Bill Bright is founder and president of Campus Crusade for Christ, International, a ministry that extends to more than 172 countries with a combined full-time and volunteer staff of over 250,000 individuals. Prior to his conversion, Bill was a faculty member at Oklahoma State University and a successful businessman in California. Among his more than fifty-six publications are *Witnessing Without Fear* and *The Transforming Power of Fasting and Prayer*. Bill also conceived the *Jesus* film, the most widely viewed film ever produced.

Dear Friend,

In response to the question, "What have you learned about leadership over the years?" I would say, "Very much," and I wish someone had told me more about the subject when I was very young.

Please allow me to share with you five particular principles I have learned which I consider especially important. All are based on God's holy Word, the Bible, which has wonderful wisdom for us on the subject of leadership.

Spiritual Confidence. The first and highest principle is to be confident that the Creator God of the universe is indeed your Savior and Lord. I have known for many years now that I have salvation in Jesus, and that I am filled with and controlled by the Holy Spirit, living in the center of God's will, fully surrendered to the Lordship of Christ. This confidence is necessary for godly leadership.

Servanthood. Our Lord gave one major prerequisite to leadership—servanthood. In a somewhat amusing encounter, one day the mother of Zebedee's sons came to Jesus and asked that He promote her sons to sit at His right and left hands in the kingdom. When "the Ten" heard about this, they were indignant. This triggered a response from the Lord that is the greatest leadership principle ever given. He said:

> You know that the rulers of the Gentiles lord it over them, and their high officials exercise authority over them. Not so with you. Instead, whoever wants to become great among you must be your servant, and whoever wants to be first must be your slave—just as the Son of Man did not come to be served, but to serve, and to give his life as a ransom for many. (Matt. 20:25–28 NIV)

In modern corporate vernacular, the Lord would say, "Look, here is the way it works in My organization. The key to getting ahead is to serve. The greater servant you become, the more you will be promoted." And what an example He set! The Creator laid aside all His glory to come down to earth to serve mere humans.

Our motivation should always be to serve and not be served. Of course we are all committed to "serving the Lord." But more is needed. We must also be committed to serving each other. For example, leaders should be committed to serving—not just directing—those whom they lead, as well as those in higher management. Nonmanagement staff should be committed to serving fellow workers in addition to those in management.

As the Lord said, "the rulers of the Gentiles," that is, those constituting the world power structures, do not have this Christ-like attitude, and instead just "exercise authority" over people with the purpose of exalting themselves. But not so for God's people. We must always maintain a servant's heart in all that we do, and work to be a blessing to all those around us.

This does not mean that leaders adopt an indecisive, Milquetoast attitude, with reluctance for making the many hard, everyday decisions needed in most jobs. But it does mean that everything we do must be from a servant's perspective. We must be servants of all.

Paul wrote that he was Jesus Christ's slave (Rom. 1:1). Let us be slaves to Him and to one another. Paul goes on to say, "Your attitude should be the kind that was shown to us by Jesus Christ, who, though he was God, did not demand and cling to his rights as God, but laid aside his mighty power and glory, taking the disguise of a slave and becoming like men. And he humbled himself even further, going so far as actually to die a criminal's death on the cross" (Phil. 2:5–8 LB).

Submission. This third leadership principle—submission to authority—is similar to servanthood, but just a bit different. The Bible teaches us that God is the author of all authority, including civil authority, church authority, and authority in the family, and that He intends this all for our benefit. "Everyone must submit himself to the governing authorities, for there is no authority except that which God has established. The authorities that exist have been established by God. Consequently, he who rebels against the authority is rebelling against what God has instituted, and those who do so will bring judgment on themselves" (Rom. 13:1–2 NIV).

This is equally important in Christian efforts and organizations. There have been dear, well-intentioned Christians who go to work in Christian organizations believing that since they are serving the Lord, they need only to submit to the Lord (as they see it); in other words, that they are an authority unto themselves and are free to pursue their own agendas. This can cause disruption of the mission that the Lord has given to that organization or department. Sometimes even open (or subtle) rebellion results. And remember, God uses strong words on this subject: "Rebellion is as the sin of witchcraft" (1 Sam. 15:23 KJV).

Proper submission to godly leaders can bring purpose, peace, and blessings; rebellion against godly authority can bring unrest and a disrupted life, missing God's best.

Recently I received a letter from a contrite and repentant dear brother in Christ who, as a college student, was on our summer staff in the 1960s. He was planning on joining staff full-time after graduation. But he now confesses that he got caught up in the rebellious spirit of the time, refusing to submit to ministry authority, and deciding to do his own thing. He says that the Lord has used him over the years but, in his own words, "I have continued to be haunted with a lack of vision. Now I believe my lack of direction is a direct result of my lack of submission to authority." After all those years, he asked my forgiveness, which he certainly has. It is a sad and touching story, but an instructive one.

There are many biblical examples of blessings from submission (such as David and Joseph) and, conversely, loss of blessings from rebellion.

Unity. In the military, they speak of organizational "cohesion"; that is, the ability of the members of an organization to work together with a common goal and purpose and with a common, cooperative effort and attitude. We usually use the term "unity." All leaders should try to foster unity among all members of their organizations, churches, staffs, or departments.

There is great power in unity and agreement. In the spirit realm, Jesus spoke of this power when he said, "Again, I tell you that if two of you on earth agree about anything you ask for, it will be done for you by my Father in heaven" (Matt. 18:19 NIV).

It also works in the physical realm. During the building of the tower of Babel recorded in Genesis 11, the people twice said to each other, "Come, let us . . ." (v. 4). God looked down on them and remarked, "If as one people . . . they have begun to do this, then nothing they plan to do will be impossible" (v. 6 NIV). God was saying because of the unity of the people and the power of that unity, that unless He intervened, nothing the people planned to do, even though evil, would be impossible! This is an incredible example of the power of unity. Of course, as we shall see below, God had other plans for them.

Communication. Another important function that leaders must cultivate and foster is good communication among members of their teams. Good communication fosters unity, and poor communication hinders unity.

Genesis 11 and the tower of Babel incident are also good examples of this. For example, God says in verse 1, "Now the whole world had one language and a common speech" (NIV). In verses 5 and 6, God said, "If as one people (unity) speaking the same language (good communication) they have begun to do this, then nothing they plan to do will be impossible to them" (NIV).

What they were doing was not in God's will, so He disrupted their communication, which also destroyed their unity! Disunity brought disharmony and the disruption of plans and efforts.

Even though our intention may be to glorify God, poor communication and disunity can also adversely affect, even destroy, our plans. To be the most effective servants of God, and for the most fruitful ministries, Christian leaders should always establish and work at maintaining an atmosphere of good communication among team members.

If Christian leaders are in God's will, with a true servant's heart, in proper submission to authority, and with good communication and unity, then "nothing they plan to do will be impossible to them."

I trust these principles will help you be the most effective servant possible in the service of our dear Lord and Savior, Jesus Christ.

Yours for fulfilling the Great Commission in this generation,
Bill Bright

Questions for Reflection

1. Is your "spiritual confidence" being eroded because of any un-
   confessed sin? If so, ask God to help you repent of that sin so that
   your fellowship with Him might be enhanced.

2. How would you describe the biblical notion of servant leadership,
   and to what extent is your leadership reflective of those values as
   opposed to the world's?

3. How effective is the communication between the various members of your ministry team? In what ways might it be enhanced?

EIGHT

Learning to Use the Pain

Jill Briscoe is a ministry leader at Elmbrook Church in Brookfield, Wisconsin, and a popular conference speaker. Among her publications are *Thank You for Being a Friend* and *Heart Strings*.

Dear Friend,

Disillusionment with fellow believers in church or mission can take many a young recruit out of ministry. It was certainly something nobody told me about. I learned to become part of the solution rather than part of the problem.

If someone had told me that just around the corner from my glad response of "Oh, yes Lord," to His invitation to enter into full-time work, I would be found in a pool of dismay muttering "Oh, no Lord," I would not have believed them! No one told me Christian institutions were full of imperfect people (like me!). Someone forgot to mention all my models were not models of perfection, but rather models of growth! Serving as a full-time worker in a Youth Center for ten years taught me that. But then if someone had told me, I would have gone ahead anyway believing it couldn't be "that bad" and maybe I could change it!

Another thing: if someone had told me how easy it would be to get too busy to be blessed, I wouldn't have believed them. Not me, with my disciplined record of quiet times, fasting and prayer, church-going and witnessing. Yet even now—forty years after entering the ministry—I struggle daily with my devotional disciplines. Knowing the little couplet "the devil trembles when he sees the weakest saint upon his knees," I should have been prepared. I don't know why I didn't expect a bad case of the "Martha, Martha" syndrome I was so familiar with in Luke 10:40ff. Jesus' beloved friend and servant Martha was "distracted by her much serving" and so was I. My daily struggle to make the choice to be found "at His feet" in the middle of the muddle continues to this day.

If someone had told me God would allow painful things to happen to our children if we ever entered full-time ministry, I wouldn't have believed them. Well, maybe little bad things; but not big things like debilitating sickness, devastating criticism, accidents, or divorce. These things happened to others of God's people in the "world," but surely we would be exempt. Of course, I knew we were all living in a spiritual war zone and the more dangerous we were to the devil, the more trouble we might find ourselves in; but somehow I expected a special dispensation. However, it wasn't long into our assignment that I found myself asking "why us?" only to receive His answer "why not?" I noticed that the Bible didn't say "a sparrow will not fall" but rather "a sparrow will not fall without the Father!" I was to reflect on that after our little girl had a serious accident. Our small sparrow testifies today that that was a spiritual high point which led to a personal knowledge of God.

If someone had told me that I would find myself like Elijah, flat on my face under my broom tree wanting to die, totally burnt out (1 Kings 19:3ff), I wouldn't have believed them. Surely God would help me stay full of the Spirit, rising up like the eagle, running and not being weary, walking and not being faint (Isa. 40:31). There have been not a few broom tree experiences for me. There have been times when like Elijah I have said, "I've had enough, Lord" (1 Kings 19:4). Yet if I'd never come to that point I'd never have known He is enough—adequate—my El Shaddai. I'd never have experienced what it takes to burn on instead of burning out.

If someone had told me I didn't have one gift that was expected of me in my role as pastor's wife, I wouldn't have believed them! Arriving in our first pastorate after ten years in youth ministries, I put paper to clipboard and naively went through the pews asking people in our congregation, "What do you expect of me as your new pastor's wife, because I really want to serve you?" To my horror, they told me! My husband, finding me devastated, suggested that because I couldn't do it well, I should do it badly! "But, I don't want to do it badly," I wailed. "I want to do it goodly!" "It's better it gets done badly than it doesn't get done at all," he pointed out. Just think, I could never have discovered gifts I didn't know I had unless I'd been willing to do it badly. Another thing. Over and over again as I muddled through my early days of ministry, doing my duty, rather then exercising my gifts, others who could do what I could not offered help! And that's the way we got all the jobs done!

Finally, if someone had told me about all the joy, all the fulfillment, all the good pain, all the pure pleasure, all the laughter, all the tears, all the friendships, and all the love there is in serving Jesus in the place of His appointment, I wouldn't have believed them. But I do now; and for this I humbly praise and adore Him!

Sincerely,
Jill Briscoe

Questions for Reflection

1. Does disillusionment with others have an adverse impact upon your attitude or morale? If so, how might you develop a more healthy and constructive response to the shortcomings found in others and yourself?

2. Do you find that serving God and others sometimes leaves you "too busy to be blessed"? If so, what adjustments do you need to make to become more like Mary and less like Martha?

3. Do you have unrealistic expectations about being "exempt" from the hardships of life because you are God's servant? Why do you think the Lord allows His servants to experience tough times so often here on earth?

NINE

Learning to Understand the Bittersweetness of Ministry

Stuart Briscoe has pastored Elmbrook Church in Brookfield, Wisconsin, since 1970. The church's ministry is extended through both a national television show and an international radio broadcast. Prior to coming to Elmbrook, Stuart served with Torchbearers, an international youth ministry. He has authored more than forty books including *Apostles' Creed, Ten Commandments, Fruit of the Spirit, Sermon on the Mount,* and *Choices for a Lifetime.*

Dear Friend,

No one tried to tell me in advance what I would experience as pastor of a local fellowship of believers. That is probably a good thing, for I doubt very much if I would have believed them. My prior experience of pastors and pastoring had been severely limited. Brought up in a very small community of believers that did not believe in the pastoral office and could not have afforded a pastor even if they had, I didn't know any pastors as a young person! When eventually I entered full-time ministry, it was in the context of parachurch activity where I met a number of pastors in a variety of situations, but only on an itinerant basis; that meant I was rarely with them for more than a week. As a result, my personal knowledge of the inside view of pastoral life was very sketchy and, I'm afraid, at times skeptical. But all that changed when I moved into Elmbrook Church still wet behind the ears! I began to learn the bittersweetness of pastoral life. And looking back over more than twenty-seven years with the same congregation, "bittersweetness" is the word that best explains my feelings.

Now you have no doubt heard the old adage that the pastor needs "the mind of a scholar, the heart of a child, and the skin of a rhinoceros," and there is a certain amount of truth therein. But I prefer to think of the pastor as a person called to be a servant of God, a proclaimer of truth, and a lover of people. And there's a bittersweetness to all three. What can be sweeter than to serve the One I love; but is there anything more bitter than the cross He sometimes calls me to bear? Is there anything more sweet than presenting the living Word of a loving God to a distraught soul, or anything more bitter than speaking a word of correction and reproof to an unrepentant erstwhile friend? And what on earth can be more bittersweet than to put your roots down in a community and allow your life to become inextricably intertwined in the lives of those around you? To share their joys? To feel their pain? To see them grow? And watch them self-destruct? Then see them restored? To laugh as they laugh, weep as they weep, rejoice as they rejoice?

In our more irreverent moments we pastors talk about some of the more formal aspects of our work as "hatching, matching, and dispatching," but beneath the jocularity we know that pastoring means being afforded the incredible privilege of joining with a young couple as they earnestly dedicate themselves and their newborn to the Lord. It entails leading a deliriously lovestruck couple into the intricacies of marriage and perhaps even the same day aiding a family in their grief as they bid farewell to a loved one summarily summoned to the world to come.

No one told me, or if they did I wasn't listening, that devoting myself to people on such a level would enrich me perhaps even more than it would benefit them! Within the confines of my own family I have, of course, known something of ecstasy and agony, but how much of both can you expect to experience if your life is limited to the parameters of genes? What I have gone through in my family has naturally changed me and hopefully improved me. But what I have been introduced to in the community of believers has taken me deeper and further that I could ever have imagined. I have been privileged to officiate (that's an awful word, but you know what I mean!) at the weddings of both my sons and my daughter. There's nothing quite like walking your daughter down the aisle, giving her away, and then stepping up on the platform to battle your emotions and lead her through the vows with the whole congregation taking great delight in watching to see if "old ironsides will finally crack!" He did! But imagine my additional joy in being God's agent in some mysterious manner whereby He joins together in marriage many of those whom I have known like sons and daughters throughout their growing years. That's sweet! But how bitter is it when some of them sadly come a couple of years later and

relate how—despite all their training and careful preparation for marriage, and all their vows and promises, hopes and aspirations notwithstanding—they have decided to "call it quits because they're not
compatible."

Can there be much greater joy than seeing the dawning of truth in
the darkened soul of a reprobate man and then over the years observing him grow in grace to become a pillar of society and leader in
the church? But then what can be more discouraging than to have a
promising young believer's ugly secret life exposed and upon pleading with him to come to repentance and experience restoration find
that he not only refuses to do so, but seeks to justify his behavior by
blaming everybody in sight (including you)?

On occasion, I must admit, I have felt like Paul when he said to the
Galatians, "Have I become your enemy for telling you the truth?" Let's
face it, none of us likes to be told what we don't want to hear, and
sometimes the pastor is the one whose duty it is to do just that. The
results can be nasty. But I must say that for every occasion that has
happened to me there have been a dozen where people have gone
out of their way to thank me for saying things that brought a word of
comfort, helped solve a problem, or perhaps simply helped dry an
eye. Their thankfulness is often so profuse I feel embarrassed, not
only because I did so little but because it was the obvious thing to do
anyway and, in my book, barely deserved thanks. But thankful they
are and repeatedly they remind me it is so.

Years ago I was called from my family Christmas-day celebrations
to a home where the father had died at the table from a massive heart
attack. There was nothing any of us could do. He was gone and the
shock and the grief were palpable. I said little; there is little to say in
moments like that. But they said much: "Thank you for coming. You
should be with your family. We're sorry we bothered you." Subsequently, whenever I met them they recounted the Christmas day I spent
with them in their grief and they told their friends about it as if they
had been visited by an angel.

Close to my home there is a small airport. I pass it regularly, but
never without thinking of my dear friend who one day took off in his
private plane and crashed in a white hot holocaust of twisted metal.
I took his funeral and I miss him all over again as I pass the scene of
his last journey. On an exterior wall of our church is a mural dedicated to the memory of one of our brightest and best teenagers. He
was killed one day while jogging on an icy road, and the dean of his
college called to ask me to inform his parents. I never see the mural
without a pang and I never talk to his parents without his name being mentioned, bringing a sad smile to our faces.

Wherever I go, the people of this fellowship to whom I've devoted many years of my life smile at me, their hands reach out to me and I hear their voices call my name. They inquire about my health; it matters to them. They ask about my kids; it's almost as if they think of them as their kids. They kid me and make rude comments about my hair (or lack thereof), they rib me about the disappearing British empire whenever I insist that the Fourth of July should be called "Rebellion Day." Yet in some strange way they let me know that I belong in their midst and they in some indefinable manner belong in my life. No one told me that being a pastor would be like this, and if they had I would never have believed it could be so sweet. Bittersweet.

Sincerely,
Stuart Briscoe

Questions for Reflection

1. To what extent does your ministry experience reflect the same bittersweetness described by the author?

2. How difficult is it for you to tell others the truth they may not want to hear but that they need to hear? If it is difficult, to what extent might you be more of a "man fearer" than a "God fearer"?

3. How close will you allow yourself to get to those to whom you minister? What will be the likely ramifications of your decision, positively and negatively?

TEN

Learning to Partner with God

Marshall K. Christiansen is Distinguished Professor of History and Culture and Executive Vice President for Administration at Western Seminary in Portland, Oregon. He also serves as provost at the Kazak-American College of Business and Humanities in Ust-Kamenogorsk, Kazakhstan. Marshall previously served as president at Warner Pacific College in Portland for fifteen years.

Dear Friend,

The practical realities of partnership with God permeate everything about Christian leadership. For me, the major lessons about those realities derive from fifteen years of experience as the president of a Christian college.

This college was my alma mater. I returned to the place where my student life and early teaching career formed an ideal model of Christian higher education. My vision of the future grew from my nostalgia about the past. Upon my arrival, however, some hard facts confronted my idealism: financial crisis, low morale, and uncertainty about the future. I asked—indeed begged—the Lord to be my partner in this daunting assignment. God's response was reassuring. I believe that the lessons I learned with God as my daily partner are applicable to Christian leaders in all sorts of situations.

Christian leaders communicate with God. Talking with God makes partnership a daily reality. Hold nothing back—your hopes and dreams, your frustrations and disappointments, your ideas and questions. Listen carefully. God is your greatest source of encouragement and your most demanding instructor.

Once, when it seemed that the pressure of securing funds to continue operations had led me to a point of unbearable stress, the Lord revealed Himself in an unforgettable way. Walking the campus late into the night, I told God that I no longer knew what to do. I could not take the pressure. His answer assured me that He cared, that He would show me His resolution, that our needs would be met until the time when His plan could be put into effect. That conversation with God is as real as any I have ever had with my wife! God's plan started to unfold within the month. Although the details would take almost two years to put into place, I never doubted that this was the work of my Partner. God's solution was one that I could not have imagined. It was perfect. The benefit of working with a partner whose strength and wisdom is unmatched becomes evident in the confidence that is essential to successful leadership.

Christian leaders respond to keenly felt needs. The burden of your heart defines your Christian call. Trust God's call upon your life. That burden directs you to needs in His kingdom work—the work that you are able to do. Under the pressure of leadership, maintaining daily focus on your call will help you stay on the main course.

My role in college administration grew from my burden for young people. How did God call people into His service? How could I be the kind of professor who could help students become all that God wanted them to be, not just great students of history? What would it take to guide this Christian college away from the brink of disaster while nurturing wonderful faculty and students? My burden led to my call to service; service led to partnership with God and with those who the Lord led to join the effort.

Many times a conversation with a student reminded me of why God had put me in this place. One such conversation occurred at our kitchen table. A young student athlete who saw the lights on in our campus residence knocked at the door. He brought all sorts of personal problems to college and, not understanding the standards of our life-style, he tested most of the rules. During a long conversation with this young man, God gave me the opportunity to share my Christian faith and the reasons for the values we affirm as God's people. He accepted the Lord as his Savior during his college years. Years later he called to ask if we still held students to high Christian standards. I assured him that we did. He was pleased, and that delighted me. His response reminded me of God's call upon my life.

Christian leaders seek the wisdom of colleagues. Trust the people who are on your team. Mistrust destroys community. Christian colleagues can handle the truth, even when circumstances are difficult. Sharing responsibilities demonstrates trust and builds a working team. Jesus trusted His disciples and they trusted Him.

One of the hard realities of the administrative tradition at my alma mater was that decisions had often come from the top down. During the first few weeks of my leadership, I recognized the problem. Once, for example, when the director of maintenance asked me what color he should use in painting an office, I told him that this was his decision. My response in this seemingly minor issue helped demonstrate the principle of trust. Eventually, in creating a management team with authority for most operational decisions of the college, this principle successfully transformed the administrative ethos of the college.

Christian leaders encourage others. Encouragement is a primary resource of leadership. When doubts prevail and hope for the future erodes, the leader bears special responsibility for illuminating the way so members of the team can see light on the path. One way to generate hope for the future is to help others see what God has already accomplished. In short, looking back may provide courage to move forward. Through our faith, the Lord moves mountains.

Expressions of appreciation in the form of a handwritten note, a phone call, or e-mail message work wonders in building morale. When employees left their positions at the college, we celebrated with them. These occasions helped us recognize accomplishments, affirm personal relationships, and demonstrate support for God's continuing call upon their lives. I can attest to the personal benefits of encouraging others. After fifteen years in office, one of my most cherished possessions is a thick file of notes of appreciation and encouragement that came back to me.

Christian leaders choose battles carefully and take risks wisely. In a culture that expects leaders to take charge, the temptation is to try to resolve every conflict. The effective leader learns to avoid petty matters and, when it is time to take risks, concentrate on those things that are for the good of the whole enterprise. God grants the gift of discernment.

A colleague from another college introduced me to a program that seemed like a perfect fit for our institution. I was convinced that this program could be developed at our college, that it was consistent with our mission, that it would increase enrollment and generate much needed revenue. A key leader of the faculty did not share my optimism about this opportunity. Rather than drawing a battle line, I withdrew. Conflict could have undermined the community we were working so hard to develop. Patience was rewarded two years later when faculty leaders endorsed the program. The outcome was a highly productive academic program, the work of a united community of faculty and administrators.

Christian leaders see the vision. Experts in business management remind us that a clearly defined mission is essential to every organization. The leader transforms mission into vision, thereby enabling members of the team to envision personal success within the context of corporate accomplishment. The Gospels show us how Jesus transformed mission into a new vision for His disciples.

A student once lamented that the campus provided no quiet place for daily prayer and meditation. His concern inspired a vision for the construction of a prayer chapel. As president of the college, it was my responsibility to envision the ways and means of fulfilling the dream of students. There were obstacles along the way, particularly among those who questioned the merit of this project among so many other worthy options. Realizing the obvious relationship between the mission of the college and the dream to build this chapel, donors caught the vision of this building. God blessed our efforts and when the project was complete our community was united in celebrating this beautiful and vitally useful addition to our campus.

Christian leaders meet the challenge. More often than not the challenges of leadership are imposed rather than chosen. Leaders select priorities and discover God-given resources to accomplish what must be done.

A former college president became an esteemed member of our faculty. Upon her advice, we requested a foundation grant that required a two-for-one matching amount by an agreed upon deadline. During the time allotted to raise the matching gifts, other priorities crowded my schedule. Finally, with just days to go it seemed like we might have to forgo the opportunity to claim this foundation gift. My responsibility was obvious—alter my schedule in order to go to see potential donors. On the last day to qualify, I was able to make a long-distance call to the foundation from the office of the donor whose contribution made the matching gift possible. The foundation president was delighted that we had met the challenge, and I knew that God had led me to donors who responded so generously.

Christian leaders put service to others first. Jesus set the example of service. Indeed, servanthood marks the unique quality of Christian leadership. The path of service is leadership by example.

My desire was that our campus would be clean and attractive. Picking up trash as I walked from place to place became one of my noticed habits. In a small way, my habit became leadership by example. It also made a statement: the president shared responsibility and no job was insignificant. My position offered daily opportunities for demonstrating the spirit of service: visiting students, faculty, staff, and friends of the college in times of illness; comforting a student who confided that she had never heard a parent say, "I love you;" writing letters of recommendation and helping those in transition discover God's direction in life. When you ask the Lord to help you recognize opportunities to serve others, your prayers will be answered.

Christian leaders practice what they preach. As the world looks on, inconsistencies between the way of Christ and our self-centered motives are noticed immediately. Consistency is recognized, only more slowly. Consistent integrity pays off in earned respect.

In devoting every ounce of my energy to the turnaround process that came with my position at the college, there were times when shining a bright light on successes and dimming the light on bad news was a major temptation. Integrity, however, demanded truth. Although it was painful, I wanted trustees to know the facts. Financial and enrollment reports, for example, had to reflect the whole truth. The same standard required a "no compromise" standard of morality, especially in interpersonal relationships.

Christian leaders discover joy on the journey. Wealth, fame, and power are idols of the world. God rewards in a relationship with Him and blesses our relationships with others. His rewards are superior in meaning and duration. So celebrate relationships.

The college environment was a gold mine for celebrating relationships. Graduation was always a time of celebration. Faculty and staff promotions generated celebration. Retreats with colleagues, banquets with students, guest lectureships, concerts, dramas, athletic events, and worship—each provided times for celebration. At times celebration was a cup of coffee and brief conversation with a friend before the beginning of a busy day. God wants us to be His joyful people. Discover joy in relationships.

May your partnership with God be the hallmark of your leadership.

Your colleague on the journey,
Marshall K. Christiansen

Questions for Reflection

1. How does your partnership with God honor the instruction of Jesus in Matthew 10:25, "for the student [you] to be like his teacher, and the servant like his master"?

2. In day-to-day leadership, how do you seek first to know God's will, then faithfully follow His direction (cf. Ps. 40:6–8)?

3. How does the Lord teach leaders to maintain their authority while building a spirit of cooperation in their community (cf. John 15:9–17)?

ELEVEN

Learning How God Develops Leaders over a Lifetime

J. Robert ("Bobby") Clinton is Professor of Leadership at the School of World Mission of Fuller Theological Seminary in Pasadena, California. He has served on that faculty since 1981. Clinton has developed the "leadership concentration," a series of leadership courses which focus on developing leaders and leadership concepts (and is unique among Bible colleges and seminaries). He is also the founder of Barnabas Publishers and the author of a number of books, including *The Making of a Leader*.

The following letter was written to a former student ("Bill") on the occasion of his thirty-second birthday. Bill was experiencing some difficulties in his church-planting ministry. Clinton sensed that he was a potential victim of "the abbreviated entry pattern," a circumstance in which potential leaders often leave ministry (typically within their first three-to-five years) due to a lack of discernment concerning God's providential shaping of their lives. Experienced mentors are especially critical at this stage, and that is the role Clinton is seeking to fulfill. In so doing he seeks to apply the leadership mandate found in Hebrews 13:7–8. The footnotes were subsequently added to enable readers of this volume to understand various concepts that would have been more familiar to Bill as a former student.

Dear Bill,

Oh, to be thirty-two again. Age is a matter of perspective, you know. From where I stand, thirty-two seems so young and fresh with vibrancy and the prospect of accomplishing so much for God. You have just begun to learn about life and leadership. And if the Lord should allow, there will be a long time of effective ministry ahead.

You have begun well. But remember the chess analogy. You must have a good opening game, a good middle game, and a good end game to come out on top. So now, you must continue well.

Over the past six to eight years you have gone through the early part of your Growth Ministry Phase.[1] During that phase of life much is learned negatively. God is doing more in you than through you.

Roles, relationships, and giftedness are often discovered via negative processing—what not to do, what you ought to do but can't yet. Early indications of the giftedness set[2] begin to emerge. That is normal and right. So cheer up and remember that God has a lifetime of processing in mind for you. You must continue well.

In wishing you a happy birthday and God's best, I wouldn't be me if I didn't also give some exhortation. So I want to pass on to you seven major leadership lessons[3] that have been emerging in my classes—and with each perhaps a probing question or two. Keep them in mind as you celebrate this thirty-second birthday and begin to think ahead to what God is going to lead you into. Age thirty-two is a good time to take stock and make some future resolutions by God's grace. Let my questions challenge you as you think of continuing well.

1. Effective leaders maintain a learning posture throughout life.

How are you doing on this one? Informal training—personal growth projects, personal research projects, reading, informal apprenticeships; non-formal training—workshops, seminars, conferences; formal training—continuing education, bringing closure on your previous program.[4] Are you still learning? Are you still in your Bible eager to learn? Are you learning from books, from people, from life? I certainly hope so. A learning posture is one of the major antidotes to plateauing, which is one of the barriers to keeping leaders from finishing well.

2. Effective leaders value spiritual authority as a primary power base.

If it is true that your natural abilities (organizational bent) and acquired skills along that line are focal[5] in your giftedness set, then this will be a crucial principle for you. One of the major problems of people who work with management skills in an organizational context is their lack of spiritual authority[6] (and consequently their reliance on positional authority). You must cultivate your spirituality—for it is spirituality from which spiritual authority flows. Are you sensing the anointing of the Lord in your life and ministry? Do you see spiritual authority in your ministry?

3. Effective leaders recognize leadership selection and development as a priority function.

Think back on your recent experience. Have you been developing people?[7] Are you alert to the potential leaders God is bringing around you? You should help people move further along in their development patterns. The basic principle underlying 2 Corinthians 1:3–4 applies: You are being taught by God in situations in order to share with others answers that carry with them your spiritual authority. God has met you. You should be able to help others see God meet them. This leadership lesson especially applies to your giftedness set. Remember that like attracts like so that people will be drawn to you who reflect some similarity to your gifting. Watch for them. Help them along. Whatever God has taught you is worth passing on to others in such a way as to move them along in their own development. Are you seeing potential leaders emerging in your ministry? Are you helping them develop? Closely related to this major lesson is the next one.

4. Effective leaders view relational empowerment as both a means and a goal of ministry.

One of the best means for developing people is through mentoring. Mentoring is a relational experience in which one person, called the mentor, empowers another person called the mentoree, by the transfer of resources (such as insights, skills, values, connections to people who can help, finances, other materials).[8] In writing this letter to you I am actually doing a mentoring activity. I am acting as a mentor-teacher and a mentor-counselor, that is, helping you learn some important perspectives that can help you in life and giving some advice that can both encourage you and give you some guidelines. I am an upward mentor for you—that is, someone older who has passed this way before you and can give perspective from my own experience. You will also need some peer mentors who recognize where you are in your development because they face the same problems, temptations, and opportunities. They can hold you accountable for your spiritual life. And you need to be mentoring some who are not as far along as you are. These multiple relationships in mentoring—upward, peer, and downward—provide a balance that can keep you on track as you persevere on in your Christian ministry. Well, how are you doing on mentoring? Do you have some mentoring relationships?

As you grow, don't be surprised that you will pick up new values that will affect your ministry philosophy. That is normal because . . .

5. Effective leaders who are productive over a lifetime have a dynamic ministry philosophy.

Three basal factors (the scriptures, giftedness, situation) define the dynamic quality of a ministry philosophy.[9] As you experience life you will see things in the Scriptures you had not previously seen that will affect your ministry philosophy. Your discovery of your giftedness set will also affect your ministry philosophy. Some of your giftedness set is just now becoming clear to you. You minister out of being—who you are. Giftedness is part of that. Your philosophy will be deeply affected by your giftedness. And since giftedness is not revealed all at once, your ministry philosophy can be expected to change as discovery prompts it. A third factor affecting your ministry philosophy involves the situation in which you are ministering. No two situations are the same. Your Baptist situation was not like your Anaheim situation. Nor is your present modified Reformed church situation like the others. Followers are different. Demands on leadership are different. These demands and situational differences will force you to alter your ministry philosophy. Focus in ministry philosophy usually begins to emerge in mid-to-late thirties. Articulation begins to emerge in mid-forties to mid-fifties. How are you doing on your personal ministry philosophy? You should be seeing hints of focus now. If you want to study someone who had focus in ministry read Charles Simeon's life. Are you seeing some major philosophy values emerging?

6. Effective leaders evince a growing awareness of their sense of destiny.

You are not in this endeavor of leadership alone. Remember God has touched your life several times in destiny experiences to assure you that He is going to use you.[10] Never take these experiences lightly. They are the divine road signs along the journey which affirm, begin to clarify the route, and open up final accomplishments at the destination. Sometimes I find it helpful to stop and go back over my list of destiny experiences and praise God and deliberately remember them before God. How are you doing on your awareness of destiny items? When you find yourself doubting or maybe even thinking of dropping out of ministry, go back to some of your foundational destiny experiences with God and let Him reassure you.

7. Effective leaders increasingly perceive their ministry in terms of a lifetime perspective.

We are back to where we started. Look at what has happened to you in terms of your whole lifetime and God's intentions in developing you. Remember that most of your Growth Ministry Phase has more to do with developing you than achieving great ministry accomplishments. So rejoice in all that God has taught you in these past six to eight years. And look forward to the coming years with a view toward seeing God bring focus to your life. In all of your present ministry don't be trapped to see just the now. Always see present ministry in terms of the bigger picture. Ask the questions, "How will this affect me in my overall development over a lifetime?" and "What is God doing in me that will affect the big picture of my life?" Remember, all of life is training you for all the rest of life.

Happy Birthday. Oh, to be thirty-two again!

Sincerely,
Bobby Clinton

As a special bonus for readers of this volume, Bobby Clinton added these additional thoughts concerning the above letter:

Five Results of Applying the Leadership Mandate

I like to interpret the command in the leadership mandate this way. "Think back on how respected Christian leaders lived and died and learn vicariously for your own lives." That is, lessons can be experienced "secondhand" and learned much more rapidly than might be the case if they were to be learned via direct experience only. I think that is the intent of the mandate.

What happens if leaders do seriously apply this command? Of course it depends on the leaders themselves. My experience with more than twelve hundred leaders who have seriously done this shows that five things happen to them. They:

1. experientially learn the providence of God.
2. sense a continuity of God's working in their past.
3. go away from the study with a high degree of anticipation that God is going to use them in the future.
4. learn vicariously through the experiences of those they study.
5. begin to perceive others in terms of the concepts learned from leadership emergence theory and thus become more deliberate in their use of these ideas in training of others.

The letter to Bill illustrates, at least in a token way, the fifth item.

We apply the leadership mandate in two major ways. One, we actually study leaders' lives and learn lessons. Two, we learn how to study leaders' lives. The methodology for studying leaders' lives is leadership emergence theory. We then apply this theory to the study of our own lives. Results 1 through 3 above are realized from the study of one's own life. Result 4 happens as lives of others (biblical, historical, or contemporary leaders) are examined. Result 5 happens spontaneously as a natural outflow of the paradigm shift[11] experienced in learning the theory.

Result 1, the providence of God, becomes real for leaders when they analyze their own past using the concepts of leadership emergence theory. The perspectives help them see "old familiar things" with new eyes. They personally perceive the providential working of God in their past. Their renewed reflection of past incidents with these new perspectives often results in fresh learning or closure which was not there previously. In short, they now see more clearly what God intended to teach them through those experiences.

Result 2, sensing a continuity of God's working, leads in turn to result 3. After the first step of sensing God's hand in many of the past incidents, a logical next step and one that many take is to begin to see a continuity between God's providential working in these incidents. There is a growing sense of destiny—an affirmation of God's working in their lives. Looking back and sensing the continual working of God up to the present naturally leads to result 3, anticipating God's hand in their lives in the future.

Result 3, anticipating God's use of them in the future, is probably the most worthwhile serendipity of the whole experience. The joy in seeing God's past working and identifying some patterns leading toward convergence gives rise to a firm anticipation that God is indeed going to use them greatly in the future. This anticipation becomes even stronger for some and becomes a sense of destiny. I have seen numerous missionaries coming to the School of World Mission at Fuller Theological Seminary in a burned-out condition or in the midst of uncertain boundary processing or in crisis. Many are ready to turn in their missionary badges and try some other vocation. And I have seen God turn them around and give a renewed sense of His presence and a holy motivation to accomplish something for the expansion of the Kingdom.

But it isn't just ability to perceive things through leadership emergence theory concepts that is helpful. God actually changes values through the principles seen in the lives of those studied. Many learn the lessons that Daniel and Joseph learned about integrity and sense of destiny and the sovereignty of God. Lessons of spiritual authority flow out of Watchman Nee's life. Those who study his life find that they desire spiritual authority to be their dominant power base. They are challenged by the word items in Nee's life. Those who study J. O. Fraser get a heavy dose of the power of imitation modeling. They get a fresh appreciation for the foundational place of power released in ministry through prayer. From Barnabas many catch the mentoring spirit. And many more will benefit from the future mentoring that will result. Those who study Titus see the value of ministry task as an informal training model that can be used to spot emerging leaders. It is amazing how many principles studied about someone of another culture have a cross-cultural application. Vicarious learning, the fourth result of seriously applying the leadership mandate, allows one to gain experience through another's life, often speeding up the process of personal development.[12]

Once you understand leadership emergence theory concepts it will be almost impossible for you ever again to look at leaders and emerging leaders in the same way as you did previously. You can't help using these concepts to help evaluate where they are and what God is doing and where they might be going next. And you can suggest lessons that God is intending with the items they are experiencing. In short, you will be able to mentor leaders and emerging leaders more effectively.

The manual, *Leadership Emergence Theory* or its popular counterpart, *The Making of a Leader* (NavPress), will help you obey the leadership mandate. By applying these concepts then you will learn how to assess good leadership and see how it emerges. You will learn how God intervenes in a leader's life to shape a good leader. You will find that you can readily apply these concepts to your life.

Questions for Reflection

1. Are you intentionally practicing lifelong learning? How might you draw greater profit from the learning opportunities found in informal, non-formal, and formal education?

2. Are you currently involved in "upward, peer, and downward" mentoring relationships? If one or more of these dimensions is currently missing from your life, what benefits might you be missing and what steps can you take to redress this omission?

3. Which of the seven leadership lessons cited by the author speaks most pertinently to your present circumstances, and what makes an understanding of that principle so timely for you?

Endnotes

1. He was in the provisional sub-phase of his Growth Ministry, the first time period after having entered into full-time ministry. I use a Ministry Time-Line to help me understand where a given leader is in his or her development. This is discussed in chapter 2 of my manual, *Leadership Emergence Theory*.

2. "Giftedness set" is a term describing the stewardship potential in a leader's life. It refers to the set of three elements that are symptomatic of a leader's capacity to influence: natural abilities, acquired skills, and spiritual gifts.

3. Not all of these seven major lessons necessarily appear in any one historic leader. They have been synthesized over many lives. Nor is there yet hard evidence that they are causal to the effectiveness in leadership though I believe there is a strong connection.

4. Three modes of learning are indicated here. *Informal* describes the deliberate use of daily activities and self-initiated growth projects as training means. *Non-formal* refers to organized yet non-programmatic learning which is experiential in focus and usually delivered via conferences, seminars, workshops, or local church institutes. *Formal* refers to programmatic institutionalized training. Historical leaders were strong in utilizing informal training. The other two modes were not that available. Today, in the light of the continuing education movement necessitated by the rapid pace of social change, all three modes are available. Learning must be a continuing process in the complex world of today. Leaders must know how to learn and must continue to learn as the dynamics of ministry change to meet the changing needs of society. Bill needed to complete a formal program that had been begun but not finished.

5. The focal element of a giftedness set refers to the dominant element of the set which could be natural abilities, acquired skills, or spiritual gifts. In this case I am suggesting that Bill's natural ability is the focal element. He is especially strong in his ability to organize things. When Bill took the leadership emergence theory course in 1982 he studied the life of Samuel Mills, an early historical leader whose focal element was the natural ability to organize and motivate people toward mission causes. If I am right about Bill, this fact of who he studied illustrates the concept of "the like-attracts-like" giftedness pattern discussed in *Unlocking Spiritual Giftedness—What Leaders Need to Know to Develop Themselves and Others*.

6. Power bases, the leader's perceived source of capacity to influence, are discussed further in my manual, *Leadership Emergence Theory*. Spiritual authority is one power base. It flows from perceived spirituality. Positional authority flows from an office held by the leader.

7. Charles Simeon (the wonderful Anglican church leader, 1759–1836) demonstrates this attitude superbly and certainly stands as one who should be imitated in the truest sense of the leadership mandate. Charles Simeon's life and ministry is treated in my book, *Focused Lives*.

8. See the book *Connecting—Finding the Mentors You Need to Succeed in Life,* coauthored by myself and Paul Stanley. This book introduces eight types of mentor functions and the Constellation Model, the kinds of basic help you will need: upward mentoring, peer mentoring, and downward mentoring.

9. The three basal factors (Scriptures, giftedness, situation) will result in a

ministry philosophy which is dynamic. That ministry philosophy can in turn be traced to the interplay of three ministry philosophy variables: blend (an integration of past and present leadership values—both of these the result of processing), focus (giftedness flowing toward destiny convergence), and articulation (the movement from implicit to explicit organization of leadership values into a strategy for ministry which has the ministry philosophy focus as its driving force). I discuss this in depth in my book, *Strategic Concepts—That Clarify a Focused Life.*

10. "Destiny Processing" is discussed in detail in my booklet, *Strategic Concepts.* A sense of destiny is an inner conviction that God's hand is on a leader and God will use that leader to accomplish His purposes through that leader. In essence, it is that touch of the Divine onto a life which gives ultimate purpose to a life beyond the finite.

11. A paradigm shift is a radical change in one's mental perspectives such that new things can be seen even from previous experiences. This is discussed further in chapter 6 of *Leadership Emergence Theory* in the processing section dealing with God's means of expanding a leader.

12. The Response Premise is an articulation of this fact and is one of the powerful motivating factors for studying this manual. This premise is a theoretical formulation worded as follows: The time of development of a leader depends upon his or her response to processing. Rapid recognition and positive response to God's processing speeds up development. Slower recognition or negative response delays development.

Learning from the Lessons of Others

Clyde Cook has been president of Biola University since 1982. Not only is Clyde an educator and administrator, but he is also a fourth-generation missionary. From 1963–1967 he and his wife served in the Philippines. He returned there for six months in 1971 to help establish theological education by extension programs. Additional leadership roles include the presidency of O. C. Ministries and trusteeships for Biola University, the Christian College Coalition (including one year as its chair), and the American Association of Independent Colleges and Universities (an organization for which he also served as president for two years).

Dear Friend,

In over eighteen years as CEO, I have learned a number of important lessons. Some of these were told to me and others I discovered the hard way.

The first lesson was learned early in my tenure, at a conference for new college presidents sponsored by the American Council of Education and the Association of Governing Boards. One of the speakers was Donald Walker, and he exhorted us as new presidents to be like a person in a snake pit. He said we should "keep moving but don't make any sudden, jerky movements."

As I reflect on my years as a president, I would say that his advice is excellent, not just for new presidents, but for *any* president. The people in the organization need to sense that you are providing leadership and direction and that the organization is moving ahead. However, particularly in academic institutions, they don't like sudden, jerky movements. I have found that faculty and staff appreciate consistency and are unhappy with surprises.

The second lesson I learned was that I am the *temporary* office holder of the presidency of Biola University. It would be easy to become enamored with myself and feel that I am "Mr. Biola," and that the whole organization revolves around me. This is a deadly perception, as the organization can function quite well without me. There have been other presidents before me, and there will be other presidents after me until the Lord returns, so it behooves me to hold the office lightly and to realize that it is temporary.

The third lesson that has stood me in good stead is realizing that this is *God's* appointment. I never had any aspirations to be the president. There are only thirty-two hundred of us in the United States, and it is difficult to declare oneself a candidate for the office and try to map out a career path to the presidency. In fact, by doing so it might assure one's quick removal from the list!

I look back and realize that being chosen for this position had nothing to do with my talents or gifts. It was the sovereignty of God. This realization liberated me, as I knew that He appointed me and I would serve Biola as long as He wanted me to serve.

Of course, this doesn't mean that I just sit in my office meditating on the sovereignty of God. He expects me to work and to work hard, and the demands of the office require a great deal of energy, wisdom, and commitment. But I realize it is because of the grace of God that I am there, and knowing this is both liberating and assuring.

The fourth lesson I'd like to share with you includes some thoughts on leadership that have helped me tremendously. In fact, I have them on little cards that stand up on my office shelves so I am reminded of them regularly.

The thought that I perhaps use the most comes from Herbert Bayard Swope: "I cannot give you the formula for success, but I can give you the formula for failure, which is: try to please everybody."

Only the president has a 360 degree responsibility for the organization. Everyone else has a slice of it, but the president has the whole. So every decision I make as president has perceived negative consequences for some part of the organization.

So as presidents we must realize that we cannot please everybody; after you have been in the office for a while, you will have offended almost every department as some decision you have made for the good of the whole is perceived negatively by a particular part of the organization. Since you cannot please everybody, it is futile to try to do so.

Under Swope's quote I have added a word from our Lord: "For I do always those things that please Him." I have to keep in mind that every decision I make and every action I take should be done to please the One who is really in charge of Biola University, our Lord Jesus Christ.

I have also learned a great deal from Peter Drucker and his insightful works. Here is a statement of his that I also keep in my office: "Results are obtained by exploiting opportunities, not by solving problems."

Solving problems just brings you back to neutral. As a president, I have to be careful that I am not spending all my time just solving problems, because if I am, I will miss the wonderful opportunities that God continually gives us.

David Alexander, president of Pomona College, echoes this same theme when he says: "It's the president's job to see that current problems don't completely obliterate future planning. That's one of the tasks of anybody in charge of an organization."

What both Alexander and Drucker are reminding us about is that we are not just managers but leaders, and we have to provide the leadership necessary for the college or university to accomplish its mission. This leadership demands exploiting opportunities, not just concentrating on problems.

There is much more that I could share, but I trust these central thoughts might be of help to you.

Sincerely,
Clyde Cook

Questions for Reflection

1. To what extent is your leadership characterized by "sudden, jerky movements"? What principles might help you become a positive change agent without creating unnecessary frustration in those you lead?

2. How well are you resisting the temptation to try to please everybody? Have you learned to place the greatest priority in pleasing the Lord as you serve Him and others?

3. Is your leadership properly focused on "exploiting opportunities" more than "solving problems"? What indicators might you watch for to discern an imbalance?

THIRTEEN

Learning the Components of Biblical Leadership

W. Robert Cook is professor emeritus at Western Seminary. He served in a variety of key roles at that institution before his retirement in 1994, including Professor of Biblical Theology from 1965–1993 and Academic Vice President and Dean of Faculty from 1969–1986. His teaching abroad includes ministry in Israel, Kenya, Holland, and Ukraine. He has authored *The Theology of John* and many journal articles.

Dear Friend,

God has called you to join a very ordinary company of brothers and sisters in carrying out an extraordinary task—serving the body of Christ in a leadership role. The privilege of such a calling, like your salvation, is a provision of sovereign grace; the responsibilities that accompany this privilege are anticipated by James when he writes, "Not many of you should presume to be teachers, my brothers, because you know that we who teach will be judged more strictly" (3:1 NIV).

What follows is not intended as a treatise on leadership. Rather, this is a series of maxims or proverbs which grow out of personal experience, observation of other leaders, and reflection upon biblical truth.

Start by being a good follower. This is what Paul had in mind when he said, "Follow my example, as I follow the example of Christ" (1 Cor. 11:1 NIV). Do not expect anyone to follow your leadership if you are not following His. Also, it is a good thing to serve under someone before having others serve under you.

Relating to character

Faithfulness is more important than success (1 Cor. 4:2). Keeping this in mind is a good ego manager, but should not be construed as an excuse for slipshod service.

Adhering to principle should transcend the desire for popularity. Ethical and moral standards as well as theological conviction should be based as much as possible on objective standards. This is not a license for meanness or pettiness, but it does give you a firm place to stand.

Respect grows from integrity rather than from rank or position. You can command obedience but not respect. It must be earned (see Matt. 20:20–28, especially vv. 25–26).

Do not forget that while you may function as a shepherd you do it as a sheep. What a tragedy if you were to lose touch with those whom you are leading. Further, that tragedy would be compounded if you ever forget that you, too, have a Shepherd (1 Peter 5:1–4).

Relating to speech

Listen before you speak (James 1:19–20). Too much counsel is given that was not asked for or needed. One of the reasons for listening carefully is to determine what is meant, not just what is said. In making this judgment do not rely on intuition alone. Instead make use of probing questions.

Do not make promises you cannot keep. One of the gifts of the Spirit to various members of the body of Christ is the gift of faith (1 Cor. 12:9). In the contemporary church this is sometimes called "vision." If you are a visionary, the church needs you. Remember, however, that all other members of the body are also gifted and all together are to complement one another with checks and balances. "The eye cannot say to the hand, 'I don't need you!'" (1 Cor. 12:21 NIV). Faith must be tempered with wisdom. Vision is not equal to groundless promises.

Keep confidences. A confidence is like a trust, and only the trustworthy are called upon to be trustees. Betraying a confidence is a sure way to lower your credibility and undermine your ministry (Prov. 13:3; 21:23).

Learn to pray in all circumstances as well as in the privacy of your prayer closet. Your days should be an ongoing conversation with your heavenly Father. Even in the midst of a busy schedule there are strategic moments of opportunity to give Him thanks, to express your adoration, to acknowledge your need, and to seek His help. "Pray continually; give thanks in all circumstances, for this is God's will for you in Christ Jesus" (1 Thess. 5:17–18 NIV).

Relating to discipline

Deal with problems in a timely manner, with both sensitivity and courage. In a timely manner does not necessarily mean immediately, although sometimes that is needed. It does mean deal with the problem sooner rather than later, after you have prepared your heart and mind to do so. Remember that you are often coming from a position of strength and authority as a leader, which may be quite intimidating. Therefore, be sensitive. On other occasions the person or problem may be most unpleasant. This will call for courage on your part to stand firm (see Matt. 18:15–17; Gal. 6:1–5).

Doctrinal correctness needs to be seasoned with graciousness. Avoid being offensive in defending the faith. If there is an offense let it be the offense of the cross. Be sure your zeal for truth is not misguided (Luke 9:54–56).

Follow through on your responsibilities as soon as possible. Putting things off is ultimately an act of showing lack of consideration for other people. Dereliction of duty is unbecoming to the servant of Christ. While you cannot manage others people's time, you can manage yours. For a businessman, time is money; for you, time is opportunity of which you should make the most (Eph. 5:15–16).

Never cease to be a learner. Before he called you to be a leader God called you to be a disciple (Matt. 11:28–30). As His disciple be open to learning more of His Word and His world.

Relating to balance

In an age of extremes between anti-intellectualism and intellectual snobbery avoid yielding to either. One of the curses of the contemporary church is a tendency toward mindless faith. Too often, how one feels determines how one thinks and acts. Yet our Lord said in Matthew 22:37 that we are to love Him with our mind as well as heart. We are to "think about" (evaluate with the mind) the true, noble, right, pure, lovely, and admirable (Phil. 4:8). In other words, feelings should yield to thought rather than vice-versa.

On the other hand, the mind that is so captured by rationalism and skepticism, that will accept nothing that cannot be proven empirically, has a deadening effect, at best, on the Christian enterprise. It eliminates any place for the spontaneity of the Spirit and childlike faith. Since faith is based on revelation (the God-breathed Scriptures) it is not irrational; since the revelation is divine, faith is supra-rational (Rom. 10:17; Heb. 11:1; cf. John 20:29).

Do not put too much stock in your press clippings, but never demean your worth as one created in God's image. Remember, "'God opposes the proud but gives grace to the humble.' Humble yourselves, therefore, under God's mighty hand, that he may lift you up in due time" (1 Peter 5:5–6 NIV). Remember also that false humiliation is a libel on God. Every human being is *imago Dei* and hence of unspeakable value; every believer is foreordained to be *imago Christi*, heightening that value to an infinite degree (Gen. 1:27; Rom. 8:29).

You will destroy your ministry if you only see the dark side of things. One who walks with God must be a realist but cannot be a pessimist. Both pessimist and realist see the world for what it is—godless—and mankind for what it is—totally depraved. The realist, unlike the pessimist, sees that fallen world seasoned with the salt of God's common grace, and looks for the redemptive work of His sovereign elective grace in the life of the unbeliever.

Do not become overly specialized in your ministry of the Scriptures. This is not a warning against having an area of personal expertise. The very fact that the Lord gifts us variously says that the body needs specialists to function in a healthy way (1 Cor. 12:7). Rather, this is a caution against letting your specialty become the tail that wags the dog. Put another way—avoid hobby horses. Emulate Paul's example and "proclaim the whole counsel of God" (Acts 20:27).

Relating to priorities

Seek to be known by what you are for rather than what you are against. The gospel is good news and thereby sets the tone and gives a framework for all of our ministry. While we are against sin, such a stand should be taken in light of God's invitation to repentance and offer of forgiveness. Do not extend the list of things that God specifically proscribes, or overlook the fact that many things are *adiaphora,* or abridge the things He approves.

Look for those few into whose lives you may make more personal investment. Some things can be done effectively en masse while other things must be done individually. Discipling falls into this latter category. Jesus, who ministered to multitudes, only selected twelve from among the many to, "be with him" (Mark 3:14 NIV). Paul gave a pattern for discipleship to Timothy, his "true son in the faith" (1 Tim. 1:2; 2 Tim. 1:2), which he himself followed with men and women (e.g., Timothy, Titus, Barnabas, Phoebe, Lydia).

If you are interested in making a name for yourself, get out of the ministry. Even the Holy Spirit, the third person of the Godhead, has a self-effacing ministry. He functions to glorify the Son (John 16:13–14). It ill behooves us to seek the spotlight when the focus should be on the Savior. As Paul said, Christ should have supremacy in all things (Col. 1:18). John the Baptist's motto should be ours: "He must become greater; I must become less" (John 3:30 NIV).

Relating to wisdom

Being decisive does not preclude seeking wise counsel. Two of the things that should characterize your leadership are that you must be a consensus builder and then, having done that, you must take the lead in pursuing the task at hand. If you expect people to follow you there must be evidence that your judgment is sound (Prov. 3:21–24); that where you are leading them is a good direction to go; that you are willing to accept the cost and risks of leadership (cf. Paul's example in 1 Thess. 2:7–9 and Phil. 4:10–13); and that your ideas have been tested at the bar of wise counsel (Prov. 12:15, 13:10). How will you know that the counsel you receive has validity? James tells us that wise counsel will be "pure; then peace loving, considerate, submissive, full of mercy and good fruit, impartial and sincere" (3:17 NIV). And, how will those you seek to lead know whether your counsel is valid? By using the same set of guidelines.

As you set out on the adventure of leadership in the body, do it with the servant mind of Christ (Phil. 2:1–11), considering Him, "so that you will not grow weary and lose heart" (Heb. 12:1–3 NIV).

Your fellow servant,
W. Robert Cook

Questions for Reflection

1. What have you learned from being a follower that can help you become a more effective leader?

2. Examine yourself in the various dimensions of wise leadership cited by the author. In which of those dimensions are you the strongest? The weakest? What steps might you take to address significant weaknesses?

3. Are you vulnerable to "growing weary and losing heart"? If so, how might "considering Jesus" strengthen you?

Learning from Biblical Images of Leadership

Robert E. Cooley is the chancellor of Gordon-Conwell Theological Seminary, having recently retired from that school's presidency. He has also served as senior editor for *Christianity Today,* chairman of the World Relief Corporation, and president of The Association of Theological Schools in the United States and Canada. His special interest in the fields of archaeology and biblical studies has prompted him to make sixty trips to the Near East.

Dear Friend,

Leadership is a world of action as well as a world of knowing. It is one thing to understand the meaning and nature of leadership, but quite another thing to live it.

Recently, I retired from the position of President of Gordon-Conwell Theological Seminary, South Hamilton, Massachusetts, and now serve that institution as Chancellor. I have been in transition from "work to service." Transitions are a very real part of the human experience. They represent movement from one state of being to another and involve separation at the front end and reincorporation at the back end. All human passages involve these three dimensions: separation, transition, and reincorporation. Such experiences as birth, marriage, or death are marked by these characteristics.

Retirement is one such transition. It involves movement from one state of activity to another. I prefer to view retirement as the transition from work to service—from formal expectations, responsibilities, accountabilities, and regular fulfillment to informal relationships, relaxed status, and new time categories. The biblical book of Numbers (8:23–25) explains the retirement of the Levite and helps us to understand leadership transition. At age fifty, a Levite retired from daily work in and around the tabernacle to render varied forms of service throughout the ceremonial complex. Such a procedure allowed younger Levites to enter into the sacred work, and yet retained the experienced Levite within the community where he could continue to contribute to the "system." This sustained the stability and continuity of the people of God. One way to view this movement of Levitical retirement is to see it as a transition from the world of work to the realm of service.

In a personal way, the transition from President to Chancellor is movement from full-time work to part-time service, from initiative and intense pressure to being contributor of helpful and meaningful service. But what is a Chancellor? Such an office is quite common in today's world of higher education and there is a range of position descriptions. Historically, the position is rooted in European history. The term comes from the Latin *cancellarius* meaning "doorkeeper." Chancellors can be found in many settings such as the chief secretary of the king of England, an officer in an embassy, one of the chief dignitaries in Anglican cathedrals who arranged services and lectured on theology, a Roman Catholic priest serving a bishop, the titular head of a British university, and in many European countries, those who act in the duties of the Prime Minister. In American higher education it is a person of high rank who may even serve as chief officer over a state system of schools. In some cases it is used as an honorific title. In my instance, I serve the Seminary's President as adviser, and assist in the resource development and representation of the institution. Together, we seek to advance the mission of the school. Although the call to service still burns bright, my human limitations are now more noticeable. I am long past fifty! As the "old Levite" continued to function by serving his brothers, it is a joy to serve at a slower pace and at the boundaries of the institution.

The subject of leadership has engaged much of my thinking in recent years, especially during this time of leadership transition. It is such a needed dynamic in the church and the world. We examine and evaluate leaders; yet, at the same time, we ignore leaders. It seems to me that four qualities are essential for effective leadership:

Integrity. Being true to God is at the heart of Christian integrity. Being true to His commands and to His call are involved. This is a work of the Holy Spirit. You cannot buy integrity at a local workshop. It comes as we submit ourselves to the Lordship of Jesus Christ. It is not the result of our personal agenda. Integrity results in credibility— a credible leadership.

Love. The leader who loves God will love people. Leaders are moved with compassion. Their actions are motivated by love. A burning love has a warmth that draws people into the leader's circle.

Vision. A leader without a vision will wander in the desert of confusion. Strategies, goals, and direction flow from vision. Vision operationalizes the mission. I believe that a vision is born of God. It will have holding power, sustaining a leader through hard times. Visions are nurtured in the devotional life.

Humility. Our calling is the basis for humility. A driven leader is often rude, showy, and pushy. Jesus said that those who humble themselves shall be the greatest in the kingdom (Matt. 5:5). Christian leadership depends upon the denial of self. In this way we find ourselves.

The standard for Christian leadership is not power, money, status, or worldly acclaim—it is servanthood. "Whoever wants to become great among you must be your servant" (Matt. 20:26 NIV). It is my prayer that you will always serve God's people in integrity, love, vision, and humility.

As I reflect upon a lifetime in leadership, I wish someone would have told me about the need to balance "leadership knowing" and "leadership doing." There must be balance! Theory needs to be informed by practice, and practice must proceed on a foundation of coherent theory. There are libraries filled with works on leadership theory and thought. After reading leadership book after leadership book I realize how important it is to study models of leadership in action. I struggled for years to understand fully the practice of leadership and in so doing observed many leaders in action. I learned much from watching leaders in the world of politics, business, the professions, and society. This was helpful, but more insight and better models were needed.

My many years of travel and study in the lands of the Bible awakened within me an understanding and appreciation for images of leadership that provide a clearer conceptualization of the defining nature and roles of ministerial leadership. Contemporary images of leadership do help in understanding traditional roles of ministry—wounded healer, practical theologian, theological liberator, or executive leader. However, my discovery of biblical images has allowed me to understand and practice leadership in a more profound way in keeping with the light of the gospel and the purpose of Christian ministry. The image of shepherd, servant, steward, and seer focuses on activities that illumine the world of leadership in action. So often we as leaders are called upon to function in multiple roles.

Before we look at the biblical images for leadership we need to agree that *leadership is a relationship.* Our activity is one of persuading for a voluntary response, of helping a group to focus on its mission. Relationship underscores everything that we do. *Shepherd, servant, steward,* and *seer* are images that take on rich meaning in the context of our relationships.

The biblical image of shepherd suggests a peaceful, pastoral picture of a person who cares for the sheep. Makmud was just such a shepherd. I became acquainted with Makmud, a local shepherd, during my periods of excavating ancient Dothan. He taught me many things about the life of a shepherd. Shepherds love their flocks, call sheep individually by name, search for the lost ones, and risk their very lives to protect the flocks from predators and danger. Leaders in the ancient world were known as the "shepherd of their people" (Ezek. 34:1–10). But not all shepherds were called "good." There were many who were thieves and hirelings (John 10:8–13). A first-century shepherd was often viewed as being unreliable and lacking responsible action in all relationships. Jesus, with purpose, modified the image of the shepherd with the adjective *good*. He is saying that shepherds do not need to be self-centered and focused on self-advancement and selfish concerns. Loving, knowing, caring, are the essential dimensions of the good leader. Leadership life finds focus in a concern for the welfare of others. The leader who will be the shepherd of people will help them grow and through this relationship empower others.

The biblical image of steward involves management and money. The various words used in the Bible mean delegated responsibility or managerial oversight. It is a powerful image for care and responsibility. The steward was one who acted on behalf of an owner, and this action required the supervision of others and the management of products and money. Responsibility was always delegated to the steward, and there was a high level of accountability. As it relates to the resource realities of an organization or an institution, an effective leader must be able to manage and control the raising of money and the spending of money. The leader, as a steward, implements a vision in practical ways. These ways involve the legal responsibility for the oversight of the conduct of people, managing policies in an orderly fashion, establishing orderly relationships for decision making, and engaging a planning process if goals are to be achieved. This imagery is a powerful symbol for the leader's life of stewardship, care, and responsibility.

The biblical image of servant underscores the essential mission of leadership—service to others. It is all too easy to be caught up in the leadership trappings and circumstance and in the dangers of self-centeredness. An effective leader will lose self in freely giving service to others. Jesus sought to instill within His disciples the desire to be servants to one another. They understood themselves to be "servants of God" and "servants of Christ." Serving others is leadership in action. We must live in balance between serving and leading. This is a good tension. In fact, the authority to lead comes through loving service.

In the ancient world, servants of different gifts and skills served in the households. Likewise, leaders serve others through the sharing of the special gifts with which they have been endowed and the expert skills that they have developed. The leader as servant seeks to serve the purposes of God and the good of others. At the very heart of ministry is service. The servant imagery is thus also central to our understanding of leadership.

The biblical image of seer underscores the visionary quality of leadership. The prophets of old brought the word of the Lord to bear upon the contemporary issues. Their visions of hope and justice energized their prophetic proclamations and actions. It seems to me that a leader stands in a similar circumstance. The leader must be a student of contemporary times and culture, and with visionary leadership guide toward response and global service. Often this will require the elimination of obsolescence and that which has either failed or been in error. Other times this will call for blazing new frontiers and walking in the unknown. Such leadership ignites into a vision that burns brightly and attracts others. We must be students of the contemporary scene and gather fresh insight, after which the data and observations need to be evaluated. Needs and trends that are determined to be significant must then be acted upon. Like the biblical seer the leader leads with a vision of hope—transforming dreams into reality.

The biblical images of shepherd, steward, servant, and seer provide an understanding of unique qualities that are formational and descriptive of the effective leader. No single image is adequate to describe the full task but rather the task requires the interaction and demonstration of all of these qualities and images. They are blended and bonded together through God's call to leadership service. Obedience to that call is in living out the hope that is both personal and communal. Hope, after all, is a gift of God.

On a beautiful fall day in November 1984, Dr. Harold John Ockenga, my predecessor as president of the Seminary, invited me into his office for a sermon. Little did I realize this would be his last one—preaching to a congregation of one. His text was Titus 1:5: "The reason I left you in Crete was that you might straighten out what was left unfinished and appoint elders in every town, as I directed you" [NIV]). The sermon topic was "God's Purpose in Your Life," and the main points were:

  I. You have unfinished work to do.
 II. Prepare pastors for every town.
III. You have been prepared to lead.

Dr. Ockenga shared with me his life and ministry, his dreams and vision, and his heart for world evangelism. We prayed together and he handed me the outline. I cherish that document as an expression of "the man who plants and the man who waters have one purpose, and each will be rewarded according to his own labor. For we are God's fellow workers; . . . For no one can lay any foundation other than the one already laid, which is Jesus Christ" (1 Cor. 3:8–9 NIV).

It is really of little consequence whether you "know" leadership; it is all important that you "live" leadership. Leadership is faith in action.

Sincerely yours,
Robert E. Cooley

Questions for Reflection

1. As you reflect upon effective models of "leadership in action" you have observed, what contributed to the effectiveness of those leaders? How might similar attitudes and skills be nurtured in your life?

2. As you think about the four biblical images of leadership described by the author, which come easiest for you? Which are the most difficult? In what ways might you build upon your strengths while addressing any critical weaknesses you discern?

3. If your predecessor in the leadership role you occupy offered you any advice during the transition, review what was shared with you. To what extent has that advice been "on target"? What counsel might you desire to share with your successor?

Learning a Marathoner's Mentality

Bert Downs is President of Western Seminary in Portland, Oregon. He earlier served as Executive Director of Pine Summit Christian Conference Center in Big Bear Lake, California and was Executive Vice President of Walk Thru the Bible Ministries, for whom he continues to teach seminars.

Dear Friend,

In 1983 I participated in an event that would radically change my life and the way I view leadership. It wasn't a particularly spiritual event, at least on the surface, but it definitely turned out that way.

Nineteen-eighty-three was the year I ran my marathon. Well, actually, it was the Portland Marathon. I just consider that year's event to be mine!

The prior year's speaking schedule led me into a study of perseverance in the faith, especially as that applies to leaders. It quickly became apparent that a "marathoner's approach to life" is called for—a leader must be a finisher, not of sprints, but of marathons. And what better way to learn about the marathon attitude than to run in one! So, following a year's worth of training, I donned the gear of the runner one bright September morning and joined about three thousand other runners not just in a marathon, but in a life-changing adventure.

It's from that adventure that what I'm going to share with you took shape. Actually, it continues to take shape. Learning about the marathon is a lifelong growth experience. My guiding biblical passage has become Hebrews 12, as it unlocks so many facets of the marathon mind-set. Credit for finally bringing these thoughts together belongs to a group of missionaries-in-training who asked me to present a seminar answering this question: "What have you learned in twenty-five years of ministry leadership that can help us finish our ministries well?"

The result was a workshop entitled, "Living Life with a Finishing Touch," a summary of which I wish to share with you in this letter. In a culture that values the initiator's approach to leadership, it's important to grasp that God is looking for leaders who are finishers. It's vital, therefore, for those who are called to Christian leadership to begin their respective races with that reality clearly in view.

1. Train to be a marathoner

Hebrews 12:1 urges those who would be mature in following Christ to ". . . run with endurance the race set before us" (NASB). The word translated race is the Greek word *agōn* from which we get the English word agony. This race is filled with struggle, contention, and conflict. The primary ingredient it requires of a finisher is endurance. We who would take on this race must do so by understanding its basic demands and realities, and then actively train for it.

This is not a once-in-a-while training, but a disciplined, everyday kind of approach through which the runner purposes to build spiritual muscle and stamina for the stages of the race ahead. This is the point at which the runner personalizes the principle popularized today by writers like Kenneth Blanchard and Steven Covey: begin with the end clearly in view. The leader-marathoner must envision the stages of the entire race and prepare for each.

In an actual marathon there are several stages in the race: there's the euphoric stage of the beginning when adrenaline and excitement prevail—when enthusiasm and energy are plentiful. That stage will eventually fade into a routine stage where the body and mind are functioning smoothly and the race is going as planned. The routine will eventuate into a struggling stage where some runners will hit the proverbial wall. During this stage, the urge to quit will try to dominate the runner. Many would-be leaders stop at this stage and begin to look for another race to start. However, the true marathoner fights through and enters a finishing stage. In this stage, the finish line comes clearly into view, the struggle is once again replaced with a joyous anticipation of the finish—and satisfaction and fulfillment become the dominant feelings as the finish line nears.

As the finish comes into view, the runner must stay diligent and on the alert. The marathoner's greatest danger will be letting his guard down during the final stretch and stumbling before he reaches the line. Five elements essential for the finisher's training kit are: truth (a deep commitment to and growing practice of God's Word), prayer (a lifestyle of intimacy with the Ultimate Encourager), pace (an understanding of how God has wired you regarding gifts, talents, personality, energy, and relational tendencies and how you'll need to manage those to be a finisher), rest (sprinting an entire marathon isn't possible, so learning how to renew oneself without stopping the race is critical), and finally, laughter (defeat the grind of the *agōn* with an open joy for the race, the road, and the reward at the end).

2. Build endurance (perseverance)

Endurance grows from a steady determination to be a finisher and adopting a corresponding approach to life. After a year of hard training for the 1983 Portland Marathon, I learned this critical truth: endurance only comes when you're willing to persist through the discipline, pain, joy, laughter, tears, and determination that training requires. And even though I trained well and finished at my projected goal (four hours), I realized that I hadn't touched my potential for developing endurance.

For the spiritual marathoner, endurance is something always being developed—he trains as he races, always getting ready for the next stage of the race. Paul directs the leader-marathoner in 1 Corinthians 9:24–27 to "Run in such a way that you may win. . . . But I buffet [train] my body and make it my slave, lest possibly after I have preached to others, I myself should be disqualified" (NASB). There is a constant disciplining of oneself (training) that's required of the Christian leader who would build endurance to make it to the finish.

3. Internalize the truth that endurance has a purpose in your life

The agony of the endurance-building process is pointless unless there is a purpose. Providentially, there are two purposes: one directed Godward and one very attached to the runner himself. The first is that the enduring runner who finishes his race brings glory to God even as Christ brought glory to Him. Joyfully, we follow in the footsteps of the Master in honoring the Father.

The second purpose is ordained by God to cause something to happen to me. James puts it this way: "Consider it all joy, my brethren when you encounter various trials, knowing that the testing of your faith produces endurance. And let endurance have its perfect result, that you may be perfect and complete, lacking in nothing" (1:2–4 NIV). Do you see it? What happens to you as you build endurance? God does something; He takes you through a process of becoming perfect, complete, lacking nothing. If leaders are known by maturity, then this is how maturity arrives—through God's building endurance in the leader as he purposefully trains to run the race God has set before him.

4. Develop the focus of a finisher

During my marathon, I hit the wall—at mile 18—8.2 miles from the finish. Every body part hurt. Even worse, my mind had just one thought: "Are you crazy? Just quit and the pain will be over!" I ran two more miles in that kind of torture, and would indeed have quit except for this: At my worst moment, another runner ran up along side me. He was running with ease and grace—but when he saw my condition, he slowed his race to bring me along. I basically fixed my eyes on him, followed him step for step, carefully heard his words of encouragement, and guess what? I made it to the finish. The spiritual finisher fixes his eyes on Jesus, hears His words of encouragement, runs as He ran: focused on the purpose, not distracted by the inevitable distracters, and aiming for the reward.

5. Systematically shed everything that can hold you back

Get rid of the encumbrances, the writer to the Hebrews says (12:1). The true marathoner knows there are things that, left unattended, can hold him back—even cause him not to finish the race. Unproductive habits, poor self-discipline, ineffective relational styles, expectations that are too low or too high, poor work patterns, material possessions. Whatever your list of possible encumbrances, it's an important one, and it must be realistically faced and purposefully dealt with.

When I began my travel down this leadership road twenty-five years ago, one of the big encumbrances for me was related to possessions. While pay wasn't big in my chosen field (education), I had been promoted quickly and learned to enjoy the perks of those promotions. When I began actively to follow Christ, many new priorities collided with those possessions. To run the race, I had to shed myself of those possessions that were holding me back. Interestingly enough, that process never stops. Just recently, my wife and I sold our house and moved into an apartment. Why? Because the house and what it demanded in terms of time and resources was getting in the way of long-standing spiritual priorities. Was this change easy? No, in many ways, it was a lot like hitting the wall in a marathon. However, Alice and I, after the fact, agree on this: with the dropping of this encumbrance we are both enjoying a renewed sense of freedom in the Lord and in our race. You never outgrow the need to be active in this process of freeing yourself for the race God has set before you.

6. Welcome the discipline of the Lord as a friend helping you to the finish

Paul writes in Romans, "For we all have sinned and fall short of the glory of God" (3:23 NIV). Yes, we all often aim as well as we can, and even so, miss the mark. Unfortunately leaders, if they are not careful, can begin to think they can't miss the mark. Often a series of successes will cause the leader to think everything will be a success. To accept the disciplining hand of God under such circumstances can become a difficult thing.

The marathoner develops a life characterized by recognizing the need for—and the welcoming of—discipline. He wants to waste no energy or time by heading in any direction that isn't toward the finish. He eagerly receives direction from the Coach—direction that gets him back on target when he has strayed, direction that keeps him on target and focused on the finish. Proverbs associates this welcoming of discipline with a life of wisdom: "My son, do not reject the discipline of the LORD, or loathe His reproof, for whom the LORD loves He reproves, even a father, the son in whom he delights" (3:11–12 NASB) A soft, moldable heart that is willing to receive discipline is rare among leaders, but absolutely essential for the leader who is committed to being a finisher.

In my early days of leadership in public schools (I was twenty-three when I became a high school principal), I experienced a lot of success, and with that success developed an attitude with a capital A. I didn't receive discipline well. One day the superintendent of the district called me into his office, closed the door, and confronted me regarding this attitude. His final words to me were: "If you don't come to grips with this and change, you'll have ended your growth as a person and a leader." I thank God for that man who cared enough to risk the relationship to make an eternal difference in me. His words have helped me continue the race when, left to my own nature, I would have self-destructed many times over. Learn to welcome discipline.

7. Run for the crowd

As I finished that 1983 marathon, a discovery awaited me at the tape: The spectators had gone home! So who was at the finish line to greet those who endured? Not the spectators, but the ones who had finished the race before us. As we crossed the finish line they cheered as if they had just finished. I hung around and cheered for some myself; it was a wonderful experience. In finishing the race, we shared in something very special.

Days afterward, it came to me that the spiritual race has the same quality. A great throng of winners, finishers, has gone on before us (Heb. 12:1). Not only that, there is a great crowd running with us, right now, even though we don't often think of fellow believers in that way. Further, should the Lord delay His return, an even greater group may follow. And in a very real way, I'm running for all of them;

I don't want to let them down. On the tough days I think of them: the ones who set the pace in front of me, the ones running beside me watching and following my pace, and the ones who will follow. And I run for them so like Paul I can say, "Imitate me, even as I imitate Jesus Christ."

My friend, aspiring to Christian leadership is a wonderful thing—being called to it even more so. Remember, it is a call to a race—not a sprint, not a 10K or half-marathon, as challenging as they can be—but to the *agon*, the marathon which will test every fiber in your being.

Have I ever known anyone who ran the race as I've described it? Yes, thankfully, I know many such marathoners. But let me tell you specifically about one. Call her Pat. She wouldn't describe herself as a leader. Hardly! In fact, for most of her life she'd describe herself as a loser—an obnoxious, hateful person who, next to herself, hated God most of all. Yet, by a work of His grace and the persistence of a loving nephew (a marathoner himself), Pat was introduced to Jesus and eventually received Him as her Savior. For her, the race was intense, only to last a few years. It began with great energy and enthusiasm, but soon became a struggle. Years of personal neglect and self-abuse began to take their toll as Pat's body began to self-destruct. She had several heart attacks, lost both of her legs below the knees to the results of diabetes, and experienced failure of both kidneys. By the end of her life, her body was one huge surgical scar.

Yet through it all, Pat endured and God did what He says He will do: He brought Christ-like qualities to her life that neither she nor others believed could ever be there. During her final days on this earth, Pat led many people to Christ as nurses, doctors, and caregivers were all touched by the majesty God had invested in this woman. At her funeral, several described her as the most beautiful woman they had ever met; hers was a beauty not of this world, but of the eternal God. He had, through the race, the *agōn,* made her into His bride. It was said of her by all who came to say good-bye on that day, "She finished well!"

My fellow Christian leader, that is one of the most important things that can be said of you and me in this world. It's my goal—and it's my prayer for you—that together we would finish well, to the glory of God! I look forward to running the race with you.

A fellow marathoner,
Bert Downs

Questions for Reflection

1. How much prayerful thought and preparation are you putting into "finishing well"? What elements should be added to your training program to help you complete your spiritual marathon? What encumbrances are complicating your running that need to be discarded?

2. How well do you receive discipline? What attitude adjustments might need to be made in order for you to become more open to constructive criticism from others?

3. To what extent are you helping fellow marathoners run well? How might you become an even greater encouragement to your brothers and sisters who are running with you?

SIXTEEN

Learning to Make Prayer a Priority

Dee Duke has pastored Jefferson Baptist Church in Jefferson, Oregon, for the past twenty-one years. When he first came to the church, it consisted of approximately twenty-five believers. Today the church averages nearly eight hundred in weekly attendance, even more amazing when you consider that the entire community has a population of less than two thousand! Dee attributes this growth to the faithful practice of individual and corporate prayer, and it is about this emphasis that he writes the following letter.

Dear Friend,

I grew up on a dairy farm in Washington State. My three brothers, my sister, and I were raised by a dad and mom who had both gone through the Great Depression and who believed strongly in the principle that hard work was a key to being successful in life. Naturally, we too were taught to work hard and to enjoy it. Even today I find myself regularly thinking about all that I should get done in order to be faithful to my responsibilities, and repeating "thoughts" that I had heard from my father many times as I worked alongside of him trying to get ahead in life. I consider this strong sense of responsibility a great legacy from my parents.

As I began pastoring twenty-one years ago I brought with me the work ethic that I had learned from my parents on the farm. My basic philosophy of life was, "There is nothing I can't accomplish if I just work hard enough." My favorite verse was Proverbs 14:23, which says, "In all labor there is profit, but mere talk leads only to poverty" (NASB). Our church was a new work, meeting in the public grade school gym with about twenty-five people, but I knew that I could build a great church if I worked hard and was faithful.

Things went very well for the first seven years of our ministry, and we grew to an average attendance of two hundred people. We had purchased some land and built a new sanctuary, all with donated labor from our congregation and paid for with cash. We were dreaming big ideas, setting big goals for the future and were planning on building a great church that would bring much glory to God. It all seemed so noble, and I was feeling so successful because all the long hours of labor were paying off.

At the end of the seventh year (about January of 1984), things began to change. I found myself experiencing some intense times of depression that I couldn't explain and that I couldn't "work" out of as I had always done before. I was having very severe headaches that no amount of aspirin would fix, and as I became more and more tired I began to lose my fire and passion.

At the same time I began to receive more and more criticism from people in our congregation who had been so loyal and had worked so hard with me to accomplish all that we had done together. People began to leave our church, and when I would ask "why?" the response would often be, "We just don't feel that you love us." It was a frustrating response because I didn't know how to fix it. I didn't know what kind of work was needed that I wasn't already doing, and I began to feel bitter toward people because they didn't appreciate all that I was doing for them. My response to those leaving was that they were just uncommitted, lukewarm Christians who weren't willing to pay the price of true discipleship.

I should have caught a glimpse of the problem from the response of a lady in our congregation after one of my sermons. I was preaching on Ephesians 4:11–12 which says, "He gave some as apostles, and some as prophets, and some as evangelists, and some as pastors and teachers, for the equipping of the saints for the work of service, to the building up of the body of Christ" (NASB). I was emphasizing how I needed to equip them to do the work, and I really emphasized the need for work. She had heard the word "equip," and sincerely thought I said, "whip." Her response to me was, "I knew that was your style, but I didn't know it was in the Bible."

Over the next five years we had some good things happen but the fruit didn't last, and I got more and more weary with the work of ministry. By the end of 1988 I was almost completely burned out and exhausted. I was feeling discouraged, disillusioned, confused, and guilty. I knew that all the problems we were having in our church must be my fault, but I just couldn't figure out what it was that I needed to start or stop doing to turn it all around. I felt like a total failure as a pastor, and I was making plans to resign and go back to farming.

About that time, I received a form letter from Dr. Joe Aldrich, then president of Multnomah School of the Bible. He was inviting all the pastors in and around Salem, Oregon, to the Coast for four days of praying. I didn't really want to go, but the thought of four days away from the pressure was appealing, and I thought it would be a great time to figure out what I was going to do with the rest of my life—and also to write a letter of resignation from my church.

So I went to Cannon Beach, Oregon, in February of 1989, and those four days completely turned me upside down and inside out. I came face to face with what I was doing and my motive for doing it. The words of Jesus to Martha in Luke 10:41–42 burned in my mind, and for four long days I felt Jesus saying to me, "Dee, Dee, you are worried and bothered about so many things; but only a few things are necessary, really only one."

I spent those four days at the first ever "Pastors' Prayer Summit," praying and crying. On the bus ride home I thought and thought about the previous twelve years of ministry, and the thought that kept coming to my mind was, "I wish I had known, I wish someone would have told me." I knew that I needed to make a drastic change in my life, and I was determined to do that. After I got home I wrote out a simple "personal mission statement" that I reviewed over and over: "I will be devoted to prayer, and I will make it the highest priority in my life."

Through the rest of 1989 I struggled with truly making my time with Jesus in prayer the highest priority in my life and ministry. I felt so lazy just sitting "doing nothing," but by the time the second Pastors' Prayer Summit rolled around in February of 1990, I was almost a completely renewed and revived pastor. My joy and fire were back, I was dreaming again and I was excited about our church and the future.

The biggest change that began to take place was my attitude and feelings toward the people in our church family. I began to pray for everyone in our church by name, every week. Without realizing it, a genuine love for the people—even if they weren't high performers—was growing, and they were sensing it. No longer did I hear that terribly frustrating line, "We don't feel like you love us any more." Today, our church mission statement is, "Jefferson Baptist Church is the 'I Love You' Church." We are continually saying, "I Love You" to God, to each other, and to the world. *Prayer has truly turned my life and our church around.*

I still believe in hard work, being responsible, and being faithful, but now it is in the context of total dependence on God, demonstrated by a devotion to prayer. I am a praying pastor, and our church is a praying church. "Ask and you will receive" is now much more my motto than "work and you will accomplish."

Prayer is the hardest work I have ever done. It is so hard to sit and pray when I would rather be up and doing something. It is so hard to wait and listen when I am inclined to be going all out to accomplish some noble goals. It is so hard to spend hours talking to someone I can't see when I feel continually pressured to talk to people I can see, and who can help me build our church.

Dear Christian leader, I understand your desire to be successful. I understand the pressure to perform, to lead, to be a vision caster, to preach. I live in the middle of that pressure from inside of me and from those around me. But in spite of those continuous pressures I do not want to go back to what I once was and did. I now truly enjoy working with Jesus, pulling a yoke with Him that is both easy and light. It is my prayer that you will not need to experience what I did before you learn to value prayer.

Sincerely,
Dee Duke

Questions for Reflection

1. Might people think of you more as a "whipper" than as an "equipper"? If so, what adjustments need to be made in your leadership style?

2. Does your ministry properly balance "ask and you will receive" and "work and you will accomplish"? If unbalanced, what correctives need to be made?

3. Why do you think that so many people feel that they aren't doing anything when they are praying? How might the activism valued by our culture cause us to neglect the contemplative dimensions of our walk with God?

SEVENTEEN

Learning to Blend the Best of the Past with the Best of the New

H. Crosby Englizian is senior professor at Western Seminary in Portland, Oregon; he has been a faculty member there (specializing in church history) since 1966. His ministry overseas includes lectureships in Australia, Singapore, Germany, and a two-year stint as a missionary in The Netherlands. He is the author of *The History of Park Street Church, Boston.*

Dear Friend,

You have recently entered into what you trust will be a God-honoring lifelong pastoral ministry, and have asked me to share some thoughts on lessons I have learned over my nearly fifty years of serving Christ as pastor, educator, and short-term missionary.

If only because of the older generation to whom you will also minister as a leader (do not trivialize them), you must remember that since 1950 America has markedly changed and so have its evangelical churches. Things were simpler, gentler, and more civil a generation and more ago. Church members were largely submissive to their leaders. They remained loyal to their home churches and did not flit about as in today's consumerist society. They were not as demanding; they were satisfied with their religious lot.

As for Christian families, most were unmarked by divorce, abortion, and promiscuity. Church leaders experiencing moral failure were few. Orthodoxy in doctrine and its practice was held to be of high importance. Worship was simple, unadorned, reflective, dignified, and fully God-honoring. Leonard Payton has made an interesting observation in *The Coming Evangelical Crisis* (p. 191): after examining the entire worship music repertoire of his congregation, of some four hundred choruses and hymns, he discovered more that 350 fit within what are classified as songs of thanks, and fewer than ten fit in the admonition category—a reflection of the widespread notion that no person can tell another person what to do. Feeling good, he wrote, has become an inextricable component of orthodoxy. As I said, things have changed.

But not all the changes have been negative by any means. I must say that at the same time many positive influences have served to enrich and enliven the church, and have fitted her to the more wholesome dimensions of our culture and time.

You are entering your profession during a period of considerable quandary wherein the very infrastructure of church life is being widely debated and discussed. Thus you will be obliged to face certain questionable marketplace forces which have filtered into church life; to fend off methodologies which tend to introduce entertainment, comedy, and "fun" into the worship service; and to stand your ground against an embarrassing mediocrity in doing church. Not to mention the most severe issue of all: the unworthy re-imaging of God, which is the source of our ills. Your mettle will surely be tested beyond seeming endurance. It may be you will struggle to retain your faith in God.

Your chosen profession being as difficult as it is, great skill will be required to maneuver through the minefields, to handle criticism well, and to know how to deal with troublesome people. At the same time you will experience many joys, rewards, and pleasures equal to the pains. God is greater than man. The church is greater than the culture. Righteousness is greater than unrighteousness.

I pray that these simple thoughts which follow will prove useful to you as you embark upon your journey.

While activating your strengths, work to overcome weaknesses

The religious atmosphere in which your were raised, the theological orientation of your formal and informal training, together with some understanding of your spiritual gifts and skills will largely determine the direction and character of your ministry.

Having taken an inventory of your strengths and weaknesses, you will quite naturally begin to build a ministry upon those strengths that God has given you. At the same time, you will more than likely postpone giving attention to the weaker areas—whether spiritual, social, emotional, or professional. I am suggesting that this postponement would be a mistake.

For example, if we were raised and trained in settings marked by dynamic, visionary leadership, and then discovered in early adult life that we were blessed with the necessary gifts, we would most likely want to emulate that kind of leadership. But to do so without also taking some time—admittedly a secondary pursuit—to improve or sharpen areas of ministerial or personal weakness would make you an incomplete leader. There are some things we do well. There are other things we don't do well at all; hence we place them on the back burner of our interests and activity.

As another example, there are those who were raised to believe that a high level of congregational spirituality is more to be sought after than visible, numerical success; and whether or not they are visionaries as well, they will choose to bend their people's interests in that particular direction as a primary focus. In other words, quality over quantity. But again, while pursuing their primary goals—increasing attendance at prayer services, encouraging a love for God, and true fellowship in a heightened spirit of community, fostering a vibrant evangelistic out-reach locally and abroad, enlarging a benevolent spirit towards the needs of the neighborhood—other areas of legitimate and needful attention could easily be omitted because of disinterest.

It is natural to gravitate in the direction of your power, for there is where results occur and people heap praise. But as you continue—and this is my point—you must not overlook your weaknesses. And be certain that we all have them; sometimes glaringly so. Rather than investing all your time and energy activating your skills, work at the same time in overcoming or improving the diminished areas of your personal talent pool, however unappealing that task may be.

Consider this repeated instance which has led hundreds of young ministers to forsake the ministry altogether. Stan was a successful pastor of a midwestern local church, having raised the congregation out of its doldrums after several years of diligent struggle and fidelity to his task. But then the roof caved in on him. Because of malicious, underhanded dealings by some of the members and their insensitiv-ity to his many years of faithful service—not to mention his personal feelings—he was obliged to resign. Many in the church were stunned; his family was outraged. As difficult as this experience was to en-dure, it proved all the more so because of certain emotional traumas the pastor had experienced earlier in life, the residue of which now hounded him and made it seemingly impossible for him to rise above this stunning setback.

While engaged in building up the church, he neglected to seek helpful counsel toward the healing of his private bruised emotions. Had he done so, the church's action would have been less painful. Furthermore, he would have been in a better position to recover and to reset his future.

You might plan to enroll in a course or attend a seminar dealing with your shortcomings, or at the very least avail yourself of wise counsel. A successful leader—though well-reputed and lauded—who is yet deficient in a major dimension of his life, still has much work to do. As Thomas á Kempis put it, "Let us strive to be in life as one prays to be found in death" (*Imitation of Christ*, chap. 23).

Cultivate a high view of God

Among twentieth-century writers who have recognized the supreme importance of a high view of God, none was more in the forefront of this concern (at least among evangelicals) than A. W. Tozer (1897–1963). His no-nonsense Christianity flowed from a lofty understanding of a royally majestic and awesome God. And I desire the same for you. To the degree that your concept of God is flawed, both you and your ministry will suffer a measure of loss; gains otherwise possible will remain unrealized.

The closest I have come to having a mentor or discipler occurred only indirectly during the year I attended the Southside Alliance Church in Chicago in the years immediately following the Second World War. There I listened intently to Tozer as he demolished evangelical idols while building holy altars to a high and holy Sovereign. More than a generation ago, he warned the church in America that she was slowly surrendering her awed consciousness of God. Were he alive today, he would shake his head in utter incredulousness, for the cautions of yesteryear have come to confused fruition. The sacredness of the preaching platform is being turned into a theatrical stage where performing ministers humor and entertain their congregational audiences. Have no part of this ecclesiastical show. As Brennan Manning declares, "The gospel of Jesus Christ is no Pollyanna tale. . . . It is a cutting knife, rolling thunder, and convulsive earthquake in the human spirit" (*The Signature of Jesus*, p. 186). Neil Postman, in his *Amusing Ourselves to Death*, has concluded that when Christianity's demanding faith "is delivered as easy and amusing, it is another kind of religion altogether" (p. 121).

The manner in which you present yourself before your people relays a message about how you perceive God. As Tozer put it, "The Church cannot escape the self-disclosure of her witness concerning God" (*Knowledge of the Holy*, p. 1). Marva Dawn, in her excellent book *Reaching Out Without Dumbing Down*, expresses some perturbation "that the awesomeness of God is repeatedly swallowed up by coziness. Not only the Church but God himself is dumbed down, made too small, trivialized" (p. 97). It makes little sense to ape our increasingly godless culture while seeking "to snatch from sin and the grave" those embroiled in the same cultural patterns.

So I implore you, "have done with lesser things" in order to reacquaint yourself with the Majesty on high. Our problem is not the culture so much as it is the way in which we confront it. We will not deal well with modernity by clasping it to our bosoms and cuddling it. Recognizing clearly its idolatries, you must resist them with the passion of an Old Testament prophet and proclaim with vigor, "I am the LORD, and there is no other; beside Me there is no God" (Isa. 45:5 NASB).

Be a Scripture-driven leader

You would think it was more than a little trite to caution you against being other than a Scripture-driven leader; however, a recall of church history and a brief glance of the church in America today suggests a renewed reminder.

I would imagine that most people prefer to follow than to lead. "Let not many of you become teachers . . . knowing that as such we shall incur a stricter judgment"(James 3:1 NASB). Knowing this, you as a leader must be wisely guided not only in choosing where to lead them but in choosing the means by which you will attract their following. Paul sets several options before us, only some of which he commends: superiority of speech, professional smarts, the force of an impressive personality, persuasive rhetoric, as well as personal abandonment to a crucified Christ and the demonstration of the Spirit's power (1 Cor. 2).

There are general leadership values of a kind that will work well in any organization, secular or ecclesiastical: training expertise, an amiable and caring personality, conflict management skills, etc. But there are values that must never find a nesting place in any sanctified church of God, though you will be sorely tempted to employ them. You will see others among your colleagues doing so—and with some visible success.

I have in mind what are called market-driven values. "Market-driven" suggests to me anything that works, which draws people, which produces results (in the business world, whatever eventuates in profits)—thus opening kingdom life to entertainment, warm fuzzies, coarse humor, religious toys, and the eventual dumbing down of inspired doctrine and God-honoring worship. This all reflects the "bigger barns" mentality.

To what end are we leaders in God's vineyard? Why do we do what we do? What do we wish to accomplish? Does an approved end justify aberrant means? Is it to attract crowds only, or that the "faith of our followers should not rest on human (market-driven) wisdom but on the power of God"? It is because the latter demands more of us that it is not so much in exemplary evidence as much as it should be.

The current attraction of the secular corporate model of leadership is in my view an indication of the diminishing attraction of a more biblically warranted model.

Better to be owned by a Scripture-driven and Spirit-empowered mentality than to be impelled by borrowed secular forces. Let your ministerial excellence flow from the excellent nature of God. G. Campbell Morgan observed that "the spirit of the city of Corinth had entered into the church." And he further cautioned, "Our work is not to catch the spirit of the age; it is to correct it" (*The Corinthian Letters of Paul,* p. 27). To be caught by that spirit is to face being gradually overcome by it. The temptations of this modern spirit are incredibly subtle in their luring appeal, to the easy acceptance of means which once we eschewed. As Manning concludes, "The seduction of counterfeit discipleship has made it too easy to be a Christian" (*The Signature of Jesus,* p. 186).

Thomas Brooks, seventeenth-century Puritan divine, in his classic *Precious Remedies Against Satan's Devices,* warns that Satan presents the world "in such a dress to the soul, as to ensnare it and win its affection." Satan, he writes, "represents the world in its beauty so as to bewitch us . . . and eventually to destroy. Where one thousand are destroyed by the world's frowns, ten thousand are destroyed by the world's smiles" (p. 102).

Think larger thoughts

At opportune points in your ministry—the Holy Spirit will identify them for you—you will want to think larger thoughts. Pray grander prayers. Dream bigger dreams. And with an intimidating fear staring you down, be bold to expand your faith. It is a God-like thing to do.

A settled local church situation, a stable church membership, and thriving programs all contribute to our professional comfort and well-being, to a sense of security in our position. Change, on the other hand, though hopeful of fresh excitement, has a reputation among some people as disruptive and threatening, especially to older saints whose oft-intoned motto recalls the famous Seven Last Words: "What has not been shall not be." Do not allow yourself to be hamstrung by this sentiment, whatever its source.

To bolster my faith on occasion, I have often referred to Acts 4:24 where I am reminded of a large God who not only made heaven and earth and the sea, but "all that is in them." He wondrously populated the heavens, the earth, and the sea. He creatively filled them with abundant good. A *Reader's Digest* (March 1966) article on the world's oceans, for example, informs us that "in 320 million cubic miles of water . . . intricate food webs support more life by weight and greater diversity of animals than any other ecosystem. The oceans also have vast resources of nickel, iron, manganese, copper, and cobalt." The incredible Person who created all this is big. He is beyond replication. His productions are on a huge scale. He produces large results with small beginnings. He turns tasteless water into delicious wine. He takes a paralyzed organization of people and makes it a source of wonder. A. W. Tozer reflects, "Since a source must be at least equal to anything that emanates from it, God is of necessity equal to all the power there is" (*Knowledge of the Holy*, p. 66).

On a day when your thoughts turn to planning the future for yourself and your ministry, do not limit yourself to the ordinary and the safe, doing year after year the same things, the same way, with the same results. To break out into uncharted waters is certain to raise new problems, new criticisms, and not a little trepidation. The temptation to retreat into a "remnant mentality"—fewness, littleness, sameness—will confront you. Something will remind you that the Scriptures speak favorably of remnant people who are "few" in number. And a board member is sure to tell you God does not despise smallness. But because God is infinite, and because your faith constantly needs refurbishing and challenge, take on goals and objectives that are worthy of a lofty view of God. Do not fear to enter unfamiliar territory if you do so with your hand in the hands of God.

Many years ago I was invited to serve a New England congregation composed entirely of unregenerate members. My first thought was: how could I, raised in fundamentalist circles, even think about pastoring a "liberal" church, where Christian doctrine meant little, where services were held only ten months in the year, where the hired organist was an unconverted Jew, and where the people's sole concern was to keep the organization alive? Nevertheless, because at that unique opportune moment I needed employment in keeping with my professional training, I accepted the invitation. For two years (after which, happily, the church went out of business, and we moved elsewhere) we got along famously. They were generous and respectful; our three young children loved the large manse; and within the first three months, some four or five persons confessed Christ as their Savior.

I could cite other instances wherein the Spirit led us to think beyond our comfort zone, although I don't initially tend to think that way. In each case, God richly honored our efforts with a sense of happy accomplishment.

The recently installed pastor of Boston's historic Park Street Church, somewhat overwhelmed by the awesome demands of his new post—but ready to accept the challenge—observed that "it is far more lethal to our spiritual lives to attempt nothing unless it seems guaranteed to succeed whether or not there is a God in heaven" (*Park Street Church PULSE,* Summer 1997).

Allow this holy ambition to enter into your prayer closet as well. Dare to pray for large victories—for the Spirit's presence and power beyond the normal, to amaze, surprise, and enrich the work under your care. Morris Inch writes in his commentary on the book of Job, "There is more going on in our lives than the little we see and are aware of" (p. 47). You might want to ask God to pull back the curtains to show you more of what He is doing. Think what it will do for your faith! And for your work!

A twofold task

Whatever our ministry, we have always a twofold task according to Paul's testimony in 1 Thessalonians 2: "We were well pleased to impart to you not only the gospel of God but also our own souls" (vv. 7–8 NASB).

Early in my ministry I was struck with the tenderness displayed and the gentle manner in which he spoke, even to the choice of his word pictures: "nursing mother, tender care, fond affection, dear to us"; and in succeeding verses, "exhorting, encouraging, and imploring you as a father would his own children," concluding with "you are our glory and joy."

I was drawn to this autobiographical paragraph for two reasons: my own failures in this regard, and certain manners I observed in pastors and leaders who were my seniors, who had been engaged in their ministries much longer than I and from whom, therefore, I expected more in keeping with the apostle's history. We learn in life that ugliness of whatever kind can be as attractive as beauty. Both draw our attention, but for differing reasons.

Strangely enough, those leaders who were the most ugly in behavior were often those most committed to truth. Their doctrinal convictions which were commendable and salutary made them hard (not gentle), bristling (not affectionate), and sometimes hateful (not blameless), all of which pained me and led me to conclude that these brothers were ignorant of the fundamentals of the gospel of Christ which they loudly proclaimed.

I determined, therefore, that wherever God would take me, and whatever positions I would fill, I would make at least this much my aim: to be faithful to proclaim the whole gospel and to be equally faithful to do so with the affection of Christ toward those who heard me. I would imagine that for most leaders less effort is required to proclaim boldly than to impart their own souls. The former is learned in school in a period of a few years. The latter is learned in life over many years; hence it's the more difficult lesson, yet at least equally important.

You will draw more people to the Savior by your firm and loving pastoring than by your convictionist preaching or your authoring of books. You can be a strong preacher of the Word and a storehouse of biblical knowledge, and even wow your listeners without being a caring person. Gene Getz has written, "There is no way to circumvent the people and be a good pastor" (*Sharpening the Focus of the Church*, p. 123). You must impart always—and at the same time—the message of the gospel and a pastoral kind of affection as you minister the grace of God.

Build a team

During the years of my professional training for the pastorate in the 1940s and 1950s, the general understanding imparted to us students was that we would bear the full responsibility for the leadership of our particular charges with all their departments and programs. The pastor did it all with the help of a few lay volunteers. None but the largest city churches in those days could afford to hire staffs. In the circles in which I was raised and educated, not much was said about "team building," whether with volunteers or with paid staff.

Today it's different. On every hand leaders are encouraged and advised to build and to train teams; whether a team of elders, or of key lay men and women, what is in view is something more than the traditional board made up of well-meaning but uninstructed parishioners. Here are a few of several reasons why you may want to consider team building.

It makes for accountability. Apart from such accountability, a leader becomes his own boss, his own judge. Should he, on a day, face a review of his work, he would not be obliged to accept it if not to his liking. In addition, accountability makes way for personal growth and the improvement of skills. It enhances responsibility and encourages change where needed.

Second, a team with integrity will forbid "turf building" by a single individual. I don't know of anything which is as troubling to observe or as painful to experience (outside of moral failure) than a leader gone amok pursuing his own ends in his own way, running roughshod over the God-given minds of his colleagues. Every definition of *koinonia* or biblical community argues against such egocentrism.

And third, in keeping with the aforesaid, keep your hands off the work of other team members. Be an encourager and a mentor, not a controller. As our Lord gave His disciples the freedom to serve—though not without an occasional caution—you must grant your partners a like freedom to occupy their positions of responsibility and to utilize their Spirit-given creativity and individuality. Let the free air of the Holy Spirit be the environment for kingdom service. Anything less is unworthy of the kingdom.

Avoid comparisons

Throughout your ministerial career you will find yourself comparing your personality, your assets, your family heritage, your gifts and accomplishments with others of your profession. However natural this impulse may be, take my advice and forget it.

If you find that you are approving yourself as better and more gifted, this can serve only to sculpt an ego. On the other hand, if your comparisons tend to lessen self-confidence and to depress your spirit, again you are the worse for the effort. When one thinks about it, such comparisons partake of so much childish silliness.

Given the infinitude of our Creator, seen in the variegated handiwork of His creatures—of many colors, diverse personalities, numerous cultures, skills and lack thereof—why measure yourself against others? It seems to me that a measureless God would surely wish His sainted children to refrain. We speak in terms of great and small, high and low, plentiful and meager. We measure space and time, atoms and molecules, energy and speed, all of which give expression to normal, natural diversity. In the physical world, such comparisons have a necessary and appropriate place, but when it comes to the gauging of strength against what someone else has, it is all very ungodly. Some things are beyond the need for discovery. Comparisons tend to reinforce prejudice and to close the mind to wider horizons. They make for unsavory have/have-not dichotomies. "Let everyone be sure that he is doing his very best, for then he will have the personal satisfaction of work well done, and won't need to compare himself with someone else" (Gal. 6:4 LB).

Have you come across the little tract "Others May; You Cannot" which has been around for the better part of this century? Its essential message is this: God will permit others to be and to do and to become what He will not permit you. So why fight it? Why indulge? Why play "footsie" with His will?

Remember that while you are measuring yourself against others and perhaps coming out an unwanted second, there are others who unbeknownst to you are measuring themselves against you and deciding in your favor. So cheer up! Like I said, it's all a bit silly.

Nurture a global mind

I was raised in a church with large missionary vision. Over the years I listened to numerous missionaries in church and at summer camp. I participated in hundreds of prayer meetings on behalf of overseas kingdom work. Missionary conferences highlighted the annual church calendar. This same kind of emphasis continued to mark college and seminary years.

When I became a pastor, the prayers, the missionary guests and conferences continued. My own prayers, however, though genuine, were offered with only a little feeling. I rarely preached on mission themes, except for an occasional evangelistic message. You might say, I was simply *missionary-minded.*

But then all this changed. I became *missionary-hearted* as well. Please note the distinction. A major catalyst in this change, for us, was a global missions trip covering more than a dozen nations, some twenty metropolitan cities, a dozen Christian schools, and mission agencies. It even included a two-month interim pastorate at a local church in suburban Brisbane, Australia. Over an eight-month period we found ourselves among masses of people alien to us; while visiting a number of usually small Christian assemblies we viewed the power of idolatrous religions, walked shack-lined ghettoes and third-world slums, and were accosted by pleading beggars and inner city ugliness. Combined with several other factors, these served to make me missionary-hearted.

I think you will find that most Christians who occupy church pews these days are missionary-minded only. Their missionary involvement is at an emotional distance from where the action is, and is largely cerebral in kind. I would suggest some ideas that you might want to think about to change this elemental condition.

1. Encourage your people to increase their knowledge of the worldwide task. This can be accomplished by a variety of means: through the introduction of carefully selected readings and biographies, becoming a pen pal with a missionary family, or organizing mini-missions events suited to different age levels. Some might wish to consider a study course, visit a foreign field, or become identified in some way with one of the many ethnic peoples who fill our cities. Even as American industrial and financial institutions keep abreast of overseas markets and trends, so the Church must do the same with its global kingdom interests.

2. Our hearts must be moved and our emotions touched by some kind of substantive involvement. In Matthew 9, Jesus displayed his heart for people: "He was moved with compassion" (v. 36 KJV).

He not only saw and passed by as a tourist might do, he did something to alleviate need. He identified with them, making their cause His own, making their suffering His own. He connected with them emotionally.

3. A natural question to ask at this point is, "From whence comes such compassion?" In Jesus' case, it came while He was *with* the people, with the lost and needy; while He was serving them, while He mingled with them, while He felt their pulse, as it were. These comfortable enclaves we call "our local church" make a great hideaway from a compassionate concern for the spiritually deprived "out there."

In an inwardly turned society, your feelings and prayers must have a vibrant overseas focus as well as a local one. America is not the world, nor is the American church the only one God is building. God's church is a global church. You and those to whom you minister need increasingly to get in touch with it.

In all things, finally, your standard for the kind of leadership you desire is the Word of God. You are not to sidestep it. You are not to use it selectively as so many do, nor substitute for it the opinions of your teachers, your friends, or your mentors. The mind of the Spirit is your best source and strength for this awesome responsibility. "Let this mind be in you which was also in Christ Jesus" (Phil. 2:5 KJV).

Yours affectionately,
H. Crosby Englizian

Questions for Reflection

1. A. W. Tozer has written, "What comes into our minds when we think about God is the most important thing about us." Why is this so? What comes into your mind when you think about God, and how accurately does this reflect His self-revelation?

2. Why is it difficult for ministers to follow Paul's example and "impart their own souls" to others? To what extent are you currently doing this as you minister to others?

3. To what extent are you more "missionary-minded" than "missionary-hearted"? What might you do to move more toward the latter?

EIGHTEEN

Learning to Pursue Integrity and Excellence

Ted Engstrom is President Emeritus of World Vision, an organization he served for many years as president and chief executive officer. Before joining World Vision, Engstrom was president of Youth for Christ International for six years. He has also served as Interim President at Azusa Pacific University. He is much in demand as a board member, and was the first board chair for the Evangelical Council for Financial Accountability. He has published over forty books, including *The Making of a Christian Leader* and *The Fine Art of Mentoring*.

Dear Friend,

I salute you for your interest in being an effective leader in the Christian community, to the glory of God. As the apostle Paul said to Timothy, his son in the faith, "to aspire to leadership is an honorable ambition" (1 Tim. 3:1 paraphrased).

Many years ago, as I sought to prepare myself for what I trusted might be a significant and redemptive career path, God gave me what I have claimed over these years as my life verse. It is Psalm 32:8 where God says, "I will instruct you and teach you in the way you should go; I will guide you with My eye" (NKJV). This promise has been such an encouragement to me all these years, and I trust it will be a promise you too can claim for yourself and your leadership responsibilities.

On occasion I have been asked, "What are the most important ingredients for Christian leaders in their responsibilities?" As I have reflected on this, two words, or concepts, have continually come to my attention. They are *integrity* and *excellence*. In fact, I have felt so strongly about these biblical concepts that I have authored two books on these themes.

Let me explain the theme of Christian integrity in leadership to you.

Integrity means wholeness, completeness, consistency. It is related to the word *integration,* which comes from the same root word as does the word *integer.* Integrity is a values-related term and it is an important biblical concept. It is used nineteen times in the Old Testament alone.

The lack of integrity has infiltrated not only business, industry, politics, and government, but also our theology. For example, the "health and wealth" gospel has become, in my judgment, a serious heresy. "Name it and claim it" is certainly not a biblical doctrine.

The Word of God is replete with appeals for integrity. Let me share just a few examples.

Following Solomon's completion of the temple and royal palace, God said to him, "As for you, if you walk before me in integrity of heart and uprightness . . . I will establish your royal throne over Israel forever" (1 Kings 9:4–5 NIV).

Again, in Psalm 7, the psalmist declares, "Judge me, O LORD, according to my righteousness, according to my integrity, O Most High" (v. 8 NIV).

The wise man in Proverbs 11:3 says, "The integrity of the upright guides them, but the unfaithful are destroyed by their duplicity" (NIV).

As I know you understand, God has ordained three, and only three, institutions—all three of which, because of the lack of integrity, are under attack. These are the family, government, and the church.

God has ordained these for the ordering of society: the family for the propagation of life; the state for the preservation of life; the church for the proclamation of the gospel. A sense of integrity must be reinstilled in each of these institutions.

As my friend Howard Hendricks has said, "The test of integrity is how you behave when no one is watching." Joseph showed integrity when he resisted the seduction of Potiphar's wife, even when he was far from home and his sexual urges may have gone unsatisfied for a long time.

Daniel, who also became a great leader in a pagan nation, showed integrity when he refused to defile himself with the royal food and wine. He showed integrity when he continued to worship God openly because he knew this was right, even though he knew, too, that he would be thrown into a den of lions because of his public prayer.

People of integrity can be trusted to be faithful. If they promise something, they will do it. Their actions are built on high moral principles. Their words are not spoken for gossip, spreading rumors, tearing others down, or for distorting the truth. People of integrity discover what pleases God—then they do it. Christians with integrity are committed both to hearing God's Word and to doing what it says.

One cannot force integrity onto someone else; we can only develop and model it in our own lives. Integrity needs to be at the very core of our being. Integrity is basic both to effective leadership and to effective difference-making. Without integrity in our lives, our work, our family, and our organization, our church will not make much of a lasting difference.

Integrity demands courage. People of integrity stand for their convictions, even at great personal cost. Biblical integrity involves not merely acting according to one's own beliefs, but acting according to scriptural teaching.

The foundation for integrity lies with God. God's standard for integrity is nothing short of His own nature.

Leaders, of course, are to be held to a stricter accountability, but they also need forgiveness and restoration when they repent of any failures.

As you look forward to your leadership responsibilities, determine within your own heart and spirit to live straight and true—even when no one is looking. We need continually to renew our own commitment to the satisfying lifestyle of personal integrity. God bless you as you make this an integral part of your life and leadership.

Second, let me talk to you a bit about what I call "the pursuit of excellence." It seems to me that striving for excellence in one's work, whatever it may be, is not only a Christian's duty, but also a basic form of Christian witness. This could be called the foundation of "nonverbal" communication that supports the verbal.

A friend of mine, Dr. Melvin Lorentzen, says in an essay: "We must stress excellence over against mediocrity done in the name of Christ. We must determine to put our best in the arts so that when we sing a hymn about Jesus and His love, when we erect a building for the worship of God, when we stage a play about the soul's pilgrimage, we will not repel individuals but attract them to God."

Excellence is not the pursuit of a lifestyle, or the pursuit of education, or the pursuit of dollars. Excellence is the pursuit of Jesus Christ. It is a journey. If we want to be excellent we need to seek to be like the "Excellent One!" We must remember that excellence is never an accident.

In Colossians 3:17 the apostle admonishes us, "Whatever you do, in word or deed, do everything in the name of the Lord Jesus, giving thanks to God the Father through Him" (NKJV). No higher standard for us could be found.

As Christian leaders, you and I should be passionate champions of quality—advocates of the first-rate. In Ecclesiastes 9:10 the wise man writes, "Whatever your hand finds to do, do it with all your might"

(NASB). It is my contention that nothing less than the pursuit of excellence could possibly please God.

Somewhere along the line a strange idea has developed that in order to be humble we also have to be mediocre. Spirituality and excellence are seen as opposite ends of a pole. Where we get this idea is a mystery to me. Certainly not from Scripture! Over and over God selected people marked by excellence for His work. Whether it was Moses of the Old Testament with his excellent heritage and palace training, or Paul in the New Testament with his excellent knowledge and organizational ability, God chose the best. And He still does!

The Word of God is filled with references to this matter of pursuing excellence and indicates that the excellence of God is the basis for our excellence. For example, in Psalm 36 we read that "God's loving kindness is excellent." In Psalm 150, "God's greatness is excellent." In Deuteronomy 12, "God's salvation is excellent." The psalmist in Psalm 8:1 writes, "O LORD, our Lord, how excellent is Your name in all the earth" (NKJV).

As Oswald Chambers has written in his wonderful book *My Utmost for His Highest*, "Acting slovenly is an insult to the Holy Spirit."

In the first chapter of his Philippian letter Paul writes, "It is my prayer that your love may abound more and more, with knowledge and all discernment, so that you may approve what is excellent, and may be pure and blameless for the day of Christ, filled with the fruits of righteousness which comes through Jesus Christ to the glory and praise of God" (vv. 9–11 NKJV).

Young friend, give life your best shot. Go for the gold! Remember, you have just one pass through this life. Make it all that it can be with the sense of excellence to the glory of God. And, God bless you for it.

Your Friend in Christ,
Ted W. Engstrom

Questions for Reflection

1. How might your ministry help rebuild integrity in the key institutions of family, government, and church?

2. "The test of integrity is how you behave when no one is watching." Do you pass this test? If not, might it help to remember that an omnipresent God is always watching?

3. Are you appropriately passionate about pursuing quality and excellence in all that you do? How might one still pursue genuine excellence without falling into the trap of unhealthy perfectionism?

NINETEEN

Learning Proper Priorities and Perspectives

Hans Finzel is Executive Director of CBInternational, a missions agency based in Wheaton, Illinois, that oversees the ministry of over 750 missionaries. Prior to assuming his present position, Finzel and his wife Donna spent ten years in Vienna, Austria, with CBI working throughout Eastern Europe to provide leadership training for pastors behind the Iron Curtain. Among Finzel's publications is *The Top Ten Mistakes Leaders Make.* The following letter was originally sent to a couple who had asked him for counsel.

Dear Friend,

It is an awesome responsibility to be considered your mentor. I am humbled when I think that you put so much weight in my opinions and perspectives on life and ministry. I appreciate you so much and consider it an honor to have a small part in guiding you into your future.

Thanks for asking for my advice on some of the things that I think you should know about as you look forward to a life of ministry. Life is certainly full of changes for you this year. You've just completed your seminary training and had your first child after being married just a little over a year. Your whole life lies before you as a blank check that has not yet been written. I guess I am about twenty years ahead of you, looking back to the time when Donna and I first married, completed seminary, and embarked upon the road of ministry. Someone told me not long ago that only one out of ten people that go into ministry actually retire from the pastorate. That dropout rate is truly discouraging.

I am happy to say that at the midpoint place where I find myself, which some people refer to as "halftime," I can look back on twenty years of ministry and thank God for His faithfulness. And, as I look forward to twenty more years before I retire—if Jesus doesn't come back or call me home before then—then I have every intention to finish well.

"What have I learned about Christian leadership that I wished I had learned earlier?" I'm glad you asked. Actually, the short answer is that there are many things you just have to learn through experience that they can't teach you in seminary. Knowledge is one thing, but experience is something else. You can't front-load all the knowledge before you go through the experience of ministry. You simply have to take the knowledge you have and learn along the way. Even though there is no substitute for experience, let me give you some of the lessons that I've learned that I wish someone had told me earlier. I'll cover them in random order and elaborate just a bit on each point.

Let me begin with your life partner. *Never shortchange the spouse God has given you for your ministry journey*. I have always given priority to my marital relationship. Through the years we've made it a habit of getting away on the average of once a quarter for at least one overnight stay in a hotel away from our children. These nurturing times have made a huge difference in our marriage. Once children come along, it is so easy for them to become the focus of the marriage and the relationship. Then one day you find that you've lost the spark that originally brought you together. Keep the spark alive and don't fall into the trap of putting God's work before your responsibility to your spouse and family. Everything I have said about your spouse applies as well to your children. As God gives you children, be sure that you don't sacrifice them for the sake of ministry. What does it profit a man if he gains the whole world and loses his children because of neglect?

Next, *seek out mentors*. One of my greatest disappointments as I look back over twenty years of Christian ministry is the lack of mentorship in my life. I have had a few men along the way that have had a significant impact in my life, but even with them I was disappointed that there wasn't as significant a relationship as I wanted. I find that very few people who you want to mentor you will actually take the initiative with you. It seems that those people you admire the most are the busiest and therefore don't have time to mentor. If I had to do it all over again, I would have been much more aggressive at seeking times with people that I wanted to be mentored by. I highly recommend that you develop mentoring relationships with people that you want to be like.

Third, *recognize that some people will let you down*. If I had to predict who would let me down, I would have missed every time.

The people you think are always going to be there are the ones that may very well totally fail you. And then at times you are surprised by the people who stand with you that you never expected. I have learned through the years not to put my faith and trust for my future in people. This is not to say we should be renegade individualists, but that we should keep our eyes on Jesus, the Author and Finisher of our faith. I have had two very dear, close friends (in fact, two of the closest friends during my years of ministry) who both bailed out of their marriages through illicit affairs and tossed aside their spouse, children, and the faith to follow the wiles of their flesh. That hurt very deeply. Of course, there also have been many other Christian leaders who have crashed and burned, some of whom I used to look up to with great admiration. Not only might those people you look up to from a distance let you down, but also those people who work very close to you. Expect it, anticipate it, and try to treat everyone with a foundational principle of grace and forgiveness. When others let you down, you can always rely on your spouse, your family, and hopefully your closest friends. And remember that Jesus will never let you down.

Fourth, *recognize that you can rarely volunteer for leadership*. Don't set out with the intention of being a leader. Set out with the intention of being willing to serve Christ's church in any way you can. Leadership is something that you have to fall into after you've proven yourself as a follower. Don't fall into the trap of not being willing to do the dirty work because you feel God has called you to be a leader. I find that leadership involves a tremendous amount of dirty work and details that followers frankly don't want to mess with. You have to earn the right to lead, after proving your ability to be a gracious and cooperative follower.

Fifth, *recognize that accountability is not optional*. There are two sides to accountability. Personal accountability involves having a small cadre of friends that you can be transparent with about every detail of your life. This is another area where I have failed in my life and would encourage you to do better than I have. Always try to have a group of the same gender with whom you can experience genuine accountability. It will go a long way to helping protect you from the wiles of the world, the flesh, and the devil. The second area of accountability is to the authority God has placed over you. I think it is imperative that people are accountable to someone. For me, as the director of my own organization, I am accountable to the God-given authority of the board of directors that is above me. I have noticed certain people in ministry who have had a spirit of independence, refusing to be accountable to anyone. It is not a healthy thing and can create dangerous imbalance and irresponsibility. Submit yourself to those whom God has put in authority over you.

Sixth, *don't forget to nurture your soul*. The older you get the busier you get and the more the battle rages to find time to nurture your own soul. Always make time to spend in the Word and in fellowship with your Savior. I love the quote from D. L. Moody: "Sin will keep you from the Bible or the Bible will keep you from sin." It is simple and it is true. Make time on a daily basis to cultivate and feed your soul, because from it springs all of character, integrity, ministry, and leadership.

Seventh, *don't forget to nurture your body*. I am sad to say that the older men get in ministry, the more they seem to neglect their physical condition. Don't fall into the trap of adding a couple of pounds for every year of your life beyond the age of twenty-five. I don't think that it is a good testimony to the church or to Christian leadership for people to be overweight and under-conditioned. Take good care of your body and it will have a very positive effect on your soul and spirit. Be careful what you eat, remember moderation in all things and, in the spirit of the apostle Paul, learn to buffet your body and make it your slave.

Eighth, *put people first*. I just read a great quote from Peter Drucker that says, "Management is a social function and has mostly to do with people, not techniques or procedures" (*Netfax, #75*, July 7, 1997). Leadership is about people, so the key to successful Christian leadership is learning how to get along with people and caring about people. I have seen many young men and women try to make a mark in Christian ministry but fail because of their lack of people skills. And these kinds of people tended to be the most gifted and brilliant individuals on the playing field. In fact, it is the highly gifted who often fail with people skills because they rely on their gifts and abilities for success. I have had a lot of failures in my own life regarding this until I learned that I serve people, and leadership is all about getting along well with people.

Ninth, *don't fall into the age discrimination trap*. It is so disappointing today how organizations and churches are no longer willing to look at anybody above the age of fifty. Whatever happened to the biblical concept of age and wisdom? Don't fall into that trap yourself. You have to realize that some things will not come to you until you have gained a certain maturity in life. You can't learn everything a sixty-year-old leader knows by the time you are thirty or forty. You simply have to pay your dues and learn through years of experience. I really believe that is what the biblical concept of wisdom is all about, so learn to respect your elders—those people over fifty who still have a lot to contribute and teach us.

Finally, *pursue lifelong learning.* Never stop learning. In fact, I like to say that the two most important words in a leader's vocabulary are listen and learn. Never stop listening to people and never stop learning. Successful leaders are lifelong learners who believe that there is always something new to learn right around the next corner. This means that you should continue to develop the habit of reading broadly many different kinds of books, journals, and periodicals. It also means you need to continue to educate yourself by continuing education both formally and informally. The world changes so dramatically that we will never survive if we are not lifelong learners.

Let me finish my letter by answering the question, "How do you succeed in leadership?" I mean success by finishing well. Paul said at the end of his career, as he sat in a dungeon in Rome: "I have fought the good fight, I have finished the race, I have kept the faith. Now, there is in store for me the crown of righteousness" (2 Tim. 4:7–8 NIV). It is not over until it's over.

I believe success is measured largely by how you finish. In other words, finishing well is what success is all about. And how do you finish well? To me, it means maintaining personal and ministry integrity. It includes a lifelong positive outlook on your work. Certainly it means you have developed mature relationships with those with whom you have worked. And it is also measured by the quality of your relationship to your spouse and what kind of parent you were to your children. It really boils down to integrity and character in all the relationships that you have both professionally and personally. I would wish for you a lifetime of effective ministry and, if God grants you the opportunity, the privilege of leadership in the work of His vineyard.

Your fan in Christ,
Hans Finzel

Questions for Reflection

1. Are you inadvertently jeopardizing your relationship with your spouse and children because of your ministry to others? What adjustments might you need to make to value them properly both in attitude and in action?

2. How well are you caring for your body? Have you gained unhealthy weight in the past few years, or become less physically fit? How might you enhance your health and energy levels?

3. What two or three additional areas of practical counsel offered by the author may be especially pertinent to you, and how might you prayerfully seek to develop a specific application for each?

TWENTY

Learning How to Minister for Decades in the Same Setting

Leslie B. Flynn is pastor emeritus at Grace Baptist Church in Nanuet, New York. He pastored that congregation for forty years before retiring in 1989. For over twenty years he was heard on weekly radio broadcasts throughout the New York City area. He is the author of forty books, including *How to Survive in the Ministry, 19 Gifts of the Spirit, The Master's Plan of Prayer, My Daughter a Preacher!?!* and *Jesus: In the Image of God—A Challenge to Christlikeness.*

Dear Friend,

It's tough to be a pastor today, probably tougher than it's ever been. You may have discovered that congregations, in general, grant a lower level of respect to pastors today. Members tend to compare you unfavorably with smooth speaking TV preachers, criticize you unjustly in open meetings, and (because of the disintegration of family values) consume valuable hours in an increasing load of complicated counseling situations. The demanding attitude of many church boards has resulted in pastoral firings in unprecedented—and almost epidemic— numbers. Have you noticed that members today are often preoccupied with outside interests, lessening their commitment to the Lord's work, and making your task much more difficult? Since retirement I've often said, "I'm not sure I could take the pressures today." I don't mean to begin on a discouraging note, but you want to make sure of your calling and of your faith in the ultimate triumph of the church Jesus is building.

Through God's goodness and the support of kind people, it was my privilege to pastor the same congregation—Grace Baptist Church of Nanuet, New York—for forty years (1949–1989). After retirement I authored a book reviewing some of the principles that helped me survive these four decades in the same parish *(How to Survive in the Ministry)*. Survival, however, is not a pastor's all-consuming goal. The Sovereign Head of the church does not wish every pastor to stay for decades in the same pulpit. On the other hand, if you move after only two or three years, you may be robbing your congregation of a potentially productive ministry. A quick summary of some of these principles may help you to "stay by the stuff" long enough to see the church through to new heights of vigor and growth.

Put others to work. Ministerial duties are overwhelming, so work smarter, not harder, by deciding what is important for you to do and delegating the rest. Moses, instead of wearing himself out by hearing every case himself, chose judges to adjudicate the less difficult cases, making his job much lighter. The apostles had the early church choose seven deacons to handle the job of alms distribution, freeing themselves for their main ministry of the Word and prayer. Don't let the good become the enemy of the best. Though I did attend all deacon meetings, I didn't attend a trustee meeting in over thirty years. While keeping informed of all church activities, I did not involve myself in their operation. Learn to say no. Don't be a job collector, but follow the main thrust of your ministry. Help your people discover and deploy their gifts. A member who chauffeurs a guest speaker to or from the airport saves you a ton of time and also personally experiences the joy of service. To stay on top of your work won't be too difficult if you have helpers to keep the top from getting too high.

Know when you cannot handle something yourself. Seek the wisdom of others. You aren't omnipotent. The lone-wolf syndrome has no place in the ministry. No pastor is gifted enough, wise enough, or strong enough to live apart from others. Calling in proven teachers and counselors will aid in the edification of your flock.

Fairly or unfairly, you'll have criticism. Some conflict is inevitable. It's how a church handles conflict that counts. Properly resolved, controversy can strengthen the unity of a church. The peace of a church is a high priority, though not at any price. You cannot please everyone. Often you'll have to do what you think is right, and let the chips fall where they may. You'll need a hide like a rhinoceros and a heart like a dove.

Don't provoke trouble. You'll have your fill of conflict without looking for it. Don't fight every contentious fellow who comes along with a chip on his shoulder. It's foolish to pull rank on inconsequential matters. Some battles are not worth winning. Save your ammunition for an important war.

Though some trouble can be avoided or delayed, some must be confronted. Confrontation is never pleasant, and must be done with humility, gentle firmness, and respect of the person.

I always took major matters to the church for its vote, encouraged open discussion, and never railroaded my point through. I recall a business meeting at which the board of deacons unanimously recommended that the church secure a full-time youth minister. At the same meeting the board of trustees unanimously recommended that the church not hire a full-time youth minister. After a full, spirited, and courteous debate the church agreed with the deacons and voted for a full-time youth leader. The trustees graciously went along with the decision, making it clear that their earlier opposition was prompted by a concern about finances. The new youth leader did a marvelous job, and the money came in.

What should you do about criticisms with potshots like, "Your sermons have no depth"? Do not fire potshots back at your critics, especially from the pulpit, but carefully evaluate the barb. Try not to let your idealism be worn thin by frustrating encounters with immature members and their unfair criticisms. Whatever is unjustifiable, quietly forget. Whatever is legitimate, take to heart and try to correct. Listen to other viewpoints. Don't take criticism personally. Maybe the Lord is trying to tell you something.

I well remember, halfway through my pastorate, a letter handed me by a supportive lady in our church just as I was walking to the platform for the morning service. Thinking it an announcement for the service, I was shocked to read a critique of recent sermons, which she alleged were shallow and had too many illustrations. My first reaction in those earlier years was to go on the defensive. Then I did some soul-searching. Without mentioning the letter to anyone I took the criticism seriously and gave more attention to the quality of my messages. A year later I received a note from this same lady with this postscript: "Pastor, your recent sermons on Joseph have been outstanding. Many members have commented on them."

Cultivate a loving congregation. View your flock as friends not enemies, sheep not wolves. Treat everyone alike. Make few demands on your people. Encourage members to have concern for each other. Never harbor resentment. Never use the podium as a bully pulpit to scold. Be there when needed. Perhaps, had I to do it over again, I would devote more time and energy to people (and family) than to projects.

How thankful I was to my pastor who warned me early in my Christian life, "Never idolize human leaders. All idols have clay feet. Look to the Lord. He alone is perfect."

I had to learn the lesson of relaxation the hard way. In the early days I frequently worked until midnight, often without taking a day off. Periods of dizziness sent me to a neurologist, who diagnosed my condition as a minor weakness of the middle ear, and advised a less strenuous schedule, going to conventions, taking vacations, and learning how to relax. From then on I diligently took off one day a week, walked two brisk miles six mornings a week, continued the practice of taking a fifteen minute nap after lunch, and went on more frequent short vacations. I am a firm proponent of hard work, but I am an equally strong believer in relaxation. To roll with the punches of a demanding pastorate and avoid burnout requires a work-leisure balance. Vance Havner said, "If we don't come apart and rest a while, we'll come apart."

Avoid perfectionism. You can't win every battle. Some suggestions will be rejected. Some motions will be voted down. You cannot always have your own way. Some members will decide to join another church.

Have a good laugh. Humor helps us not to take ourselves and our circumstances too seriously. When I was a teenager, I heard my humor-loving pastor say, "When people's mouths are open with laughter, I pour down doses of truth." He who laughs, lasts.

Don't blow it when you're on top and riding high. One whale warned another, "When you get to the top and start to spout off, that's when you get harpooned." The Bible contains stories of many leaders who in later life were tripped up by pride or lust. You must be vigilant, nurture your own marriage relationship, resist temptation at the very start, schedule a daily devotional period to strengthen your inner life, and keep growing. Practice integrity. If you preach tithing, you'd better tithe, or else you'll weaken your character.

Three final miscellaneous suggestions. Don't forget God's love for His people, the Jews. We owe them our spiritual heritage. Over sixty Jews attended some time or other during my forty years' pastorate. Both my ministry and my life were much blessed by their presence and support.

Honor women in the leadership of the church. I was brought face-to-face with the question of women in ministry when one of my daughters, successful in business and happily married, informed me of her call to seminary. Reared in a tradition that frowned on women preachers, this dilemma led to an in-depth biblical search on this issue. The result was a book, *My Daughter a Preacher!?!* Beware of treating our interpretation of Scripture as infallible and as inerrant as the Scriptures themselves. I took part in her ordination service.

Make sure that you give the reading of Scripture a prominent place in your church service. Very often churches which claim to be Bible-based read far less Scripture in their public worship than do liturgical denominations which read passages from Old Testament history, the Psalms, the Gospels, and the Epistles all in the same service. Paul wrote to Timothy, "Devote yourself to the public reading of Scripture" (1 Tim. 4:13 NIV).

May the Lord bless your ministry as you teach the Word and care for souls in your area of His vineyard.

Sincerely,
Leslie Flynn

Questions for Reflection

1. Why might a minister who constantly hops from ministry to ministry in seeking greener pastures elsewhere never experience a truly productive ministry?

2. "Never idolize human leaders. All idols have clay feet. Look to the Lord. He alone is perfect." To what extent are you looking more to the Lord than to fellow humans for an example worthy of emulation?

3. What two or three additional areas of practical counsel offered by the author may be especially pertinent to you, and how might you prayerfully seek to develop a specific application for each?

TWENTY-ONE

Learning to Build Teams

Kenneth O. Gangel is Executive Director of Graduate Studies at Toccoa Falls College in Toccoa Falls, Georgia, and Distinguished Professor Emeritus of Christian Education at Dallas Theological Seminary in Dallas, Texas. He has previously held administrative leadership positions at Dallas Seminary, Miami Christian College, Trinity Evangelical Divinity School, and Calvary Bible College. Among his many publications are *Feeding and Leading*, *Team Leadership in Christian Ministry*, and *Communication and Conflict Management in Christian Organizations* (coauthored with Samuel L. Canine).

Dear Friend,

Like many in my generation, I grew up in churches in which the pastor was the dominant leader. In almost every case the congregation could have voted him out (just as easily as they voted him in), but while he was there he determined events—unless, of course, a strong elder or deacon board decided to rise up and wrest control. Such situations usually ended up in church fights and church splits, all too frequent bruises on the body of Christ.

Thirty-five years ago I began to reflect on my own leadership style, already ten years into full-time ministry. What emerged over the next quarter century was a clear awareness of team concept in ministry, leaders working together, mutual responsibility for outcomes—even though one of them might be a "leader among equals." Slowly I have tried to purge my vocabulary of cosmos-laden words like *power, control, success, in charge,* and their numerous cousins that skew us in the direction of autocratic leadership.

The culmination of my thinking produced the following definition of Christian leadership, which appears on page 64 of my Moody Press publication, *Team Leadership*:

> Biblical team leadership takes place when divinely appointed men and women accept responsibility for obedience to God's call. They recognize the importance of preparation time, allowing the Holy Spirit to develop tenderness of heart and skill of hands. They carry out their leadership roles with deep conviction of God's will, clear theological perspective from His Word, and an acute awareness of the contemporary issues which they and their followers face. Above all, they exercise leadership as servants and stewards, sharing authority with their followers and affirming that leadership is primarily ministry to others, modeling for others, and mutual membership with others in Christ's body.

Philosophically, evangelical Christians believe that all truth is God's truth. Consequently we should not be surprised when people unrelated to Christ and the Bible acknowledge truth from its pages. Through what theologians call "common grace," God allows people to invent useful machines, discover cures for diseases, and write leadership books which square with Scripture.

Such has been the case in the 1990s. A great volume of leadership literature poured off the presses for twenty years after World War II. Much of it was based on military experience or the jump-starting of industry after that global conflict. Then many of those pens fell silent as only an occasional book by Peter Drucker or others would appear. The publication of *The Leadership Challenge* by Kouzes and Posner in 1987, however, brought forth a plethora of books on leadership and administration from secular scholarship.

I offer here no empirical review of literature, but the simple observation that in its own pragmatic way, secular specialists have come around to the biblical position that leadership is best carried out among a group of people. Should there be any hesitation on that note, just read through *The Leader of the Future* published in 1996 by Jossey-Bass and the Drucker Foundation.

So let us be done with the Lone Ranger and let Tonto exit with him. Leadership in churches and Christian organizations, both biblically and scientifically described, pulls together a team of people who love each other, pray together, plan together, and accept mutual and collective praise or criticism for the effectiveness or ineffectiveness. Dump the old myths: "Groups may discuss but leaders make decisions"; "Make your changes in the first year before people feel comfortable criticizing you"; "Always let them know who's in charge."

This letter calls on you to be a team leader and to cultivate team leaders. Yes, it takes much more time than knee-jerking the decisions yourself. In the long run, however, it will not only enhance your own leadership and encourage other leaders, but it will leave a legacy in your church or organization for whomever follows you when God calls you to a new place.

I leave you with the words of Paul in Romans 12:5: ". . . in Christ we who are many form one body, and each member belongs to all the others" (NIV).

Sincerely,
Kenn Gangel

Questions for Reflection

1. In what ways might an autocratic leadership style be especially vulnerable to creating church conflict? Have you seen this happen?

2. Would others think of you as a team-builder? Why or why not?

3. In what ways might non-Christians be able to contribute insights that may be helpful to Christian leaders? To what extent are you currently benefiting from those insights? What safeguards might need to be in place to preserve the doctrines of biblical sufficiency and authority?

TWENTY-TWO

Learning to Avoid
Subtle Temptations

Carl F. H. Henry is a true evangelical statesman. He has been a key player in many major developments in recent evangelicalism, including the formation of the National Association of Evangelicals, the founding of Fuller Seminary, and the creation of *Christianity Today* (of which he was founding editor). He chaired the 1966 World Congress of Evangelism in Berlin and was program chairman for the 1971 Jerusalem Conference on Biblical Prophecy. He has written or edited over thirty books, including *God, Revelation and Authority* (6 vols.) and the autobiographical *Confessions of a Theologian*.

Dear Friend,

I wish someone had told me that you would really welcome an occasional pat on the back. It would presumably help to offset that boot in the derrière targeted by erstwhile friends who give way every now and then to a lust for prominence and power, and who walk over anyone to get it. Don't let such misguided kangaroos embitter you. Just join the Almighty in a good laugh, or keep your silence altogether.

A Welsh revivalist once told me that many American preachers don't know what to do with their silences. They feel they must fill every vacuum with words, even when preaching. Sometimes the most powerful moment in a service, he said, occurs when the Spirit's hush falls. Give God a chance to speak now and then, especially in the silences.

Don't forget to pray. I've always believed in prayer; more than that, I have prayed. But not enough. Nobody told me that in those supposedly "golden" years (when one turns over what little gold he has to doctors, dentists, and hospitals) that the loss of memory and recollection would unexpectedly puncture holes in my prayer list. I start out praying for Russia and find myself wandering through Hong Kong.

My petitions get shorter while my prayer list gets longer. I wish I could be steeped in prayer even if I can no longer easily shift my knees from first to overdrive. But God sees me, and He is not hard of hearing.

Don't aspire to leadership. If it comes you will lose a lot of friends. Aspire to be "Number Two." You will have the field to yourself. When the right time comes the Lord will call you up higher. And you more likely will be ready.

Beware of money. Give away some of it, lest it burn a hole in your pocket. Designate it for ministries you know you can trust. You are moving into a century when self-promotion will be slicker than ever. The mail will be preempted by city slickers, country slickers, and just plain slickers. They want your savings. Invest in devout individuals, twice born, who can bring along some friends that Christ has redeemed or whom the prophets and apostles would have welcomed.

When on the road, don't take a laptop computer; take an extra towel. You may unexpectedly happen onto a fellow believer and, overjoyed, feel impelled to wash his feet. He in turn may unwittingly think he has been overtaken by an angel. That sort of fellowship is risky business; it might start a revival! Let me know if that happens. I'd like very much to get in on the action!

Your friend,
Carl F. H. Henry

Questions for Reflection

1. How often do you take time to encourage other Christian leaders? Do you actively seek out opportunities to serve other believers in general with the equivalent of "washing their feet"? How generous and strategic are you in your financial giving to others?

2. Have you learned how to allow God to speak to you (and others) in times of silence, or do you quickly fill that vacuum with noise?

3. Do people think of you as being inappropriately ambitious for leadership? If so, in what ways might that hinder your ministry to and with them? What adjustments in attitude or actions might need to be made to be less vulnerable to that reputation?

TWENTY-THREE

Learning How to Handle Criticism

J. Grant Howard is Director of Faculty Development at Phoenix Seminary. He served for many years as Professor of Pastoral Theology at Western Seminary's Portland and Phoenix campuses. Among his publications are *The Trauma of Transparency, Creativity in Preaching, Knowing God's Will—and Doing It!* and *Balancing Life's Demands.*

Dear Friend,

"Criticism is the manure that makes the plants of the Lord grow strong." Those words were penned by Joe Bayly some time ago, yet they still remain pungently true today. Hear the words of the following young, well-fertilized pastors.

"The past few months have been difficult for me. I have been criticized by a number of important people in the church. Frankly, some of it was justified, but I wasn't prepared for the stinging bite of it and the depression that came along with it. There have been times when I was ready to pack my bags and leave."

"After five months I feel as though I have experienced the whole gamut of emotions: from great enthusiasm, excitement, and joy to great disappointment, anxiety, and discouragement."

My own entrance into ministry was similar. A couple of hours after I preached my first sermon a member called to comment on the message. He said it was good, "but . . ." Then he proceeded to rip it to shreds. At least it seemed so to me. He said my main points were not clear, and my illustrations and applications were poor. Furthermore, I spoke too long, mispronounced "adult" (look it up!), and unbuttoned my coat six times. I got a large load of criticism unexpectedly dumped on my ego. How did I handle it? Days of angry depression, fortified with the fact that a few months prior to this I had been given my seminary's Senior Preaching Award. How could he do this to me? Well, he did and they (your people) will. I am not saying that all criticism is wrong. Some of it will be quite valid. Some invalid. Some debatable. But all should be dealt with as soon as possible. If we are going to deal with criticism adequately we must understand how it relates to leadership.

First, *recognize that criticism goes with leadership.* You're a leader. Your leadership will be scrutinized, idolized, and criticized. Scrutinized, because your work is done in public. Idolized, because your work is done on a pedestal. Criticized, because your work is done with people, whom you can't please all the time. Therein lie the ingredients for criticism. Visibility creates vulnerability, which means you are open to attack and susceptible to getting hurt. If you are one of the warm, relational type of leaders, that will put you into even closer contact with others, making you an even more visible and vulnerable target.

If you are an aggressive leader, you will often visibly challenge the status quo and set yourself up for the criticism you will endure when you are seeking to effect change.

I have strengths in the area of creative preaching. Consequently I am often experimenting with ways to preach the Word more effectively. Those who are comfortable with an innovative preaching style tend to put me on a pedestal. Those who aren't tend to criticize me. To summarize, criticism is the inevitable and necessary by-product of leadership.

Second, *understand the nature of criticism.* Who will criticize you? Anyone and everyone. Young and old. Men and women. Boards and committees. Members and visitors. Friends and strangers. Even fellow staff.

When will they criticize you? Anytime. Right before or after a service; or weeks or even months later, after you've forgotten the incident, but after they have had time to build a major case against you. Some may be reacting to their own problems, and you're getting the backlash. Often it comes at unexpected times, from such unlikely sources. Some people are "chronic criticizers." At best it is a hobby for them, at worst it is a vocation.

For what will they criticize you? Everything. Anything. Your marriage. Your family. The way you talk. The way you work. The way you dress. Your use of humor. Your manners. Are you always on time? Any distracting habits? Friendly?

How will they criticize you? Behind your back. To your face. Oral. Written. Signed. Unsigned.

Third, *understand your reactions to criticism.* You will have a mixture of two reactions: anger and depression. You will be mad and sad. You will be preoccupied with your critic's words. You will find it difficult to concentrate on your Bible study and sermon preparation. Instead you will replay over and over in your mind the critical comments aimed at you.

Fear moves in on you. Perhaps you are not really where you ought to be. You shouldn't have taken this position. Maybe you shouldn't be in the ministry. Decisions that seemed so right now seem suspect. Could it all be a mistake? Self-depreciation starts paying you unwelcome visits. You can't do it right. You can't do it well. Others don't appreciate your efforts or your dedication. You try to counsel yourself out of this negative mind-set, but begin to discover the truth of the saying, "He that hath himself for a doctor, hath a fool for a patient." You begin to lose objectivity.

Procrastination seeps in. Things you used to handle quickly, you now put off indefinitely. You ponder more. You produce less. Your motivation is down. Your mulling is up. Self-fulfilling prophecies begin to occur. You did not do it well the last time, you probably won't do it well the next time.

It was just a few months ago that you accepted the challenge and call to this new ministry. Things were going well. Then it happened. Criticism! It came swiftly, immediately inundating your total being, touching down like a Texas twister with devastating ferocity. Now you are totally disillusioned and confused, wallowing in misery and self-pity. Even the thought of quitting has crossed your mind. Before you get into the resignation phase, I want to give you some principles on how to deal with criticism to stabilize your thinking.

Expect it. It's inevitable. You will be criticized. Don't assume you are going to be such a nice guy and such a smooth operator and such a dedicated, discerning, congenial, wise, winsome, and positive person that you are going to have everyone 100 percent for you all the time! That's unrealistic. Only a perfect person can live up to those criteria. We don't qualify. We are imperfect persons living in an imperfect world.

See God in it. His plan is for members of the church to help each other grow. This is basically accomplished by teaching and admonishing one another (Col. 1:28, 3:16). Teaching deals with ignorance. We need to know the truth. Admonishing deals with disobedience. We need to do the truth. Romans 15:14 indicates that all believers can and should carry out this teaching/admonishing with regard to each other. Like it or not, God will use others to criticize our ignorance and disobedience. Synonyms for this double-thrust discipling underscore its confrontive, aggressive nature: warn, rebuke, correct, discipline, confront, test, provoke. Don't forget, all of this is to be done in love (Eph. 4:15).

Develop a healthy self-concept. If you don't have this, you will be like a yo-yo in the hands of your critics. You will be up when things are going okay, and down when you are getting low approval ratings. If you don't have a healthy, growing self-concept, one that is keenly aware of strengths and weaknesses and is working on them, then you are at the mercy of the critics, well-meaning as they may be. If your self-concept is essentially dependent on the constant approval and approbation of the flock, you are in serious trouble. If your self-concept is being built on and balanced by the Word, then you will be able to think more accurately about yourself. Romans 12:3 will help you think correctly about your uniquely gifted self.

Carry on consistent self-evaluation. Criticize yourself. Base it on legitimate standards, the Scriptures. This helps to prepare you for the criticism of others. If you are highly threatened and defensive with regard to criticism from others, it is a good indication that you aren't engaging in meaningful, consistent evaluation of yourself. Self-criticism will prevent a lot of criticism from others, because when they call the problem to your attention you can tell them that the Lord has been dealing with you already with regard to this matter and you would appreciate their prayers on your behalf. In a sense you "beat them to the punch." But watch out for the temptation to be too introspective. We may dwell almost morbidly on an issue. This is not healthy, nor is it biblical. The same Bible that motivates us to internal investigation also tells us that the general tenor of our thought life is to be positive (Phil. 4:8).

Invite criticism. Tell people you want it and need it. Facilitate feedback using comment cards in the pew racks, attitude and need surveys, distributed as bulletin inserts. Make definite appointments to meet. Explore the use of e-mail, the fax machine, telephone, the written letter. Read them all, signed or unsigned. Discover the potential of face-to-face conversation in dealing with criticism. The pastor should have an annual review by the board.

Small groups are vital to the church. Included would be Sunday school classes, boards, committees, ministry staff, office staff, and growth groups. They can help the church and the pastor evaluate the criticism to see if it has any merit. It behooves the pastor to stay close to small groups.

Schedule periodic question and answer sessions for segments of the membership, e.g., one-fourth of the members meet in an open forum with the pastor every four to eight months.

When appropriate and profitable you may choose to share portions of critiquing letters with the congregation.

Rely on congregational resources. You have school teachers with expertise in spelling, punctuation, vocabulary, grammar, logic, etc. The bulletin should be perfect, no errors, every Sunday.

Furthermore, you should never hear "That's irrelevant . . ." nor should our ears ever be assaulted with, "It was me . . ." The point is this: there will always be people listening critically to what is written and spoken. Harness that skill.

The individual who sells clothing may provide insight on color coordination, fit, fashion, and style. A local florist may provide a rich reservoir of experience in enhancing platform beauty. The graphic artist critiques your dull, drab bulletin every Sunday. Why not ask her to submit some creative new proposals?

It's not easy to invite criticism. Nor is it easy to receive it when it is given. The critic can be unkind and hurt our feelings. But there is no growth without pain and God may choose to use the pain of criticism to get our attention and change our life-style. The above suggestions are designed to keep the pastor in contact with as many of the people as possible. We want them to develop their critical thinking skills. The key to the development of critical thinking is to ask questions.

Here are four ground rules that I suggest for critics: (1) Don't criticize right before or after a worship service; (2) Don't criticize when you are angry. Calm down, cool off, and then talk; (3) Don't criticize weeks or months after the incident; and (4) Don't just criticize—offer solutions.

I also want to encourage you to set specific personal goals. Do this for your life and ministry. Share them (when appropriate) with your leaders and your congregation. This kind of goal setting will help to create a healthy context for criticism.

Finally, remember this: Never fear criticism when you are right, and never ignore it when you are wrong.

Sincerely,
Grant Howard

Questions for Reflection

1. In what ways have you already experienced your leadership being "scrutinized, idolized, and criticized"? How did you respond to each, and how pleased were you with that response?

2. "He that hath himself for a doctor, hath a fool for a patient." How might others help you to process criticism in a more healthy and constructive manner? How might a better use of the expertise of others leave you less vulnerable to valid criticism?

3. How faithfully are you practicing self-examination and self-criticism? Do you invite input from others? Do you respond to that input from a biblically balanced self-image?

TWENTY-FOUR

Learning to Maximize Human Relationships

David Jeffery is Vice President for Advancement at Western Seminary in Portland, Oregon. Prior to this he served as Chief Marketing Administrator at Seattle Pacific University, Executive Vice President at Western Evangelical Seminary, and Executive Vice President/Chief Operating Officer at Northwest Medical Teams.

Dear Friend,

Whether you manage an institution or an organization, work for a corporation, or have a leadership role in your church, be sure to spend time with people you love. Your most pressing need (next to maintaining a relationship with God) is knowing how to maximize your human relationships.

I encourage those I work with to try to understand more and more the simple but powerful concept of building deep relationships. By building relationships, we can accomplish almost superhuman feats. Each of us brings to our organization great talents, skills, resources, and caring concerns; but life's highest achievers are those who best understand and most skillfully utilize the process of inter-relationships. They are the ones who know where and how to find the greatest fulfillment, happiness, and achievement.

Ephesians 3:14–22 is my life text. In this prayer of Paul's, he proclaims that the God of the humanly impossible is able to do exceedingly abundantly above all that we can ask, think, or imagine. Often God does these spectacular things through ordinary people. In spending most of my professional career directing, training, and supervising a marketing team for Christian institutions, I have seen God do this time and time again. These people were willing to step out in faith and fulfill a vision.

Connecting with other people is risky business, but it's the only way we can ever hope to become high achievers. One of the by-products of our technological orientation is that we have come to rely almost fanatically upon so-called specialists such as social workers, psychotherapists, encounter group leaders, coaches, etc. to help us connect with others. We pay big money for motivational tapes and self-help messages. We use sophisticated equipment to conduct conference calls and communicate with increasing numbers of people through Internet technology. Yet with all our sophisticated trappings, we are the most disconnected people of any generation. I have watched many of the people that I have worked with experience divorce. Many are disconnected from their children and extended families. Addictions and depression have touched many of their lives. Conflict, anger, resentment, and workaholism have caused untold amounts of suffering. How can we be so progressive on the one hand and yet so inferior when it comes to our relationships? What good is progress if we are faced with broken homes and disenfranchised coworkers and friends? What good is interactive technology if we cannot interact with those who live in our own homes? What good does it do to reach out around the world if we cannot touch someone next door? A great tragedy we face, as an advanced society, is that we underestimate the intrinsic value of deep and lasting relationships. When love is reduced to one-night stands or live-in arrangements shaped by "what's in it for me" attitudes, we can only expect to come up empty in our human relationships.

High achievers understand that everyone has value. People and relationships are not predictable. If I have learned anything over twenty-five years in marketing, it is simply that you cannot lump all people together in convenient little categories or segments and accurately predict their reactions and responses. Many of us have big jobs with great responsibilities, leaving us less time than we would prefer to spend with each individual; but our success depends largely upon the degree to which we recognize that each person is an individual with unique needs, concerns, histories, and desires. In my field (marketing), a high achiever must invest in person-to-person relationship time. Personal relationships make *all* human endeavors possible.

Over twenty-two years ago I was working with a major donor couple. This couple had the ability and willingness to make a major capital campaign effort a success. In the course of my cultivation work with them, I asked the wife some personal questions about significant dates in her life such as birthdays, anniversaries, and deaths of parents. She was very kind and yet a little curt by saying, "Oh, you are just a fundraiser; you won't pay any attention to these dates anyway." Well,

I love a challenge and I am proud to say that over the past twenty-two years I have never missed calling Reva to wish her a happy birthday on St. Patrick's Day and sending cards of either sympathy or congratulations to remember other key events in her life. She and her husband have indeed made a difference for the college I then served, but that came from the efforts to build a lasting relationship—not because I had mastered the fine arts of closing a sale.

Anyone who sets out to relate successfully with people must start from the position that all relationships are essentially person-to-person relationships. Our success will come from a willingness to invest in building deep relationships. One of the most difficult challenges I have faced is shifting my management style from that of an entrepreneur/"lone ranger" to that of a professional coach and manager. The following principles have guided me in changing my style.

First, make loving God and spending time with Him priority number one. In so doing I can value every person I meet in my daily life—no matter if they are a donor with a considerable net worth, a prospective student with a tremendous IQ, or just a stranger that we pass on a busy sidewalk—and take time to smile and greet them. We demonstrate that we truly love God by loving those He loves. We must learn that to reach our full potential as leaders the best investment we can make towards high achievement is to inspire, encourage, pray for, and enable others to become high achievers themselves.

To give up our demands for the world to do our will and instead dedicate ourselves to doing God's will is a leader's act of faith. It is not easy to empty ourselves of our "rights" and the motivation for success.

I find it difficult to take time for prayer, running, Bible reading, music, building relationships, and meditation. I am too busy "doing"—evaluating alternatives, making decisions, setting up and keeping appointments, talking on the phone, going on fundraising calls, processing e-mail—these all seem more productive. I appear to value those activities so highly that I rarely take time for matters of the heart. But God faithfully teaches me to remember my family and my staff. When He does, I again pledge to get my priorities straight.

The second principle is that if you want to be loved, you have to love others first. I think of my friend, Doug Pennoyer, a Rhodes Scholar and successful university professor and administrator, who spent six months living in a tent outside the village of a head-hunting tribe in the Philippines. They had never let an outsider into their area. He did it because of God's love for him. God has given Doug a love for these people. To build a relationship it took him six months and a bad case of malaria. Only then did this tribe trust Doug. Only then could Doug begin to learn their language and document their customs. Doug's love for these people has, in subsequent years, taken him back, and he has reaped the joy of loving.

The third principle is that of achieving greatness through service. I learned this principle from Jim Hurd at Seattle Pacific University. I would get annoyed at Jim sometimes because he seemed to be everywhere all at once—doing this and that for everyone. He would always be the first to clean up or pick up, demonstrating a remarkable tenacity to serve. Then I heard Tom Skinner, an author and evangelist, speak. He told our group, "Everybody is somebody's foolish servant. I'm a servant for Jesus. Whose servant are you?" We all serve some master. If we are not serving Jesus, then we are serving another god of our own making. Am I willing, as Jim was, to be a servant?

Servants take risks for the sake of others. They can cry and laugh with us. They are vulnerable. They are willing to be misunderstood. Servants get involved when others would play it safe. Servants do not need to see the results of their work; they trust God and commit their work to Him. Faithfulness is more important than seeing immediate, visible results. Servants believe that prayer is the highest form of action, but they are willing to stop praying to serve someone in need. Jim, where did you get the internal sense of security, the comfort, the freedom, and the courage to be a servant? Did God's love for you radically set you free to live for others, to be their servant? I have to believe that this servant leadership life-style has come back to bless Jim and his wife Mary many times over.

The fourth principle is the importance of unity. Unity implies that a loving, accepting, and cooperative attitude toward others leads to great effectiveness in getting things done. During the 1988–89 year, the development staff at Seattle Pacific University accomplished a significant goal that had never been done before at that school: raising over a million dollars for student scholarships in a single year. It was accomplished by a staff of twelve who worked hand-in-hand, arm-in-arm, side-by-side; encouraging, inspiring, lifting, challenging, and believing in each other and in the plan we had developed. We had one focus—believing we were going to be successful—and it worked. We celebrated achievements as a team. What a great memory, everyone working together! It was a big accomplishment when you realize the average gift was $350. People united with us in reaching the goal.

The fifth principle is the need to take responsibility. Commitment is a critical part of any relationship, whether it's marriage, friendship, business, or education. Our natural tendency is to concern ourselves more with what others should be doing than with what we should be doing. The principle of responsibility suggests that if we are going to work effectively with people, we must express that responsibility through responsiveness to their needs first. A senior vice president at my first job after graduating from college, Ray Allen, taught me this principle. I worked for a financial institution and began in the collections department, dealing with people who had experienced financial reversals in their lives. I will never forget my first house call to a client. The debtor lived approximately two hundred miles north of our office. Mr. Allen had told me to bring back a specific amount of money as a payment on the client's account. I returned to the office four hours later with the client's promise to pay ten days later on the first of the month. I was met at the door of the office by Mr. Allen with a broad smile and an outstretched hand: "How much money did you bring back?" When I told him the "whole story" he promptly sent me back out the door with the instructions not to return without the payment. I learned again the lesson of responsibility (by the way, the bank had already charged off this account to bad debt and I ultimately collected the total balance). Being responsible and holding people responsible has become a lifelong principle.

The sixth principle is the importance of expressing praise and gratitude. "We are all excited by the love of praise," wrote Cicero. Praise encourages people to achieve, gives them inner confidence, and makes them grow. I have heard it said that there is no mystery to raising healthy children—just praise them continually. Former President George Bush made it his practice to write thank you and recognition notes every day at 10:00 P.M. For many years, I have done a similar exercise with my associates. We begin by compiling a nearly exhaustive list of the many good things about each other. What a joy! We have found these pieces of paper that contain words of praise and thankfulness end up achieving a status in our lives that even the most prominent writers never achieve. These lists will never be thrown away. These words of praise and thanksgiving strike deeply. They satisfy, nourish, soothe, and stir us to greater accomplishments. So, say it! Write it! Live it! Don't hold back; praise, thanksgiving, and gratefulness will be tremendously cherished. Give generously whatever and whenever you can.

The seventh principle is learning to persevere. When a situation around us is not good, we can turn it around through persistence, understanding, and untiring effort. In 1993, I was working for a Christian institution that was facing its most challenging hour. A series of overwhelming situations had to be solved for this institution to be solvent and survive. Each one of these situations, by itself, seemed an insurmountable challenge to face—a most difficult marathon. However, each morning the ten of us who made up the staff determined that we would persevere. We prayed and we continued to do the right things. Who can even imagine how many other people were praying and offering moral support? I cannot begin to answer that question, but I can tell you that at the exact time when hope was almost gone, God stepped in and rewarded our perseverance.

The real race of life is more like a marathon than a hundred-yard dash. Many people fail to develop the perseverance that running the marathon requires. Giving up on situations and relationships is certainly much more simple than sticking with it and trying to make it work. When it does work, you will be glad that you persisted and you will have built lasting bonds with the people around you who assisted you in reaching your goal.

Five easy-to-learn, practical components summarize these principles: (1) Value people; (2) Give of yourself; (3) Make cooperation and affiliation a way of life; (4) Be grateful; and (5) Practice persistence.

In Kevin Mannoia's book entitled *The Integrity Factory: A Journey in Leadership Formation,* he makes the point that there are two dimensions of leadership: the visible activities of the leader and the unseen foundation in the leader's character. The foundation is like the 90 percent of an iceberg that is below the surface. People see the 10 percent, but the stability of the iceberg is below the surface. That challenges me to build deep relationships with God, family, and friends who love me and desire to hold me accountable.

Consider the faith of a successful leader: "success" is less in doing than in being. Building deep relationships is never wasted. Only by giving all areas of our life back to God can we receive it rightly again with the power to make a difference in our world.

Sincerely,
Dave Jeffery

Questions for Reflection

1. How much time and effort are you investing in building deep, quality relationships with others? Are you loving others first, and experiencing their love in return?

2. Consider following George Bush's example and writing daily a series of praise and gratitude notes to those with whom you serve. You might best begin by reflecting upon the strengths and virtues of these colaborers.

3. How does the doctrine of God's faithfulness help build perseverance in us when prospects seem otherwise dim?

TWENTY-FIVE

Learning the Significance of Decisions

Don Jensen is Director of Pastoral Training at Western Seminary in Portland, Oregon. He was senior pastor at Village Baptist Church in Beaverton, Oregon, for twenty-eight years. He earlier served as pastor of Grace Baptist Church in Glendora, California, for ten-and-a-half years. Don has also served as president of CBFMS (now CBInternational) for five years. He is the author of *Your Church Can Excel in Global Giving* and *Encouragement for God's Servants*. Don's letter was originally sent to a young pastor who had asked him to share what he had learned about pastoral ministry.

Dear Friend,

Based upon my having served as a senior pastor for over thirty-eight years (over ten years in my first pastorate and over twenty-eight years in my most recent assignment), you asked me to share with you what lessons about pastoral leadership I could pass on to you as you begin your career as the lead pastor of a congregation. I suppose your question could also be expressed by asking what mistakes did I make in my first years that you want to be sure to avoid repeating? However one might frame the question, I know that if I had to do it over again, there are some decisions I would make differently. I use the word "decisions" simply because *we are the kind of leaders we decide to be.* A. W. Tozer put it like this: "Before God every man is what he wills to be." When I first read that statement, I immediately realized how true it is. There are many issues over which we have no control. These include our family background, our gifting, the growth and demographics of the community where God may place us, the history of the people we are called upon to serve, and countless other circumstances that converge upon our lives and ministry. But we do

151

have control over what kind of person we choose to be, how we will respond to the issues we will face each day, and what leadership character we will exercise in the midst of these variable circumstances.

To fulfill the assignment of pastoral leadership, there are five essentials that must be properly addressed: the heart, the family, the church ministry, the development of leadership skills, and the training of future leaders. Each of these will be impacted by the decisions you make because the decisions you make will determine the kind of pastoral leader you will be. Numerical size of your ministry is *not* part of the equation we are responsible for. We must be willing to leave those results to God. What we are responsible for is the kind of leader we will choose to be. Do we have a heart to follow after the Lord Jesus? Will we give our family high priority? Will the church we are called to pastor achieve the goals God wants it to achieve? What will we do to ensure that our world will be a better place because of the leadership we exercise?

In each of these areas I made some wrong choices. I hope my sharing some of my present insights will give to you a better start and a greater finish. If it does, I will be gratified.

A heart to follow the Leader of leaders

Solomon put it simply: "Above all else, guard your heart, for it affects everything you do" (Prov. 4:23 NLT). If your heart isn't right, your leadership capabilities will bring no eternal value. Today you are a leader; the haunting question is, what kind? Do you remember how Moses sent twelve men, each from one of the twelve tribes, to explore the land of Canaan? A number of times in the thirteenth chapter of Numbers, they are all called "leaders." But ten led God's people away from God's blessing and only two toward it.

One greater than Solomon said, "Love the Lord with all your heart." Follow the Lord wholeheartedly and you will lead your people to discover God's special grace. These are truths that you already know and teach, but we also know how easy it is not to do what we say we do (and should do). Above all else guard your heart, your time, your priorities to ensure that you are prayerfully listening and responding to God's voice daily. Meditate on His Word day and night. Establish holy habits and tenaciously practice them. Psalm 78 ends with the beautiful statement about King David that you want said about your own pastoral leadership: "David shepherded them [God's people] with integrity of heart; with skillful hands he led them" (v. 72 NIV). David basically did what he knew he should do. But in the same Psalm, there is also the record of those who "ended their lives in failure." These were the people who did not do what they knew to do.

Several years ago, after an eye examination, my ophthalmologist said I needed surgery. Because I have always had a phobia regarding anyone doing anything to my eyes, I asked, "What if I don't?" He replied without a bat of his eyelash, "You'll go blind!" I quickly got healed of my phobia and made immediate arrangements for surgery. The impact of that event caused me to ask myself a lot of hard questions. Were I to go blind, could I continue in the ministry? And why hadn't I memorized more of God's Word? I realized that I had left my heart vulnerable. If we are to be godly leaders, we must above all else guard our hearts. *The first and foundational principle of pastoral leadership is godliness.* Everything depends upon it. If you have not already done so, decide now upon your priorities. How many Scriptures will you memorize each week? How much time will you set aside to listen to God each day? When? How? Sadly, most pastors pray less than ten minutes per day. No wonder there is a leadership crisis! Be careful to be a prayerful pastor. Decide now to lead your congregation from a kneeling position. Determine to lead your people to pray. God's promise to bless His people awaits those who call upon Him. A humble calling on the Lord comes out of a relationship with the Lord. Develop that relationship listening to His heartbeat and sharing yours.

Because you will encounter pressures on many fronts to combat and defeat your good decisions, take whatever steps you need to ensure that you will follow through all the way. Don't try to do it without the support of a trusted friend and accountability partner(s). To help ensure that purity is maintained, having an accountability partner of the same sex is a requirement Village Baptist made of all our pastoral and board leadership. It is a "must" relationship. Not to have one is an automatic reason to resign.

If you do not now presently have such a partner in the work of the ministry who you can count on to pray for you and hold you accountable for godly living, begin today to ask God to provide one for you. Jonathan encouraged David, and God has a Jonathan to encourage you as well. Do everything in your might to ensure that your belief system (what you say is important) is the same as your value system (what you show by your actions is important).

Leading your family

The leaders from Issachar who were under the command of King David "understood the temper of the times and knew the best course . . . to take" (1 Chron. 12:32 NLT). Characterizing them was their "single purpose of making David the king" (v. 38). They not only spent time with him learning from him, they did it with their family members

(v. 32). We too must serve with and lead our families. The apostle Paul explicitly wrote to Timothy that the elder "must be faithful to his wife" and "manage his own family well . . . for if a man cannot manage his own household, how can he take care of God's church?" (1 Tim. 3:2–5 NLT). The bottom line is simply that we have some kind of spiritual blueprint that we can follow so that we build the lives of our family members well. What kind of character qualities do you want your family to possess? How do you plan to go about helping them to possess these qualities?

In the first years of my ministry, I sinned against my family. I spent an inordinate amount of time with the church family away from my own family. From time to time, I was convicted and said to my wife, "We're going to establish a family night each week." We did this for one or two weeks, but then I allowed other things to take priority. Again, several months would go by and I would make another half-hearted (or quarter-hearted) effort and again failed to live up to my word. I'll never forget how one night I was home and overheard my three-year-old daughter ask my wife, "Mommy, how come Daddy's home? Is he sick?" I lamented to my wife, "Is the only time my kids see me at home is when I'm sick?" I again said, "For sure, we're going to have a weekly family night no matter what!" But tragically, what I said was priority really wasn't my priority in practice. My belief system wasn't aligned with my value system.

Several more months went by. The oldest of my three children was now about eight. One of my sons asked me one evening if I would help him build his model airplane. I responded by saying that I had a meeting at the church, but I would do it the following night. The following evening came and my son asked me with great expectancy, "Daddy, are you going to help me build my model tonight?" What do you think I said? I explained that since the previous evening, a very important issue had come up that required my attention and then asked, "Do you understand?" With tears running down his cheeks, my son said "Yes, Daddy, I understand, but you promised!" Well after I helped build his model that night, we had a family night every week without fail. If you were to ask my adult children today about the highlights of their upbringing, one of them would be "family nights." By the way, I can't even remember what that "important issue" was. What I do know is that my family was far more important. I didn't want to lose them and I thank God that I learned my lesson before it was too late.

Spend time with your family members. If God gives to you sons, spend special time with each of them. If God gives to you daughters, "date" them. If you are going to know the special bents God wired into your children, you must spend time with them. And when you spend quality time with them you will help them become all that God wants them to be. Regularly, date your wife and spend time just with her. Remember that a godly leader of a church is a godly leader of his family. When all the dust settles, what really counts is that we made a strong, happy, and godly contribution to the lives of our family members successfully passing the baton of truth and holiness to each of them.

Leading your church

A leader leads and if we are to lead a church congregation, we must know where we want to take them. There is only one place where we can discover this and that is in the presence of the Lord of the church. If I had to do it all over again, I would not assume the role of the leader until I had discerned from the Lord what He wanted for that local expression of His church to do. I would then articulate this purpose in a succinct form. You can call it a mission statement, vision statement, or purpose statement; the name makes no difference. You may even find it necessary to sharpen it more precisely over time, but it is essential that you know where you are to lead the church over which you are to be the overseer. Next, I would make sure that you have a leadership team who are all in agreement and who will support you to accomplish this mission. Let me underscore this again: if you are to give leadership, you *must* know where you will be leading the people.

Once, you know where you want to go, then comes the task of knowing how to best get there. This also needs to be articulated with both objectives and tactical procedures spelled out so all responsible personnel are reading from the same page. This kind of document is what I call a "Master Plan." Such a document is larger than any one person and needs to be developed cooperatively by the entire leadership team. Then it must be made known to all the constituency so everyone will know where they are going and how they will get there.

The Core Values/Philosophy of Ministry also needs to be written so there will be no misunderstanding by well-meaning people on how best to accomplish the objectives in the Master Plan. Unlike the Master Plan, which is a living and changeable document, the Core Values that govern the way you will go about your ministry reflect convictions that you will go to the wall for.

Another brief document we have found to be very helpful in our leadership dynamics is what we call our "Church Policy." This articulates the respective roles of the congregation, board, pastoral staff, and Senior Pastor. This furnishes us with a clear definition of who does what. It has both kept us from stepping on each other's toes and given to us a smooth operation in the discharge of our respective responsibilities.

Had I had these basic documents in print at the beginning of my ministry, I would have been spared many hours of needless meetings and would have freed all the members of those meetings from the same frustrations. More importantly, we all could have been involved in *doing* ministry instead of *talking* about it. Today there are many splendid and helpful resources available to help you formulate these kinds of documents, but be careful to remember that it all begins with a spiritual ear tuned in on what the Spirit is saying to the churches. Time spent listening and responding to the Spirit of God is essential. That is where you must begin and that is where you must continue. In addition to your daily time alone with God, I urge you to set aside retreat times (one to three days) on a regular basis, monthly, quarterly, or some other arrangement. As you surround yourself with leadership staff, require that they do the same. Without those times, stagnancy can too easily set in.

Learning to develop the skills of leadership/Learning from leaders

We all learn to lead by leading. The leaders of Issachar not only had a heart to lead, they spent time with the master leader, David. They observed his skills and learned from him. David "led . . . with skillful hands." In modern terminology, the leaders of Issachar were mentored by a master leader. Get one! Get several! Don't try to lead without one!

The best place to secure a mentor is the local church. I wish I had been privileged to serve in an internship learning from proven staff who could have walked with me through the multifaceted aspects of church life. If one wants to know what church is really all about, attendance and participation in staff and board meetings are essential. Merely observing a few such meetings doesn't cut it. You've got to be there on a somewhat regular basis. That's where decisions are made and that's where church is done. When I was in seminary, I was an assistant pastor of a church. The title was misleading. I received assignments, but no instruction or critique. I was never invited to attend any of the meetings where the decisions were formed. My work was appreciated and I received a stipend that unfortunately was a primary incentive to assume the responsibilities of that office. If I had it to do over again, I would have sought out a church with a proven history of training and would have offered the leadership a salary to train me for a minimum of one year (and ideally for three years).

Now you may say, "I agree. I wish I had done that as well, but here I am already in charge of a church and I have all kinds of questions. How can I get good counsel for the situation where I find myself today?" You can make up for lost time by seeking out help available to you. Several years ago, a young pastor made a lunch appointment with me to ask some questions from me about the ministry. When we sat down, after a short time of exchanging congenialities, he whipped out his laptop and started to ask me questions already formatted in his software. I was one among several he interviewed. As he asked me a number of personal and ministry questions, I thought to myself, "What a good idea!" As a matter of fact it was such a good idea, I wondered why I hadn't thought of doing it? He was intent on maximizing his time and avoiding mistakes. He was from out of state, but knew he was going to be in the area and took advantage of the opportunity to meet with me. I was pleased to give him my time and so would most other leaders. There are a lot of ways to get mentoring and nearly all of them are available to you.

Another way of saying this is, "Network your resources of godly leaders!" Hardly any problem comes up in our ministries that someone hasn't already handled.

Leading leaders

Mentoring is a two-way street. We take in so we can give out. We give out and need to take in. The leader who is mentoring needs to be mentored. The person who is being mentored needs to mentor.

Included in the role of a pastor is the need to bring healing to the hurting. This will often be done by the pastor himself. If, however, the pastor is the only one who does this, the flock will depend entirely upon him. With this scenario—which by the way is the most common in the U.S.—the pastor's time will be stretched and limited. To prevent this bottleneck, concentrate on developing leaders who will make a positive difference. Regularly ask yourself the hard questions: (1) Whom am I developing into godly and skillful leaders? (2) How am I going about it? (3) Whom are they leading? (4) How effective are they? (5) What can I do better next time? (6) What kind of difference is being made in the world as a result of these leaders? These are the kind of questions that naturally flow from the instruction given to the young pastor, Timothy. In his last known letter, Paul wrote: "You have heard me teach many things that have been confirmed by many reliable witnesses. Teach these great truths to trustworthy people who are able to pass them on to others" (2 Tim. 2:2 NLT). Paul put four generations of leaders in this one sentence. How successful we are can easily be confirmed by asking the third and fourth generations about the leadership skills they have learned from the leaders we have helped develop and are now in the process of passing on to others.

There will always be more to do than time to do it. For this simple reason you need to be careful to ask yourself, "Is what I am doing making a difference for the kingdom of God on the people out there?"

You will make the greatest contribution to the world that our Lord wants to reach by developing leaders who will develop leaders. Jesus chose to invest His time and energy in certain potential leaders. His choice of men was the result of prayer. You will make no mistake by asking the Lord to give to you direction in choosing from your reservoir of leadership. They are probably already on your leadership team: staff and board members, key laymen, new converts, and a number of others who have a heart to serve God and need only to be challenged and encouraged to meet with you.

Another way to say this is develop an "apprentice" mentality. An assistant to a leader will help make the leader look good but an apprentice is in training to be a leader. Work at encouraging all your leaders on your board, pastoral staff, small group leadership, teaching and support staff to have an apprentice. This is doing what Paul told Timothy about passing the baton to others who can pass it on to others.

The list could go on, but from my perspective and experience these five areas are essential to develop under the hand of God. There is a world of people for whom Christ died that need to hear that they are loved and can be forgiven. I know that our Lord will honor every effort you put into incorporating these qualities into your life and ministry. As a result you will finish well, knowing that you have made a difference for the kingdom of God in a world of need.

Let's keep in touch,
Don Jensen

Questions for Reflection

1. In what key areas and relationships of your life might your beliefs and value system not be properly harmonized? What factors might be contributing to this discrepancy between what you think you believe and what your actions reveal about what you truly value?

2. Do you have a clear sense as to the direction in which you should be leading your people? If not, what can you do to correct this?

3. Ask yourself the six "hard questions" posed by the author with respect to our development of leaders. Are you satisfied with your answers to each question?

Learning How to Lead
When the Honeymoon Ends

John E. Johnson has for the last five years served as senior pastor of Trinity Baptist International Church in Wassenaar, The Netherlands. Prior to this, he pastored Lents Baptist Church in Portland, Oregon, for a decade. While in Portland, Johnson also served as an adjunct faculty member for Western Seminary, and more recently has taught graduate courses in both Europe and Southeast Asia. He has published two articles in *Bibliotheca Sacra*. The following letter was originally sent to a young man whom Johnson had mentored, and who had subsequently gone on to pastor an established traditional church—only to experience significant disenchantment with his church two years later.

Dear Friend,

When my wife and I stood before our pastor to declare our marital vows, he gave us good counsel regarding the initial days of our marriage. He prefaced it with the words, "Once the sugar coating melts away under the heat of marital responsibility. . . ." From your letter, it appears that the sugar coating has indeed melted away under the heat of pastoral responsibility—and congregational expectations. The honeymoon has passed, the heat is on. Welcome to the ranks!

As I read your letter, your words drove me back to the beginning days of my ministry. I too faced similar frustrations. Right now, you would like to send some sheep to market. I understand—I've been there. So let me share what I wish someone had told me about leadership in such situations.

First, *lead with love*. Reflecting back on the interview process, people seemed generally enthusiastic about the ideas you would bring for change and the leadership you would exercise to bring the church to a new and exciting chapter in its history. Now you lie awake at night, mystified about the pastor's role in leadership. My guess is that you are trying to find your bearings, both at the board and congregational levels.

Now that you have set the tone and shared your dreams, some are voicing the opinion that you need to be firm, take charge, lead the troops, and handle any dissidents. Others, for reasons that may have little to do with you personally, are suspicious of your influence. They may even resent your leadership, considering any authority you might exercise to be intrusive, threatening, even autocratic. If this isn't confusing enough, some who want more assertive leadership are the first to be offended when you give it. No wonder Bill Hybels, founding pastor of Willow Creek Church, once said at a leadership conference here in The Netherlands, "The local church is the most leadership intensive organization in society." It is the most complex institution, harder to lead than any other one.

Imagine what he might have said had he begun where you did, with an established work. As difficult and challenging as it is to begin from ground level, there is something to be said for the efforts required when beginning on the eighth or eightieth floor. When you are building on layers of ministry, years of "we have always done it this way," you may be discovering that people aren't necessarily panting for vision-oriented leadership. There may be a sense of "Been there, done that," or even worse, "Been there, tried that, and it didn't work." The end result is that these members of an older work are not so generous in their granting of credibility and trust, and not so inclined to followership.

In a newer work, there seems to be a general sense of "We are joining you." In an established work like yours, the mind-set tends to be "You are joining us." This isn't so apparent at first, but it becomes increasingly clear (especially when the congregation is challenged to embark upon new chapters). This hit home to me one day when I was sharing the details of a possible relocation of our church building. It was going fairly well, until I began to realize they were asking questions such as, "Well, will *your* church have a large hall for the youth?" Until they know you have joined them, it is highly probable they will not be joining you.

So, can one read Barna and Warren without creating more havoc for the soul? Do you dare to attend another Church Growth and Leadership conference? I think you can, as long as you shape these ideas to your context. It's likely that some in your church will never get on board, never join you, and never accept your leadership. But some, probably far more than you think, will join the effort to be vision-oriented and purpose-driven when they know that you love them. I used to declare boldly, "The train is leaving. Get on or get out of the way." Having worked my way through the vision process and believing, as James Belasco writes, that vision alone is no solution—everything is execution (cf. *Flight of the Buffalo,* p. 31), I would urge the troops forward. Maybe it is the result of experience and the scars that often come with it, but I am increasingly inclined to say, "The train needs to leave. I would really love to have you aboard. But if it takes a bit more time, I'll be there to help you. In the meantime I will do my best to win your trust."

If I can put it one other way, it's being willing to go through leadership's preliminary stages. Aubrey Malphurs, in his book *Values-Driven Leadership* (p. 134), observed that within an established work there are two necessary stages before the leadership stage. The first is the chaplain stage. Preaching and caring are the chief functions of this ministry. At this point, one's influence as a leader will be limited. Plan for one to three years. The second stage is the pastor stage. In these three to five years shepherding, gaining credibility, and establishing trust are the main points of focus. For visionary men like yourself, these stages will require a mix of restraint, tenacity, carefulness, wisdom, and patience, enabled by a heart that is in love with God and His church. And hopefully, in submission to such a process, you will have gained credibility as well as authority invested by the congregation to act on its behalf.

Second, *create the capital.* Your letter tells me that you are tired. Ministry can be draining, and if you are not careful you will not have the strength to give the necessary leadership. Once, in describing the rigors of working in the White House, Henry Kissinger said that the days are "too busy to create new intellectual capital. You just consume it." This is often true of ministry as well. Now that you are in the thick of it all, you may find yourself consuming more than you are creating.

There are a myriad of demands, each exhausting a portion of you. Joseph Sittler calls it the "maceration of ministry." This is what happens to most ministers. Their time, their vocational focus, their vision of the central task, their mental life, and their contemplative "acreage" are "all under the chopper." Such fragmentation leads to a loss of bearings, a dizzying occupational oscillation, and a well that has run dry (*The Ecology of Faith,* p. 78).

If you become emotionally or physically spent in managing the present, you will not be able to shine a spotlight on the future and marshal people to create it. The pulpit will lack energy, board meetings will have all the excitement of doing tax preparations, and counsel given to parishioners will lack insight. Ministry will drift into unproductive business, of days filled with small changes to small things: reading nonessentials and checking it off as study, getting through the inbox and calling it progress. The reality is, as Pepsico CEO Roger Enrico once told his team, "Small changes to small things are a waste of time." Leadership isn't about processing papers, it's about making significant things happen.

What's the solution? There has to be a determined spirit, a disciplined approach to ministry that unashamedly and unapologetically guards time devoted to creating capital—time alone with God, reflection, and provocative reading. There has to be the discipline to say no to unproductive church meetings, the courage to willingly pay the price of disappointing others, and the wisdom to discern what really matters. Only then will there be the energy, the capital, to keep the covenant with your youthful dreams. And after ten years of ministry, it will be seen as ten years rather than one year ten times.

Third, *respect God's ownership.* As you close your letter, I sense you are considering a phone call to Jonah's travel agent. Having become a repository for people's emotional investments, ranging from resentment to devotion, other situations—especially new works—appear quite compelling. It might be timely to read a section of Eugene Peterson's *Under the Unpredictable Plant* entitled, "Buying Passage to Tarshish" (pp. 9f.). It might also be wise to reflect on Paul's words to Timothy found in 1 Timothy 1:12. It's here we are reminded that pastoral leadership is not our own. It is Christ who has put us into service. So stay under submission, knowing you are right where God wants you. Keep your vision for the future, but live in the present, delighting in what God has presently served up. H. B. London gives fair warning here: "Pastors sometimes waste years, waiting for something special to happen for them . . . and ministry passes them by" (*The Heart of a Great Pastor,* p. 72). Effective ministry does not start in the misty distance—it begins now. So in the midst of your God-given task, stop waiting and start blooming. And when He chooses to move you, it will be His prerogative, not yours. In the meantime, as the rest of the verse underscores, God will give you the strength equal to the difficult tasks. So lead, and keep on keeping on.

Sincerely,
John Johnson

Questions for Reflection

1. Where are you with respect to the "honeymoon" phase of your current ministry? If it's behind you, how do you find yourself reacting to any changes since that time of new beginnings?

2. Are you able to do the things needed to "create the capital" that sustained ministry leadership requires? If not, what changes in your priorities might be prudent?

3. Do you find yourself currently "considering a phone call to Jonah's travel agent"? If so, how might the author's counsel help you to assess the appropriateness of that feeling?

TWENTY-SEVEN

Learning to Appreciate God's Providence

Walter C. Kaiser Jr. assumed the presidency of Gordon-Conwell Theological Seminary on July 1, 1997. He also serves as that institution's Colman M. Mockler Distinguished Professor of Old Testament. Prior to coming to Gordon-Conwell, Kaiser taught at Wheaton College and Trinity Evangelical Divinity School, where he combined his faculty role with administrative duties as senior vice president of education, academic dean, and senior vice president of distance learning and ministries. He also serves as a board member for several Christian organizations. In addition to being a prolific contributor to journals, Kaiser has authored nearly thirty books, including *Toward an Old Testament Theology, Hard Sayings of the Old Testament,* and *Toward an Exegetical Theology: Biblical Exegesis for Teaching and Preaching.*

Dear Friend,

I am delighted to hear that you have sensed God's call on your life to prepare for the role of leadership in theological education. Without the call of God, I am afraid you are headed for a dreadful experience. However, your statement that you believe it is God Himself who has directed you to this leadership position will make all the difference in the world—both in the good and hard times. Christian leaders are not born; they must be called by God!

You asked about my own experience in leadership. It is difficult to say where my own preparation for leadership began. Perhaps it was as early as my junior high days in our church. Just about that time we had a young World War II navy chaplain, Rev. Robert W. Smith, and his wife come to our suburban Philadelphia town to take the pastorate. For the next ten years this husband-and-wife team poured themselves into the lives of the twenty kids in the young people's group. They discipled and mentored each one of us by taking us along for ministry opportunities in the city missions, jails, street meetings, rest homes, youth rallies, and Christian camps, as well as having us in their home for food and fellowship. We were taught how to organize our own Christian Endeavor Meetings (a church young people's organization) and take different responsibilities in each meeting. So effective was the impact of the Smiths on our lives that nineteen of the twenty teenagers from that church went into full-time Christian service—a percentage rarely achieved.

During high school, I was introduced to the ministry of Christian Endeavor, which represented over one hundred and fifty evangelical churches in Delaware County, Pennsylvania. In my senior year, I became president of Delaware County Christian Endeavor. We met once a month during the school year after Sunday night church service at a different church throughout the county, usually with some four to six hundred young people present. It was here that I learned about working across denominational lines, helping leaders work together. In addition to our Sunday evening programs, we sponsored a Labor Day weekend conference at the Downingtown, Pennsylvania, YMCA camps for about three hundred attendees.

All of this was run out of the planning, budgets, and leadership of our own personnel without any financial backing from any major donor or church. When I look back on the fact that I was only in high school, as were many of the rest of the officers, I am amazed at what we dared to tackle and how much we had ventured without any promised financial backing or official authorization (other than our own officers). However, we were sure that God had called us to this work, so what else really mattered? I covet this same venturing forth and visionary experience for you as well. It was not that we were too ignorant to act any differently; it was that we were convinced that this was a work God wanted to us to do. We could not have had more fun in any other outlet than what we were having as a leadership team in Delaware County C.E.

The Smiths urged that I go to Wheaton College. I was reluctant, for Wheaton was a long way off from the farm on the outskirts of southwest Philadelphia. But I went in obedience to the call of God.

Quickly I learned about the Sunday ministry among "people of color" on Chicago's south side. Over a dozen Sunday schools had been set up, financed, and run by three hundred Wheaton students. For the next five years (including the first two years at Wheaton's Graduate School of Theology), I learned more about leadership from working with—and eventually leading—the team of sixty college students at the Sunday school we ran at Thirtieth and South LaSalle Streets. Not only was there the responsibility of caring for six to eight hundred children that we personally picked up in the Projects, but eventually there was the responsibility of praying for and working with all of the student teachers to ensure that they too were maturing while they were ministering to others. The task I had been divinely prompted to assume regarding the spiritual development of the teachers would play a large role in shaping my concept of leadership.

Particularly memorable times of growth in my own life were those weekly sessions on Saturday afternoons when I would slip into the small chapel upstairs in the Memorial Student Center of Wheaton College and pray specifically for each of the college teachers working in our Sunday school. Many an interpersonal conflict was carried to the Lord in those sessions as I sought wisdom, relief, and harmony among the brethren.

As I completed my graduate seminary training, a teaching opportunity opened up on the college faculty at Wheaton. I was now married and working part-time as an assistant pastor at a church in Geneva, Illinois. After three years of teaching, President V. Raymond Edman told me he wanted me to go on for my Ph.D. in Old Testament and Archaeology. He offered me a summer scholarship to begin a program at Brandeis University in Waltham, Massachusetts. I told him I could not accept his gracious offer, for the Lord was coming back soon and I had to be busy winning people to Christ in the meantime! Dr. Edman pushed back in his chair and said thoughtfully, "Walter, I know the Lord is coming back soon, but what God requires of His stewards is faithfulness. If God is sending you to parse Hebrew verbs, then you had better be doing that when He returns rather than any other good work He has required of others, for faithfulness is what is necessary if we are to follow the Lord!"

How could I argue with that? I learned another great lesson about leadership: it is more important to be faithful to our Lord and His calling than to be busy about a thousand other good projects. Dr. Edman picked up the mentoring job begun by my pastor in my teens and impacted my life greatly; for had I not had his counsel at that point in my life, I would never have received the training I was going to need.

In the midst of enjoying my college teaching experience, God made me most restless about the ineffectiveness of a lot of careless ministry and non-biblical preaching in the church. The slogan in the sixties was, "The church has had it." Thus it was that God called me to teach at Trinity Evangelical Divinity School. I hated to leave the college classroom. I had just been voted "Junior Teacher of the Year," our home was a hang-out for the class officers that we were sponsoring, and we were house parents to thirteen freshman at Wheaton College. What more could my wife and I wish to do? This was it. Yet God led us to leave all of that and go teach at the seminary level; for what good would it do to train Christian leaders at a Christian college if they were not able to return to work in the church, the institution Christ said the gates of hell would have no chance in defeating?

The seminary teaching years turned out to be wonderful years of service. After finishing the doctoral work, we began a ministry on weekends in churches around the country during the school year and conducted about five to seven summer Bible Conferences each June to August. When I reached forty years of age another unexpected ministry opened up: writing. I had not planned on doing this either, but there was a divine compulsion that I could not deny—even though I did not think that this was a particular gift or interest of mine! But as each idea would jell, it was an obsession I could not rid myself of until I got it down in print.

After I had been teaching at the seminary for some fifteen years, I was asked if I would submit my name as a candidate for the position of Academic Dean of the seminary. I declined to do so on two separate occasions in 1978 and 1979. I was approached for a third time, and I finally agreed to let my name stand and to take the position if my colleagues, who by this time knew me well, would vote unanimously for my candidacy. I knew that we had seldom had such a vote, so I felt more than safe in posing this Gideon-like testing of the waters. They fooled me, or so I was told—it was a unanimous vote. Could so many be mistaken about the will of the Lord? And, I had promised to abide by their decision, so I entered a new venture of leadership at Trinity Evangelical Divinity School.

The principles I had learned while leading the sixty college students in south Chicago came into play as I assumed the role of ministering to those who taught our students. This became my first and most responsible task—praying for and encouraging the faculty. In the meantime, I had been tutored by my close relationship in the previous fifteen years with Kenneth Kantzer, whom I would succeed as dean. We would spend hours together on the telephone or at his home dreaming and planning about faculty, theological education, and program objectives. In reality, my role was to act as a sounding board, a good listener, and occasionally a stimulus for everything from programs to how we could attract the world's best faculty. Unwittingly, these sessions turned out to be wonderful transitional training times for the tasks I was to assume later.

After serving for twelve and a half years as Academic Dean of TEDS, the Lord abruptly halted the wonderful time we were having at an early morning breakfast meeting on Friday, October 11, 1991. What took place, and what motivated it, is still a mystery to me; but it has since become clear that the Lord was in it, for I doubt if I would have left Trinity after twenty-nine years as my own personal choice. Suddenly I had been asked to resign from my former institution to allow a whole new leadership team to be identified and installed.

During the next five years I often inquired of the Lord for the reason for so sudden a change. I had a letter from my president that said there were no moral, doctrinal, fiscal, or leadership reasons for the request for my resignation. But five years later, to the day and almost to the exact hour, Friday, October 11, 1996, at 9:00 A.M., I was being interviewed by the Board of Gordon-Conwell Theological Seminary to be their President. As the interview began in Boston, I was startled out of my wits to realize that God had dramatically answered my five-year-old question. Thus, as I assume a distinctively new role in leadership as president of Gordon-Conwell Theological Seminary at my advanced years, I look forward to more surprises and learning experiences along the way. God is never through with us until He says so.

So what have I learned in all of this? First, people investing themselves in others' lives is no small part of leadership preparation. Second, training for leadership is a lifelong process and rarely the result of a high impact sort of lecture or tutelage. Third, faithfulness is still the key to godly and successful leadership. Fourth, as Dr. Edman was fond of quoting from others, never doubt in the darkness what God has told you in the light: He will remain faithful and will bring us the answer to our nagging questions that emerge from leadership problems in His own time.

There is much more that I could say, of course, but I can only tell you my story as evidence as to how God has worked in my life, constantly surprising me with new challenges and opportunities to serve. Walk close to your Lord and He will guide your footsteps and prepare your paths.

Warmest personal regards.

Cordially in our Lord's service with you,
Walter C. Kaiser Jr.

Questions for Reflection

1. As you reflect upon your teenage years, what experiences did you have (or lessons did you learn) that helped prepare you for subsequent leadership responsibilities?

2. When you look back on some significant and unexpected circumstances in your life, can you sense in retrospect God's providential intent?

3. "Never doubt in the darkness what God has told you in the light." What are some key principles about God and His care that you have learned from Him that you are at times tempted to doubt?

TWENTY-EIGHT

Learning How to Treat Others with Care

Dave Kelley is a business and finance consultant for Alliance 2000, a company that he founded. He earlier served as Vice President of Business and Finance at Western Seminary, Controller for Promise Keepers, Vice President of Finance at Mercy Corps International, Controller at World Vision, and Controller at George Fox University.

Dear Friend,

Congratulations on your first management job in a Christian organization. Regarding your questions, there are many things I would like to share with you about leadership that I have learned in my twenty-three years as a financial manager in several Christian organizations, things I wish someone would have shared with me early on. The key question is, "What defines quality leadership in Christian organizations?" There are many issues I could talk about, but in this letter I want to concentrate on the most visible aspect of healthy leadership: how a leader treats other people.

First, be careful never to put a leader on too high of a pedestal. When you do, you may easily become disillusioned when that person fails—and being human, he or she eventually will. We all fail at times; the key is how do we respond when we do? Do we learn from our mistakes and emerge with greater wisdom? Do we recover well from the failure? With this in mind, seek out people whose lives you can learn from, people who both succeed well and who fail well, people who are truly "servant leaders." Just remember that they are still fallible people.

Second, learn how to demonstrate your care for people. When I was Controller at World Vision during most of the 1980s, Dr. Ted Engstrom was president there. He was a quality leader who led by example. Ted always stressed the importance of being honest, having integrity, and being open with the public. He cared about staff, and used a personal approach to management. As busy as Ted was, he still made a point of regularly walking through the offices and interacting with employees. He occasionally would stick his head in my office, call me by name, and often remember something personal about me to comment on positively. In other words, he cared for people and showed it. Build these qualities into your management style.

Take time for your staff. Encourage them and build them up. If you feel you don't naturally have these qualities, you can learn them. If it is not easy for you to compliment those who work with and for you, put a periodic reminder on your calendar to stop by each key staff person's office unannounced. Use that time to give encouragement, pray together if the situation warrants, or have some fun in the workplace. You will be amazed at how this builds team spirit, loyalty, and a positive atmosphere.

A manager I worked with at Promise Keepers, Dan Schaffer, is one of the most spiritually deep people I have ever known. He is one of the four founders of Promise Keepers. Dan is a very open, caring person. He has been through deep pain in his life, but has such an honest relationship with God that he has come back from those hard times even deeper with the Lord. Though he managed a large program and staff at Promise Keepers—producing quality work and results—yet he always seemed to have time for those who were hurting. I urge you to follow his example and take time for those around you. By the way, you would do well also to imitate his determination to allow the difficulties and hardships that will come your way, both in your work and in your life, to drive you closer to and deeper in the Lord, not further away from Him.

My last—and most important—example of treating others with care is Jesus. He lived the model life of servant leadership, spending in-depth time with His followers, building them up and developing them. When His disciples were discussing which one of them was the greatest, Jesus classically defined servant leadership to them: "If anyone wants to be first, he shall be last of all and servant of all" (Mark 9:35 NASB). Continually study the life of Christ, especially how He treated people, and prayerfully build those qualities into your life and work.

Do you see a pattern in the examples I have shared? I want you to learn from people like these. You can do so if you develop the following qualities of servant leadership for both your management and lifestyle:

Openness: Leaders should be open with others and quick to admit when they're wrong, especially with staff. Instead of hiding their weaknesses, servant leaders acknowledge them and know when to ask for help (and forgiveness).

Encouragement: It amazes me how few Christian leaders take time to encourage their staff. Once a new manager asked the leader of a well-known Christian organization for an occasional word of encouragement. The leader responded, "I have never done that, and never will. It's not in my personality [to encourage]." Not surprisingly, that organization experienced a high staff turnover rate. Since you are now in a leadership position, take time to encourage your staff. This is not in addition to your work, it *is* your work.

Treating others fairly and with integrity: Do not expect staff to work unreasonable hours. Encourage them to make their families a priority. Pay employees fairly. Do not justify low wages with the excuse, "We pay less because this is a ministry." Be honest, be legal, and don't feel you are above the law. If you ask staff to work overtime who are "non-exempt" as defined by the law, pay them accordingly. If you don't, you are breaking the law. Unfortunately, many Christian organizations fail in this area.

People skills: Have some humor and fun in your workplace and in your life. Spend time with your staff, and value them.

Avoid being spiritually abusive: This is a very subtle trap and one that is unfortunately all too common in Christian organizations. Christian leaders can easily slip into using their authority to spiritually manipulate or abuse others. I once heard a vice president say to his managers, "My fear is that one day you will stand before God and He will say to you, 'Why didn't you spend more time working at this job?'" This was spiritual abuse. If you find yourself spiritually abusing others, stop! If at some time in your career you feel you are being spiritually abused, I strongly encourage you to read *The Subtle Power of Spiritual Abuse* by David Johnson and Jeff VanVonderen. Chapters 20 and 21 can help you decide whether to fight a spiritually abusive situation or to leave it. There is nothing unspiritual about leaving an abusive situation.

So if you as a leader learn to value people, this will take you a long way in becoming the servant leader God has called you to be. Do not have your identity be your work, but have your identity be in Jesus Christ.

You were created in the image of Christ Jesus; what a heritage! You are a quality person with many talents and abilities. Grab the challenge and adventure that is ahead of you and run with it. Don't walk, run!

Yours in Christ,
Dave Kelley

Questions for Reflection

1. Have you ever put any other person on a pedestal by wrongly expecting perfection from him or her, only to find subsequently that those expectations could never be met? If so, what lessons did you learn? What might you want to tell someone who may have *you* on a similar pedestal?

2. In what tangible ways do you show people around you that you genuinely care about them? Would they sense that care if you asked them?

3. Do you treat others with fairness and integrity? Examine your current practice in those areas cited by the author.

TWENTY-NINE

Learning from Mentors and Role Models

Jay Kesler is President of Taylor University in Upland, Indiana, a role he assumed in 1985. Prior leadership positions include the presidency of Youth for Christ/USA, pastoring First Baptist Church in Geneva, Illinois, and publisher for *Campus Life Magazine*. Jay also serves on multiple boards and councils of reference. He speaks on a daily radio program titled "Family Forum" and is the author of many books, including *Being Holy, Being Human,* and *Parents and Teenagers*.

Dear Friend,

You have asked me to give you my insights on leadership as I look back over roughly forty years of Christian ministry.

I have been very fortunate as a young person to have had four men in my life who have taken particular interest in me and my future and who have passed on to me their experience, not only by direction but by the example of their lives. I am convinced that leaders are best developed through mentoring relationships and consider myself fortunate to have had four very good mentors.

The first is my father, who though a working-class man working in a factory, made an indelible mark on me in various areas. For one thing, though he was a product of the Depression and had his education cut short by the need to go to work and support his family, he always encouraged me toward the intellectual life and toward growing as a person and as an individual. He filled our house with books that he read voraciously. In fact, I received a great deal of personal affirmation from him as I developed an interest in reading. By the time I was twelve years old, I had read all of Zane Grey, Jack London, and everything published by Steinbeck, Hemingway, Louis Brumfield, Clarence Darrow, Dickens, Poe, Hawthorne, and Darwin; and though this particular diet was not necessarily the basis for a broad and thorough education, it did teach me to read. As I pursued higher education, therefore, reading was such a natural part of my life that it never left me as my major avocation. In addition, my father believed that one must do the best in his or her circumstances. He would not tolerate whining or blaming others for one's problems. He insisted on focusing on a particular task and finishing that task. He did not seem defeated by circumstances but felt that one should make the best of the resources available and not envy those who seem to have a better hand dealt to them. He was honest, forthright, and somewhat a champion of the underdog. He was a union leader and was extremely interested in social justice. He led civil rights efforts before the Second World War and before the civil rights issue had become a popular political topic. Though he was not a Christian, he lived out what I later discovered were Christian principles in his innate desire for fairness, industry, loyalty, and fair play. I never heard him speak disparagingly of a woman, nor did he use any crude, sexually-oriented language. He did not tolerate racial or ethnic slurs; he would not tolerate or allow any evaluation of another person based on ethnicity, looks, dress, gender, color, or religion. He gave all of his children the distinct idea that God is the judge and that ultimately the opinion of others was secondary and of lesser value than God's approval. When I later learned that God was like a father, I had few adjustments to make from the biblical model.

The second most important mentor in my life is Dr. Milo A. Rediger, at that time dean of Taylor University (and who later became its president). Dr. Rediger taught a course on Old Testament literature in which he introduced me to the inductive method of Bible study (that is, looking at the Bible not with a microscope but with a telescope). Though he certainly understood biblical exegesis and would insist on correct rendering of the individual text, he saw the Bible in a much broader way—topically, if you please—gleaning from both Old and New Testaments the mind of God on various subjects ranging all the way from family to human redemption. This inductive approach later became popular in InterVarsity circles, set the tone for my theological background and understanding, and I feel has served me very well in the midst of the confusions that often beset evangelicals. Dr. Rediger's great breadth and the inculcating of the character of Jesus Christ into his life made a permanent impact on me and helped me to develop a Christian worldview that is comprehensive rather than truncated and provincial. Though I have deep loyalties to the evangelical church, I am grateful to be able to understand the cultural and historical antecedents that form our civilization. There is a wideness in God's mercy and I am grateful to Dr. Rediger for having helped me to escape the cage of smallness that often accompanies Christians who see the Bible through their own ethnocentricity.

The third mentor in my life was Dr. Ted Engstrom, former president of both Youth for Christ and World Vision International (and currently a Christian statesman involved in world evangelization and Christian leadership). Dr. Ted was my first employer. He hired me at Youth for Christ and mentored me in the habits of leadership. Primarily he encouraged me to read and grow, and not to limit my reading to predictable devotional books but to find out where the cutting edge was in current culture. When I first entered the Youth for Christ movement, the people were largely oral communicators, excellent on their feet, and very capable of leading through public speaking. I brought, through my Taylor University education and Dr. Rediger, some understanding of written communication as well as oral. Therefore, I was able to put into writing many of my thoughts and soon discovered that the man who comes to the meeting with ideas in writing and provides the skeleton for the meeting's agenda, often ends up winning the day. I don't know that I did this as a conscious thing, though it seemed that Ted encouraged this writing and thoroughness in detail. We used to kid as young staff members that we would have a meeting with Ted and discuss our assignment, and by the time we got back to our desk it was there in writing; by the next morning there was a second memo asking us what progress we had made on our assignment thus far! One time we held a party for Ted in which we celebrated his "memopause." Nonetheless, this insistent attention to detail set the tone for my administrative and executive leadership style over the years. I owe Ted Engstrom a great deal for this leadership style that was certainly not only theologically and philosophically based, but also practical in its outreach and insistent on ensuring that an idea could be put into action. Ted Engstrom is not just a theorist but a doer, and this has been an important influence on my life.

The fourth person in my life has been Dr. Sam Wolgemuth, a former president for Youth for Christ International and a former bishop in the Mennonite Brethren in Christ denomination. Sam is a man who, more than any man I have ever known, understands process. He knows the shortcut but refuses to take it. He always insists that everyone in the room understand what they are doing and attempts to get them all on the same page. He was a consensus leader long before the Japanese began to write about that approach. Though at times he challenged my youthful impatience, over the years I have felt that his style of seeking to respect the opinion of every person in the room and making sure that all those who were going to be affected by a decision were considered provides the basis for my leadership style.

These four men—my father teaching me about the character of God, Milo Rediger stretching my worldview, Ted Engstrom sharpening my administrative skills, and Sam Wolgemuth humanizing and civilizing my leadership style—have molded me into whatever is good about my leadership. I don't give them any blame for the things that are bad; when I have failed, it is generally because I have neglected to remember their lessons.

I covet for every young person the kind of loving, caring hands-on relationship that I had as the Timothy to these four men.

Sincerely,
Jay Kesler

Questions for Reflection

1. In what significant ways (positively and negatively) have you been shaped by your parents? If you have children, how do you think they will answer this question when they are grown up?

2. In what ways might your cultural background shape how you read and interpret the Bible? Do you read and dialogue widely enough to be able to discover "blind spots" and hermeneutical biases that may distort your understanding of God's truth?

3. To what extent do you "seek to respect the opinion of every person in the room and make sure that all those who were going to be affected by a decision were considered"? Why might the failure to do so adversely impact your leadership effectiveness?

THIRTY

Learning to Observe God in Everyday Life

Since 1991 **Bonnie Kopp** has served at Multnomah Bible College (Portland, Oregon) as the advisor for the Women's Ministries major in which she also teaches courses in psychology, sociology, and leadership. In addition she directs the career counseling development program on that campus and works part-time as a career counselor and consultant for IDAK Group, Inc., an organization that specializes in mid-career advancement for individuals and companies. Prior to assuming her current responsibilities, Bonnie and her husband, Tom, were missionaries in the Republic of South Africa for sixteen years.

Dear Friend,

Nothing replaces the daily practical leadership training program that God puts us through. I am constantly amazed at our Master Teacher who teaches us through life experiences. I want to share personally with you some principles of leadership which I wish I had learned earlier in my ministry. There seems to be a gigantic gulf between knowing truths in your head and practicing them in your daily life. May you be a faster learner than I.

Live boldly! You simply cannot be a dynamic ministry leader without truly knowing your God. I'm not talking about mere facts concerning Him, but a vital, vibrant personal fellowship. Knowing your God means a practical daily living and talking like you truly believe what He has said.

My husband and I lived in South Africa during very troubled times. Every week for a couple of years we met with an Asian pastor and his wife for prayer and encouragement. During one of these times, we were informed that a mob of African youth was marching toward our area and were going to kill everyone in their path. We were encouraged to arm ourselves with whatever we could find and to gather in the church. I was totally immobilized by fear. My Asian friend turned to me and held both of my hands in hers. As she peered intently into my eyes, she said, "Bonnie, what's this? I can see and feel your fear! Remember God's word, 'I will never desert you, nor will I ever forsake you, so that we confidently say, the Lord is my helper, I will not be afraid. What shall man do to me?' Don't forget this because now is your opportunity to live it!" I began to learn that the world doesn't only need a definition of the gospel, but a demonstration of the gospel. Begin now by asking God to make you a vital demonstration to your world. Don't be surprised or afraid of tasks larger than you, or situations that make you uncomfortable. Grab onto them with both hands because you have a big God. Don't forget that you are immortal until God calls you home. He does not choose you because you are so great but because He is so great. Let the world see Him through your life. Live boldly!

Choose to remember! Every time you see God intervene in your life in a special way, keep a record of the event. I didn't start this practice until later on in ministry. I am convinced that this is a biblical principle that will give you strength when you are in the midst of confusion, waiting, pain, difficulty, disappointment, doubting, or discouragement. God is in the business of growing your faith and He often starts this by taking you through small steps of obedience. As you are faithful, He adjusts and expands the test. He desires for you to know Him practically in daily life as well as through the Word. I now have a very long record of all God's personal interventions and miracles in my life. In troubled times, I take it out and choose to remember these events. Based upon what I know about God and what I have seen Him do personally, I choose to praise Him and take action. "Those who know their God will display strength and take action" (Dan. 11:32 NASB).

Even now as I write this letter, I am practicing the discipline of "choosing to remember." During the past eight days my wonderful, godly mother-in-law has been in intensive care. I am experiencing the peace and strength of the Lord as I choose to recall what He has done in the past through similar difficulties. "Yet I will exult in the Lord. I will rejoice in the God of my salvation."

Be you and no one else! I have been so fortunate to have an identical twin sister. We began switching places in the third grade so by the time we were in high school, we had perfected the art of being someone else. Through my career counseling, I have personally worked with many ministry leaders who have also perfected the art of being someone else. They never purposely set out to be deceptive. They just mistakenly believed that they were supposed to be able to do everything well. Therefore, they never became focused or found their niche. Authenticity is vital to leadership. You simply cannot be all that God intends you to be when you are trying to be someone else. I have become convinced that one of the main causes of burnout in the ministry is not working in your own areas of giftedness.

Leadership is knowing where you need to go and persuading others to come along. However, I believe there are two distinct leadership ladders in accomplishing this goal. One ladder of leadership is overseeing or supervising the activities of others, while the second is being the expert or specialist. If you allow yourself to be placed in a position where your responsibilities do not match how God has gifted you, there is a good chance that you will join the multitude of disappointed, burned-out ministry leaders. My desire is that you remain in fruitful ministry for the long haul. God has given every one of us natural talents as well as spiritual gifts. I encourage you now, early in your leadership, to have a good assessment of your talents and gifts. Then be faithful in using them. This is not only an issue of integrity but of wise stewardship. The truth is you cannot be all that God intends you to be until you believe that God has uniquely, wonderfully, purposefully created you! Learn faithfulness in using the gifts God has entrusted to you. Enjoy being authentically you and no one else!

Lighten up! Don't take yourself too seriously. People with no humor are boring, and leaders with no humor will bury their followers. Credible leaders have a sense of humor; they are able to laugh at themselves and their troubles. I have learned that it takes faith to laugh even in the most stressful times. My African friends taught me that humor helps people to thrive.

Only several months after arriving on the African continent, my husband was asked to be the main speaker at a large church conference. He strongly encouraged me to make the necessary adjustments to my clothing for such an occasion. I sorely wished that I had heeded his advice when I stumbled out of the four-seater airplane onto the marshy ground and my white material-covered high heels sank into the saturated earth from the previous night's rain. As the missionary pilot, with twinkling eyes, waved his good-bye and "good luck," I wobbled over to the hand-made, rough-hewn, backless benches and promptly snagged my nylons. As I sat there under the hot African sun, listening for hours to the translation of my husband's messages, I had a growing sense of panic as I felt a growing need to relieve myself. It was readily apparent that there were no buildings in sight, not even a tree or an ant hill to use as a bathroom. In desperation I decided to attempt walking as inconspicuously as possible on my tiptoes (so my high heels wouldn't totally sink and trip me), past five hundred Africans, to the only waist high bushes that I could see. They were about 100 meters directly behind where my husband was preaching. I was chiding myself the whole way for wearing a straight white linen skirt and wondering just how I was going to manage in those bushes. I was just beginning to squat down after an incredible effort, when all of a sudden my foot slipped in a wet cow pie and I landed in the middle. As a response to my involuntary scream, five Africans, who were also using the bushes around me, jumped up and quickly rushed to my aid. The two embarrassed gentlemen left quickly, leaving three African women with this blubbering American. Every Zulu word that I had spent hours practicing was long gone. We didn't need words to communicate anyway. As I looked at these beautiful barefoot women, each dressed with a large piece of material wrapped around them, I suddenly had a vivid picture of just how ridiculous I must look standing there with my nylons around my ankles. I pointed to their bare feet and shook my head at my shoes. I pointed to their wraparound skirts and shook my head at my white straight one. We all began to laugh. I removed my shoes and threw them on the ground next to the discarded nylons. All three women came close and hugged me. We walked arm in arm back to the benches, bonded as sisters. Many times, we as God's servants are His greatest hurdles in reaching the world because we take ourselves so seriously, causing people to see us instead of God. Take God seriously, but realize that you are human. God is God and you are not.

Learn contentment early in ministry! Don't be surprised if early on in your ministry you struggle with a lack of contentment. You may hear about fellow colleagues who are receiving higher salaries, having greater benefits, or carrying fewer responsibilities. You may be tempted to compare yourself and your circumstances with others and wonder if it is all really worth it. Contentment is learned. Contentment is a choice based upon truth. It is choosing to believe that all you need is God and what He chooses to provide. Life is unfair. Tragically I have witnessed leaders destroy the very ministry God gave them by entertaining an attitude of entitlement. The truth is, no one owes you, and certainly God doesn't.

I recall lingering one evening over supper with my parents and graphically describing our poverty-line salary and difficult work situations during our first five years in Africa. After patiently listening for over an hour, my father graciously stopped me and asked, "Bonnie, who chose this ministry?" I answered, "Well, we did." He responded, "Then you need to learn contentment or God will not be able to use you effectively."

Only by living through either perceived or genuinely unfair situations will these truths be tested in your life. It is vital that you count the cost early in ministry. Your future leadership will be greatly affected by your choice to respond as the apostle Paul did: "I have learned to be content in whatever circumstances I am" (Phil. 4:11 NASB).

Seek God's heart more than His hands! By examining your own prayer life, you can tell what you are seeking. When we seek His hands, we generally make requests—even demands—of God on the basis of what we see. Usually we have the plan and direction in mind and we boldly ask God to agree and bless. It can sound so spiritual as the leader to be concerned about the program, the message, the attendance, the feedback. But this is not vision. True transforming vision only comes when we intently seek God's heart and thus see what He sees. This is what God was teaching Habakkuk. Compare his prayer at the beginning of the book (Hab. 1:2–4) with his prayer at the end (Hab. 3:17–19). Talk about transformation! I believe the prophet received a transforming vision of God and discovered to his amazement that God had been seeking him with an even greater intensity. Learn early in your leadership to truly seek God's heart more than His hands. Put aside your agenda and plans, and allow God to make you uncomfortable and to stretch you.

People follow a leader with vision. They are looking for a woman or a man who truly sees God. Take the time early in your ministry to follow the instructions God gave to Habakkuk. "Look among the nations! Observe! Be astonished! Wonder! Because I am doing something in your days. You would not believe it if you were told." Vision comes when you begin to see what God sees. Only then can we truly know and practice, "the just shall live by faith."

In the summer of 1997, my husband and I had the privilege of conducting a leadership seminar in South Africa organized by a group of African men whom we had taught at a South African Bible School fifteen years previously. One of the men in particular referred to us as "his mother and father." It was then that we realized afresh that someone was looking to our example. May God help us to be faithful as leaders. May God help us to fulfill faithfully each responsibility as He gives it to us so that in time He will be pleased to use us to impact the lives of others.

Learning leadership is a lifetime process. It just doesn't happen overnight or by taking some seminar course. Expect God to be doing a daily, active work in your life to bring you to that time when you will be the mentor and others will be looking to you. Until then, single out leaders whose faith you want to imitate (Heb. 13:7) so that you in turn will also become worth imitating.

Sincerely,
Bonnie Kopp

Questions for Reflection

1. How would you have responded if you were in the author's place when she heard about the threatening mob? How well are you living out the gospel by responding to life's difficulties in a manner consistent with God's promises and provisions?

2. To what extent is remembering God's faithfulness a recurring theme in Scripture? Consider keeping a record of God's providential interventions in your life if you're not already doing so, and read through it periodically to strengthen your faith and gratitude.

3. Do you have a good sense of your unique gifts and talents? To what extent is your current ministry a good fit with your God-given abilities?

THIRTY-ONE

Learning How to Reinvigorate a Well-Established Ministry

Woodrow Kroll is President and Bible Teacher of Back to the Bible in Lincoln, Nebraska. Woodrow teaches God's Word on the Back to the Bible broadcast, heard daily on 995 stations throughout the world and speaks on the daily short feature, "The Bible Minute." He is also the Bible teacher for the organization's weekly television ministry. Prior to his present responsibility, Woodrow served as president of Practical Bible College in Binghamton, New York. He has authored more than two dozen books, including *The Vanishing Ministry*.

Dear Friend,

Someone has said that it's easier to give birth to a baby than it is to raise the dead. In applying this principle to organizations, I have no firsthand experience from which I can advise you concerning either beginning a new ministry or reviving one that has failed. However, it has been my happy task on two occasions to be charged with leadership roles in well-established, vital yet older ministries, that just needed reinvigorated ideas and new vision.

One day you may have this same challenge facing you. Moving an older ministry with a godly heritage to new heights is one of the most difficult tasks of leadership. If you meet that challenge, most will likely say that's what was expected of you. If you fail to meet it, well, keep your résumé updated.

Almost everything I know about making substantive changes in established ministries I've learned from experience, and that means from successes and failures. Fortunately, to date at least, the successes have outnumbered the failures. I'm honored that you asked me to share with you what I've learned. I pray that my insights will be helpful in some way, and that you will be entirely successful in shaking out the dust and charting a new course for your ministry. Here's what I've learned about being a change agent in a respected and well-established ministry.

First, always preserve the reputation of the past.

To some extent, all change represents a critique of the past. That's why it's so important that you praise past leaders frequently; affirm them and the work that they did. They are your heritage. Your ability to build on that work depends on the strength of their foundation. If they have left you a good foundation, be vocally grateful for it and for them.

If the former leadership in your ministry is still living, keep them informed about what you are doing. Treat them special. It can be devastating to young leadership when your predecessors are openly critical of you. Keep them positive about you by being positive about them. Remember Ronald Reagan's 11th Commandment: "Thou shalt not speak evil of a fellow Republican."

Second, move slowly but deliberately.

An older organization is like a huge battleship lumbering through the open water. If you turn too hard to the right or to the left, you will simply capsize the ship. God called you to steer the ship, not sink it.

It will take ten years or more to make substantive changes in an older organization. Plan on staying at least that long. It's true that some fortunate leaders have accomplished substantive changes in less time, but many more have failed than have succeeded. Rapid change in an older organization often leads to rapid replacement of the change agent and a reversion to the old order of things. Map out a strategy for long-term change and stick to that strategy. That will be good for you too. After all, when the changes have been made, you'll find it less inviting to leave.

Don't make substantive changes your first year. Use that year to get to know your people, the corporate culture of your ministry, and the history of the organization. Learn the history well; it can be a valuable ally in corporate change.

Third, rally broad-based support for change.

Gather the support of everyone you can, but don't expect everyone to support your changes. Some support you can do without, but to make the kind of changes that last, make certain you have the support of your board and your key lieutenants. A solid leadership core is essential for substantive change.

Never go into a board meeting if you know you're going to lose a vote. Do all the necessary preparation to ensure that everyone understands the issues and agrees with what you are presenting. You may not always have unanimity in the vote for change; that's not realistic. But you should rarely have a dissenting vote. As a leader, it's your job to see that everyone is moving in the same direction, and that includes your board.

Change is painful; be ready for the pain. There will be many bad days during the change process. When you must inflict pain on your staff, do it compassionately, mercifully, and honestly. Do it personally; don't send a lieutenant to do it.

Fourth, give away your best ideas.

This is a key concept in making positive change. If you are viewed as the only change agent in your organization, you'll be viewed as a radical. Radicals follow radicals; people follow leaders.

Make "your" ideas "other's" ideas. Plant seeds in every meeting with others. Allow those seeds to germinate as "their" ideas and your staff will give you heartier support for them. In fact, they will own them and champion them. You can never expect people to support your ideas with the same enthusiasm they support their own, so make your ideas their ideas. After all, it's change that's important, not credit.

Fifth, challenge and empower everybody you touch.

I believe it is the task of every leader to challenge and empower everyone who works with him. I once thought I could accomplish meaningful changes all by myself, but I soon learned the task was too large for me and abandoned my Superman complex.

Shortly after assuming the leadership role at my present ministry I issued this invitation to my staff: "Come, help me create a working culture where your personal growth propels the growth of this ministry. Let us never be satisfied with the minimum acceptable level of quality. I want you to have the freedom to strive for maximum quality—true excellence in Christ. I want you to feel secure in the knowledge that you have been created a unique human being with a definite purpose, created in Christ with specific gifts to be God's agent to change people's relationships with Him."

Being a genuine change agent often means creating a climate in which people are comfortable being challenged to stretch themselves, to dream things never dreamed before. But that challenge needs to be accompanied with empowerment, enabling each member of your team to run with the ball when they pick it up. You are a team. Everyone has an assignment and the job gets done only when everyone is challenged and empowered to fulfill that assignment.

Sixth, every now and then look back.

Visionary leaders are always looking ahead, into the future. I suspect that vision may be overrated in today's supercharged society. Real leaders need to be as aware of how far they have come as they are of how far they have to go. Give your people the opportunity to look back every once in a while and say, "Can you believe that! Look how far we've come together." Of course you can believe it; you planned it. Allow the accomplishments of your people to overtake them occasionally, and overwhelm them always.

Don't point out the substantive changes under your leadership too often, especially if your support is not ministry wide. You will be perceived as bragging. Do your work; do it faithfully and then periodically look back to rejoice at what's been accomplished. Give your staff the joy of engaging in a corporate "Wow!" every now and then.

Seventh, prepare some change agents to come after you.

Be a model to everyone, but a mentor to those who will be the next generation of change agents in your ministry. Modeling is teaching by lifestyle and example. Mentoring is when you deliberately take aside privately some of your key team players and interact with them, instruct them, encourage them, and empower them.

Every Moses needs his Joshua. Every Paul needs his Timothy. Every leader needs his understudy. You are not predetermining who will be the next generation of leadership, you are simply ensuring that there will be a next generation by investing yourself in others consistently. After all, true leadership is not determined by what is accomplished during your term of office; true leadership is determined by what remains after you're gone. Model and mentor.

When change agents follow you, be as gracious to them as you wished your predecessor had been to you. If you've taught them well, when young change agents take over from you, don't be surprised or apprehensive when they make positive changes just as you did. That's what you've prepared them to do.

Years ago, as a young leader, I was the associate director to the founder of a fine organization. My boss told me that I was the future of that ministry and that I should feel free to make any changes I wanted. I took my time, studied the organization, and carefully planned change. But when I began to initiate some changes, the founder was surprised. If you give someone the mandate and authority for change, don't be surprised when they make changes.

You are about to experience the best of times and the worst of times. Being a change agent requires a great deal of skill, tact, diplomacy, and a healthy dose of daily prayer. Still, it is an exciting role and one

God does not entrust to everyone. The past is too important to be destroyed in charting the future. But the future is too important to be inhibited by the past. Balance is the key, and as the change agent you hold that key.

Be patient. Be bold. Be kind. Be ready. There are many minefields on the path to change, but without change there is no progress and without risk there is no change. Stay close to God when making changes. Make sure you have clean hands and a pure heart. Without them, no change you make will be blessed by God. Be assured of my prayers. You'll need them.

Your fellow servant,
Woodrow Kroll

Questions for Reflection

1. How healthy and productive is your relationship with those who preceded you in your current ministry?

2. To what extent are you needing to receive credit for your good ideas as opposed to "giving them away to others"? Reflect on the difference in motivation that you've observed when people are implementing "their" ideas as opposed to those that came from someone else.

3. Are you taking time to celebrate what God has accomplished through you and others? If not, what might your team be missing by way of enhanced morale, gratitude, and enthusiasm?

THIRTY-TWO

Learning How to Pass the Baton

Dr. Robert A. Krupp is the Director of Library and Information Services and Lecturer in Church History at Western Seminary, Portland, Oregon, as well as a freelance writer and editor. From 1993–1997 he was the University Librarian for Trinity International University, serving Trinity Evangelical Divinity School and Trinity College in Deerfield, Illinois. From 1983–1993 Bob was Library Director and Associate Professor of Church History at Western Seminary. He was a member of the Athletes in Action Weightlifting Team (Campus Crusade for Christ). His research interest is the Greek Church Fathers, specifically John Chrysostom.

Dear Friend,

If the Lord grants me three score and ten years, I am about halfway between my seminary graduation and the time when I will pass whatever baton I am holding for the last time. As I have studied and reflected on leadership in the Christian community I am more and more thrust back to very basic concepts that were taught to me early in my training.

A leader is always a disciple. There is no substitute for a close walk with God. The leader who does not make prayer a priority will drift and fall. There is also no substitute for time with God in His written word. Daily reflective times where we invite God to take His powerful two-edged sword and penetrate our facade and lead us to change and grow in godliness are essential. We must love God, godliness, and spiritual growth in our own lives. There are many temptations to focus on what we do instead of who we are. More and more I want to do a few things well—and totally as an act of devotion—instead of engaging in some game of ministry monopoly where I collect the right chips of power and position but lead an empty life of secret hypocrisy. Many leaders fall and some of those who have fallen were my seminary classmates, colleagues, and students. I believe they all wandered from a life of devotion. They cared more about power than piety; more about what they did and less about who they were.

A leader is a member of local church of worshiping, ministering disciples. Many leaders live as if they are above the local church. They act as some sort of special ministers to the universal church who don't need to dirty themselves with the concerns of one local body. This is never true. All Christians are to be members of a local church. Some leaders think God has given them a ministry to travel without accountability, serving wherever they wish devoid of responsible accountable relationships. These relationships are at the heart of a local church. Times of corporate worship and times where we sit under the teaching ministry of one who will give an answer to God for our souls are essential for spiritual growth. We never outgrow our need for them.

Christian leadership is different than leadership in other contexts. God's Spirit is present. Even if the organization looks like a secular group, it has the spiritual power to be life-transforming. This also leads to a serious caution. It can be faked. We can pose as Christian leaders but lead as if we were in a secular context and do nothing in the power of the Spirit. In Ephesians 4:12–15 Paul teaches us the purpose of leadership that is Christian. Christian leaders minister in such a way that they edify the saints and promote unity in the body. Leadership that does not build up a person's spiritual life and promote unity in the body of Christ may be efficient, it may be charismatic and powerful, but it is not Christian.

Pride is the ever present subtle enemy of Christian leaders. There are always temptations to pride and self-promotion. Many of us seem to be afraid to trust the sovereignty of God and want to be sure that we get credit for all we do. We read and teach passages about eternal rewards and about ministering in secret, but we really want our praise and our reputation to be just right and, hopefully, well-known. So many of us have manufactured images, managed and massaged to our conception of perfection. We are afraid of transparency and candor and hide behind a mask. In the end we suffer doubly. We never know and always doubt if we would be effective if we were real, and we must always have our guard up lest our real self shine through the ever present mask. We are left to wonder if anyone suspects what lies under the mask. We never know what our lives would be like if we transparently served in the power of the living God. We settle for managed mediocrity.

Leaders are not an end unto themselves. We are part of the body of Christ. We are part of a tapestry of ministry that God has been weaving since Pentecost. Our ministry is not a personal kingdom that dies with us. We are part of the body of Christ that began with the Pentecostal outpouring of the Spirit and will continue until the return of our risen Lord. Are we afraid to be part of something bigger than we are? One of the most difficult aspects of ministry is receiving and passing the baton. I was on a relay team in high school and we won and lost races by how well we passed the baton. I have seen batons passed badly in ministry. I've seen those who refused to pass it, I've seen those who dropped it during their leg of the race, and I've seen those who refused to take the pass. In a relay race, each member submits to the goal of the team, and the time for a relay race is faster than any individual could run the race. If our ministry is not part of something bigger than we can do in our own power then it is not part of the body of Christ. Regretfully there are many lone rangers in the church who don't submit to anything larger than their desires.

Success without a successor is not success. As Paul exhorted Timothy (2 Tim. 2:2), we must pass on our knowledge and wisdom so that the interwoven chain of ministry continues. We should always have a successor in training should God move us to another post in His kingdom. When we leave a place of service we should never entertain thoughts that it will die without us. Should the Lord tarry there will be faithful service after we have died. We should remember this and prepare for it.

Sincerely,
R. A. Krupp

Questions for Reflection

1. Who has passed a baton of ministry to you? How well was it passed and received? Have you passed a baton to another? How well was that baton passed?

2. Do you wear a mask while you serve? If so, what are your fears? What is keeping you from being more transparent?

3. Have you ever experienced a time of ministry where you were confident of the present power of God and others could see that power in you? How is ministering in the Spirit different than doing the exact same functions in the flesh?

THIRTY-THREE

Learning to Value People

Aubrey Malphurs is the pastor of Northwood Community Church in Dallas, Texas, the chairman of the Field Education Department at Dallas Seminary, and the president of Vision Ministries International, a ministry training and consulting organization. He has pastored three churches and authored numerous books in the areas of leadership and church ministry, including: *Developing a Vision for Ministry in the Twenty-first Century, Strategy 2000: Churches Making Disciples for the Next Millennium, Values-Driven Leadership: Discovering and Developing Your Core Values,* and *Ministry Nuts and Bolts: What They Don't Teach Pastors in Seminary.*

Dear Friend,

Though I have some years left in ministry, if I were to begin my ministry career tomorrow I would spend more time in developing relationships with people. If you were to ask the average person who sits under my ministry, either in the church or the seminary, they would tell you that I am a relational person. On a scale of one to ten, they might rate me a seven or an eight. However, the truth is that I am not wired to be a people person. Instead God has designed me to be more goal or task oriented than relationally oriented. My tendency is also toward introversion. The key, however, is that I have improved relationally by working hard at developing my people skills.

Every young pastor must realize that ministry is all about people. Ministry takes place in the context of relationships. We do not minister to pews, we minister to people, spiritually hungry people. For some this is not a problem. God has wired them to be people persons. They are extroverts who thrive on relationships. Being around people charges their batteries. If it were up to them, much of their day would be spent with people.

However, if you do not like people or value people (whether lost or saved), then ministry is not for you. The Savior valued people, even lost people. In contrast to the Pharisees and teachers of the law who devalued lost people, the Savior welcomed them and even ate with them, an act that was offensive to the Pharisees (Luke 15:2). And to illustrate their worth as human beings, He told the parable of the Lost Sheep and the Lost Coin (Luke 15:10).

Because Jesus valued people, He cared deeply about them. When He saw the crowds, Matthew says, "He had compassion on them, because they were harassed and helpless, like sheep without a shepherd" (Matt. 9:36 NIV). Jesus did not spend all His time with people, however. There were periods in His busy schedule when He slipped away to be by Himself and pray (Mark 1:35), and times where He led His disciples off to rest and be by themselves (Mark 6:30–31). However, much of His time was spent with and ministering to people, whether the disciples or the multitudes.

In his book entitled *Top Performance,* Zig Ziglar cites a study conducted by the Stanford Research Center, Harvard University, and the Carnegie Foundation. It revealed that, regardless of your profession, fifteen percent of the reason why you get a job, keep a job, and move ahead in that job is determined by your technical skills and knowledge; the other eighty-five percent has to do with your people skills and people knowledge.

Unfortunately, many pastors who have attended seminary focus primarily—if not exclusively—on technical skills and knowledge. That is not to say that theology, Bible, languages, and church history are not important. No minister should launch into ministry without these tools in his tool kit. The problem is that so little training takes place in the areas of people skills and people knowledge. The young seminarian is left with the impression that those things are not important, or that he will pick them up when he gets into ministry. These statistics announce that they are important, and waiting until one's first ministry to develop them is too late.

Relationships are vital to pastoral leadership. You cannot lead without them. In fact, your authority to lead your people will not come from your position as pastor but from the trust of your people. You will never lead people who do not trust you. Unfortunately, we live at a time when many (especially "Generation Xers") are slow to trust anyone in authority. That makes it difficult to have an effective ministry with these young men and women who are the future of the church in North America as well as Europe. It can be done, but it will take time and a lot of hard work at building trusting relationships.

Other new pastors make the mistake of spending most of their week in the study preparing for Sunday's sermon. They pop out for a short time on Sunday to deliver their masterpiece and then beat a hasty retreat back to the study. Why do they do this? Perhaps they were taught this in seminary, or a prior pastor modeled this behavior. My friend Ron Klassen, who is a seminary graduate, has coauthored an excellent book that hits this proverbial ministry nail on the head with the following insight:

> What I learned was that my effectiveness as the pastor of the Brewster church had little to do with how well I preached or led worship or administered, though those things all had their place. My effectiveness as pastor was determined by my personal relationships with people.
>
> Effectiveness came only when I started spending less time in my study and more time in the local café drinking coffee. It came when I spent less time organizing church events and more time touring members' businesses or having lunch with them. It came when I got out of the office and went to the ball games or went hunting. I learned that an hour of personal time with someone in my congregation could have more impact than a dozen sermons.
>
> Because I am a behind-the-desk person, I had to block off on my calendar several hours a week for relationships, so I wouldn't just drift toward desk work, which came easier for me. And because I am shy, I had to work at developing people skills. But the more I worked at it, the easier it got and the more I enjoyed it. Once I started regularly investing time in building relationships, it wasn't long before church members started viewing me as a member of the family instead of an outsider. (Ron Klassen and John Koessler, *No Little Places*, pp. 99–100)

As I reflect back over my thirty years or more of ministry, like Klassen, what I remember most is not the sermons I preached nor the matters I administered. What I remember most are the relationships with people. I have pastored two churches, and I am currently pastoring a third. Whenever I think about any one of those churches, it is the people that come to mind first.

I pastored my first church in the early seventies. It was a church plant located in Miami, Florida. As is typical of church planting, a lot of evangelism took place and a number of people came to faith. I have never forgotten the faces of all those people whom we baptized at Miami Beach. I also recall how my wife developed relationships with a number of the young women who lived in the same apartment building where we lived and where the church met. I remember one particular lady who showed a strong interest in spiritual things. In time, she accepted Christ. Next, I developed a relationship with her husband. Then he came to faith. What a difference it made in that family and their outlook on life. Just recently, she sent us a card announcing her graduation from a Christian university in the Northwest and her plan to pursue teaching in a Christian school.

My challenge to you is not to spend most of your time each week hidden away in your study, preparing for one or two hours on Sunday morning. Instead, spend a lot more of your time with your people. You know full well that the church is not just a building situated on the corner of First Street and Main. The church is people—it is all about people!

Sincerely,
Aubrey Malphurs

Questions for Reflection

1. In your opinion, are you a natural people person or are you more task or goal oriented? How would other people describe you?

2. Do you value people? How much time do you spend with people each week? Do you equally value non-Christians? Would they agree with your answer?

3. If you struggle with relationships, what would it take for you to become more relational? Are you willing to do this? Why or why not?

THIRTY-FOUR

Learning About Loneliness, Dryness, and Anger

James Martin has served over ten years as senior pastor of Mt. Olivet Baptist Church in Portland, Oregon. He also serves as a trustee and adjunct professor at Western Seminary. He is past president of Albina Ministerial Alliance in Portland and serves on the Board of Directors of the National Association of Evangelicals. He frequently does seminars and conferences on family life, financial freedom, and managing priorities.

Dear Friend,

It is very rare that I write to someone whom I do not know. However, I suspect that we have much in common. Since you are a fellow servant of Jesus Christ, you can identify with some of the things I am about to say. I am thankful for the opportunity to share with you in this small way.

I received Jesus Christ in 1960. After straying from the faith several years, I rededicated my life to Christ. Since then, I have had many, many life-changing experiences. One of those experiences was the subsequent divine call I received to enter the gospel ministry. The first two years of ministry I spent preaching in some jail worship services, doing volunteer chapel at nursing homes, and preaching at different churches. I had a passion to see people saved. Since I believed in a literal hell, I went about (at times, with reckless abandon) trying to lead people to Jesus Christ. I tried to persuade them by speaking about God's love and how they could end up going to hell if they did not repent. Although I was zealous and sincere in my efforts, I am sure I turned many people off with my aggressive style of evangelism. I am sure most new Christians go through a similar phase, where one believes that sincerity and a clear presentation of the gospel will get immediate results. I have since learned that conversion is a process. Those who hear the gospel for the first time, no matter how clearly it is presented, may not receive it at that moment. No one told me that back then. However, I should have known from my own journey.

In spite of my lack of sensitivity, God was gracious. I saw many people come to Christ during some of my preaching engagements. However, there were so few disciple-making churches in our area that many of these new Christians failed to grow and eventually turned back to their old lifestyle. That is when my wife and I started praying for God to give me an opportunity to pastor a church so I could be more involved in the spiritual development of God's people. Our prayers were soon answered. (By the way, I am using the term "pastor" to denote the person who is the primary teacher of the Word of God and provides strategic leadership and vision to the congregation. If there are multiple pastors on staff in a church, the person I'm referring to would probably carry the title of "senior pastor" or "lead pastor.")

One year prior to my first church assignment, I became aware of my need for additional theological preparation. I decided to enroll in a seminary. I had given so much of my life to worldly living, I was determined to give my best to this new calling. I received a sound seminary education with strong Bible teaching.

Besides my relationship with Jesus Christ and my relationship with my wife and children, nothing fulfilled and challenged me more than serving as a shepherd for God's people. However, I don't remember anything in my former worldly life that caused the types of frustrations and pains that I have experienced as a pastor. Seminary training did not intentionally prepare me for dealing with the kinds of stresses and strains I have encountered in this role. I often share with seminary students the highs and lows of pastoral ministry from my own real-life experiences. Many eager students are unaware of the constant changes and challenges they will face as professional church leaders.

Of what should I have been made aware of or warned about? It seems there are several issues I have faced that could have been dealt with a little better if I had some advance notice from someone who was an experienced professional church leader. These issues include loneliness, dryness, and anger—terms I never heard until I was in my second pastorate.

The very first uncomfortable surprise I received in my early pastoral experience was how lonely being a pastor can be. Loneliness is an occupational hazard for pastors. I have learned that this loneliness is quite unlike other kinds of loneliness because of its spiritual nature. Somehow, in spite of all the time I spend communicating with God, doing God's work, and being in the midst of God's people, I find myself lonely. It is a miserable feeling and often leads to self-pity. Far too often, I find myself focusing inward instead of upon God and my calling. This has serious implications, since this is one way our enemy, Satan, opposes God's people. Loneliness has caused me to question my value, my calling, and, at times, even affected my self-esteem. This is dangerous because I know a low self-esteem can hinder my effectiveness in serving Christ. It can also lead to depression, which in turn can lead to several bodily ills (some of which can even be life-threatening).

During the late 1960s and early 1970s, I was the leader of a popular dance band. I also played on city league championship basketball and bowling teams. In all these settings I was with people who felt that they needed each other and who looked out for each other. We valued being together. It was no big deal to use each other's things—sometimes even without asking. Misunderstandings and disagreements were soon patched up. We valued our relationships. It was a "team" thing.

I also remember the six years I spent as a police officer. There is an extraordinary bond that exists between police officers. Regardless of that racial tension that usually exists in most police departments across our nation, there is not the slightest hesitation for those same officers to put aside their personal conflicts and rush to the aid of a follow officer who is in trouble. They will use any means necessary to thwart an outside force from harming the "fraternity." Even though we must strongly oppose some of the corruption and unethical tactics found in many police departments, we must admit they really do honor their code of silence and comradeship in the line of duty.

After having experienced these kinds of relationships during my worldly days, I expected to have even more friends and deeper relationships in the pastoral ranks. I felt I had a right to expect this, since we were all serving the same Lord, teaching out of the same inspired Word, and trying to lead people to the same Lord and the same eternal life. This is the body of Christ. There was all this teaching, preaching, and talk about loving one another as Christ loved us. Surely God's ministers would present a united front and set the example for the congregation to emulate.

I soon found out how difficult it is to have close friendships with other pastors who live in the same community. I was not prepared for the divisions and individualistic spirits I found among the pastoral ranks. For one thing, there is a racial divide. Regardless of the much-promoted racial reconciliation movement being advanced in the past few years by groups such as the Promise Keepers, there continues to be a lack of unity among Christian leaders and churches. I am in no way speaking against the attempts to solve this problem in the Body of Christ. However, racial reconciliation is more than the integration of races at a worship service, where we exchange pulpits or our choirs sing at one another's church. It is more than offering public apologies for wrongs committed by one's forefathers. That's admirable but not enough. What happens outside the church walls—in the schools, in the business arena, in housing, when the worship service is over— that is what really matters.

Another contributing factor to loneliness is that some pastors of the same race compete for members in the same community. We see each other's buildings and ministries, hear people talk about what's happening at so and so's church, and allow ourselves to become intimidated or envious. We have our own "turf battles." These battles become more of a problem if the community from which we attract members is small, or if a church is doing something innovative and grows rapidly and steadily. I don't remember being counseled in seminary about the existence of this attitude and what to do to avoid or survive it. I didn't think this would be an issue among pastors. Someone should have told me.

Early in my ministry I fell for the false message of the world that "bigger is better," and "success is based on size." I found myself separated from others based on church size or theological training. The "big guys" often, knowingly or unknowingly, exalted themselves because of the size of their ministry. I saw them as the "experts" on how to raise a large budget and grow a large congregation fast by using their methods. As one of the "little guys," I became disillusioned, envious, and often felt like a failure because I lacked the skills and the opportunities to grow such a ministry. As I matured in my calling, I learned someone else's techniques will not always work well in my particular setting. The people are not the same in all locations, and pastors differ in their vision, charisma, and leadership style. My failure to understand these things produced unrealistic expectations and unnecessary disappointments. Denial and withdrawal set in. The result was even greater loneliness.

Our congregations do not understand our emotional discomforts. I have discovered that it often takes a pastor to relate to another pastor. Just like a man can never understand the pain a woman feels while in labor or during the actual delivery of a baby, neither can members of the congregation know the pain and disappointments of a pastor who has a heart for his people. They see the pastor's smiling face in the pulpit on Sunday mornings. They hear a fine sermon and think all is well. However, all may not be well. Sometimes the physician gets sick and needs the service of another physician. We experience

fear, rejection, low self-esteem, insecurity, and a host of other emotions just like any other human being. We need genuine, caring friendships. We need a place to be transparent. We pastors need to admit
this to our congregations. We must not allow them to make us more
than we really are. We are fallible. I did not want to admit or even
believe I could have such feelings, because I saw this as a sign of
weakness. If anyone had to be strong, it had to be the pastor. Lately,
I have come to see the healthiness of being more transparent at strategic times. It sure relieves me of a lot of pressure when I realize I
don't have to pretend to be the know-it-all, fix-it-all man. I have also
learned many people in my congregation are more at ease around a
leader who is not "perfect" but who struggles and has doubts and
fears at times just as they do.

Spiritual dryness is another occupational hazard for pastors. During the time I led my dance band, there were hardly any limits to our
desire to play anywhere and anytime. I remember one New Year's Eve
when we were scheduled to play for a big dance beginning at 11:00
P.M. The town was two hours away from home. About three hours
before we were to depart, a snowstorm came and dropped over six
inches of heavy, wet snow. Almost everything came to a standstill,
except us. We were determined to go even against the warnings of
our parents and friends. We didn't get underway until about 8:30 P.M.
It took us almost four hours to get to our destination. No one else
was on the road. Several times we came close to wrecking our ve-
hicles. We risked our lives for a grand total of thirty-five dollars per
person. We were crazy but committed.

Once we drove sixteen hours from West Virginia to Connecticut to
play for a dance. All we were promised was 60 percent of the ticket
sales. The promoter did a horrible job promoting the event. No one
showed up. All we received was a meal. If I had not stashed away a
few dollars for hotel and food, I don't know if we even would have
made it back home. Yet we were willing to do it again, all for the sake
of the call. It was like an addiction to set up those instruments and
play.

I couldn't believe it when I developed an even greater zeal when I
started preaching. Just as I had done with the band, I was willing to
go anywhere, anytime to preach. I turned nothing down. You may be
thinking I was in it for the money. Let's clear that up right now. My
preaching career started in West Virginia in the late 1970s. That's right,
West Virginia. The churches were very small, and they rarely gave
anything over twenty-five dollars as an honorarium. You see, money
was not the object; I just wanted to preach. It was a fire that burned
inside me. After I became a pastor, I could hardly sleep on Saturday

nights mulling over my sermon. I was up bright and early on Sunday morning, excited and ready to go. Something took over every time I opened the Bible to teach or preach. There was never a dull moment back then. I was anxious for others to know what I knew, to grow like I was growing, to serve like I was serving, and to give as I was giving. It was so exciting.

Some years ago, B. B. King, the so-called "King of the Blues," wrote a song entitled, "The Thrill is Gone." It referred to a love affair with a woman. However, something unpleasant happened in the relationship, and the attraction was no longer there. He didn't want her any longer. I can identify somewhat with that song. I developed a true love affair with my role as pastor/teacher, but then something happened. At times, I did not feel in love anymore. If I were a gambling man, I would have put up my life's possessions against the thought that I would ever lose my zeal for preaching a sermon or teaching a lesson. However, one Sunday morning in the summer of 1996, I found myself wishing I didn't have to preach that day. I didn't have that zing. I felt what I was doing was meaningless; you know, that kind of feeling Solomon described in Ecclesiastes. I had studied the Scriptures and my notes were in order, but I was not as excited to preach. This has happened several times since. I had heard other pastors say they felt this way at times, but I questioned their calling. Unfortunately, I lost a little respect for them. I suspected they were unspiritual and insincere. I could not imagine me ever feeling that way. I was proud that I was motivated and wanted to preach each Sunday. After all, I wanted to do more for God, since I had done so much on the worldly side. Therefore, when I felt that first lack of enthusiasm, I felt so guilty, so ashamed of myself. I couldn't tell anyone I had those thoughts. What would they think of me? I had always championed the call to commitment and how we can "do all things through Christ." Yet, here I was in this area of dryness. The thrill was gone. I felt like I was going to a job rather than a ministry.

I had to do some serious evaluation of myself to determine what had caused this reaction. During my search I was reminded of my humanness. I can hear you saying, "Really? So what else is new?" I say this because, even though we all know this to be true, in times of difficulties we often forget it and beat ourselves up for feeling a God-given emotion such as anger or disappointment. We have emotions just like any other human being; whether the feelings are justified or not, we cannot deny the fact that they are there.

Why do we lose our zeal at times? First, I believe we are often disappointed at the lack of progress in those to whom we minister. Do you ever feel like your ministry is in vain? Doesn't it seem like you are always pushing and pulling people? Don't you feel like the people are just not spiritual enough to understand your vision and your passion? Somewhere along the way I learned Jesus never told us to be successful; rather, Jesus called us to be faithful. There's a big difference between the two. Once we realize this, it can relieve much unnecessary pressure. I wish someone had drilled that into me early.

Second, we often lose the thrill because we are burned-out (or nearing it). Many of us need to take a rest. We are on emotional overload. We are carrying the burden of too many people. We are anxious. But ultimately that's the Lord's job. The flock is His flock. We are to cast all our cares upon Him because He cares for us (1 Peter 5:7). I used to think I was impressing God by being a workaholic pastor. Most of the time people don't even notice how much we are doing and God gets no glory out of some of our motives.

Since we are human, and on a path of spiritual growth ourselves, we need to be ministered to by other gifted people. We are always praying for others, but we need their prayer for us. We are always leading others to worship God, but we too need to worship Him. We are always telling people to read the Bible for spiritual strength, but we need to read the Bible to increase our spiritual strength. Too often we allow the busyness of ministry to cause us to neglect this prayer, personal Bible study, and meditation. We fail to nourish ourselves from God's Word, because we usually read the Bible looking for sermon or lesson material. The shepherd needs to eat. One writer said preachers must not fall into the attitude of telling people, "Do what I say, not what I do." The apostle Paul was one who directed people's attention to his lifestyle, not merely his words. He expressed this concept to Timothy when he wrote, "You know all about my teaching, my way of life, my purpose, faith, patience, love, endurance, persecutions, sufferings" (2 Tim. 3:10–11 NIV).

Another factor that may cause us to lose the thrill is that our message may not be as popular as some others. Frequently, I feel like just "a voice in the wilderness." Is there anyone else reminding people of the holiness of God and calling them to repentance and commitment? It gets tiring when there seems to be such an indifference regarding the things of God.

That was Elijah's problem. After winning the battle between God and Baal on Mt. Carmel, and hearing people acknowledge that the Lord was God, Elijah more than likely expected the whole nation (including King Ahab and Queen Jezebel) to turn to the Lord God. When things didn't go the way Elijah just knew they would, he ran away, sulked in the desert, and wanted to die. He isolated himself from people and complained to God that no one cared, and he was the only one left that was on the Lord's side. Do you ever feel that way? Sure you do. Take heart my friend, you are not alone. Few of God's prophets have escaped that emotion.

A third major surprise in ministry was feelings of anger—even anger toward God. Now, that's a concept I was fearful of saying. However, in reading the Bible I find several instances where the writers questioned God about certain circumstances. I have recently experienced some of the most painful periods in my entire ministry. The first occurred in May 1997. A small group of longtime members, claiming to be led by God, launched an attack against my leadership. It carried over into the most frustrating and unprofitable church business meeting I've ever experienced. Some of our business was made public, some members were persuaded to stop giving to the church, and some left who failed to investigate the motives of the accusers. I have no problem with people asking questions about what I do, but I do take offense when they question my motive for doing something. I may not always make the best decisions, but I certainly don't make them from selfish motives. I learned how treacherous some church members can be.

Let me be the first to say we must be careful not to quickly dismiss the complaints of our enemies. Even though they are mean-spirited, they may have a valid point. Honest evaluation is the only way to analyze whether their statements are valid or not, and how much attention should be given to the issues they raise.

In addition, we must remember people sometimes explode on others because they have a series of pressing events going on in their own lives, unrelated to the people upon whom they explode. Sometimes people have hang-ups in their own lives that they have not properly dealt with, and innocent people receive the brunt of their anger.

The second traumatic event occurred one month later (June 1997). It involved the loss of a highly popular and charismatic top-level staff member—one that I thought was an excellent ministry partner with great potential. Keeping true to my integrity, I will not mention the details of what necessitated my request for this person's resignation; I will merely mention that unkept promises and a lack of trust will surely ruin a relationship. Again, our church lost a few members and experienced a small decline in giving. One year later, I am still dealing with the aftershock of this incident.

Recently, my wife, Lyn, spoke words of wisdom about this. She felt this ordeal was the result of my selfishness. "You prayed for the wrong thing and received it," she said. "You prayed for God to send someone to take care of *you* instead of praying for someone to help you care for His [God's] *flock*." Now that I look back over it, she's right. My friend, be careful what you pray for. You just might get it.

While all this was going on, one of our most loyal older leaders strangely sided with the opposition and turned on our elder board and me. This person had given seven years of outstanding service. This person personally took care of most of my needs at the church and oversaw the caring ministry of our church without hesitation. This broken relationship was more shocking and painful than the other two incidents.

I had heard the stories of betrayals and defections from other pastors, but I thought I was safe. After all, I had taken all the precautions. I had been careful of my friendships. I thought I had surrounded myself with those who would "watch my back." I also thought that if I just lived a morally clean lifestyle, and preached the Word of God without compromise, my pastoral career would be relatively pain free.

However, for the first time in my life, I found myself angry, and I was angry at God. "How could He allow all this to happen? How can people get away with such things? Where is the justice?" These thoughts swirled over and over in my mind. There were times I was so low that I felt God did not care about me at all.

I found myself losing sleep and being snappy at times with family and staff. In the past, I have told our congregation that none of us should feel too proud to seek professional assistance when we are dealing with emotional things that seem to be too much for us to bear. Therefore, I followed my own advice and visited with a Christian psychologist to help me sort through some emotions I am having trouble releasing. I have been told I am going through a healing process, and it will take some time to complete it. The pain is deep and like an open wound that gets disturbed every time I walk into our sanctuary or see certain people. It is very noticeable that certain once-loyal members are no longer here.

Several times last year, I found myself contemplating leaving the ministry and looking for a secular job. I sometimes think leaving the area would rid me of any kind of contact with the things that continue to remind me of this ordeal. However, I knew that I could be getting outside of the perfect will of God. Most of us know what happens when we get ahead of God. We may get blessed but never the way God would like to bless us. If you want proof, just ask Abraham and Sarah. Israel is still paying for the mistake those two made when they failed to wait on the son God had promised to give them.

You may feel my story is not all that traumatic. Maybe you have had worse things happen to you. While that may be true, we must remember that not all people are affected in the same way by similar problems. Some can endure more than others.

So what have I learned from all this? I wish I could give the "happily-ever-after" story. I am not completely healed, and I still struggle with certain issues. I still wrestle with whether or not I am making a difference. I still have thoughts every now and then about giving up the pastoral ministry. At times, I feel completely hopeless and don't even know how to help myself. At times, I don't know how to pray. At times, I don't want to pray.

I have had to repent for my short periods of blaming God for these uncomfortable events. I realize my selfishness. God is not unfair. He always does what is right. His plans and ways are far beyond my understanding. I knew all this, and it's right there in the Word of God; but somehow I just rationalized my way to a conclusion that satisfied me. God's prophets did what was right, yet they suffered much greater than I have or ever will.

I have learned being fully devoted to God is no guarantee we will avoid the fires of life. As part of His plan for us, God sometimes allows us to go through the uncomfortable trials of life in order to test our faith and to help us acquire endurance (James 1:2–3). It makes us better witnesses, because we know a God who provides in all of life's situations. Even though God is silent and seems distant, He is with us. He will not allow us to be destroyed by our circumstances, and He is working everything out for our good (Rom. 8:28). Even though I know this myself, I still find myself, just like Job, fluctuating between the darkness of hopelessness and the light of faith. Many years ago, this would have caused me to question my salvation.

I have also learned that just because God is silent, it does not mean that He does not care. The Book of Job is proof of that truth. I know God is worthy of praise and honor regardless of how I may feel spiritually or otherwise. I have never stopped believing that.

Allow me to end with this. Do you recall David's experience as an outlaw and fugitive? Even though God had anointed him king (1 Sam. 16), most scholars believe it was at least sixteen years before David actually took the throne. He spent most of those years on the run from the wrath of a jealous King Saul who was trying to kill him. In 1 Samuel 22, we find David hiding in a cave at Adullam. Notice the people who joined him there. In addition to his family, there were four hundred distressed, debt-ridden, and mistreated men. This is hardly the kind of people one needs when in such dire straits as David. However, David became their captain. He ministered to them and trained them. He helped them reach their potential. Those same men later became David's men of valor. Wow! What a change! While on the run, David never stopped seeking God, even though he questioned God.

While he was in the cave, he wrote Psalm 142. In this psalm David is honest with God. He admitted his pain, but he realized his only source of strength was in the Lord. Many other psalms were written during times of struggle and stress. These are the Scriptures that millions upon millions of God's people have used in times of their own struggles and depression.

Could it also be that God sometimes uses our "cave experiences" (e.g., loneliness and injustice) to give us a new ministry, while we wait on the ultimate ministry? I have come to believe this is a great possibility.

If you ever find yourself in a similar situation, I caution you not to be too quick to doubt yourself or push others away who try to get close to you. In our attempt to protect ourselves from further pain, we may actually reject some of the very people God places in our lives for us to mentor and develop, to help become whole again, and to become servants of valor for Christ.

I highly recommend that seminaries continue to offer certain strategic courses that are taught by local church leaders, who will be transparent with their spiritual journey and can give a practical side to the theoretical teaching that is so predominant in much of the seminary course work. Seminary students need to know what it's really like to serve in the kingdom of God in times like these. God help each of us to do our part.

Grace, mercy, and peace,
James Martin

Questions for Reflection

1. To what extent are you seeking to promote racial reconciliation within the Body of Christ both inside and outside the four walls of the church building?

2. In what ways can you relate to the author's struggles with ministerial loneliness? With dryness? With anger? What lessons have you learned through similar struggles?

3. How might one discern whether ministry struggles are an indication that it's time to move on to a new ministry or a testing designed to refine you for more effective ministry in your present setting?

THIRTY-FIVE

Learning to Be Successful in God's Eyes

James Means is Professor of Pastoral Ministries and Homiletics at Denver Seminary in Denver, Colorado. Prior to assuming this position in 1978, Jim pastored various Evangelical Free Church congregations for twenty-one years; he has also served in various interim pastoral roles since joining the Seminary full-time. His teaching ministry extends overseas, as James has ministered in Uganda, Kenya, the Philippines, the People's Republic of China, Italy, Ukraine, and Australia. Among his publications are *A Tearful Celebration, Leadership in Christian Ministry,* and *Effective Pastors for a New Century.*

Dear Friend,

Entering a new millennium certainly must be an exciting—and somewhat confusing—experience for young servants of the King of Kings! Opportunities and resources have never been greater; yet, despite the long overdue modernization of methodology and our technological advantages, nothing has yet effected any retardation of our culture's rush toward secularization. The church that we, the older generation, now bequeath to you young leaders is, for the most part, institutionally healthy but widely criticized for its insipid theology and flimsy piety. Serious discipleship is not the norm, and in many cases has been replaced with a privatized form of religion that refuses to submit to biblical mandates that seem outmoded and far too restrictive for the majority of our citizens. The consumer orientation of our culture has invaded the church and bears ominous implications for the future of evangelicalism. The most compelling question facing Christian leaders at this crucial time is: will we be satisfied with institutional prosperity or will we possess a passion for spiritual renewal and vitality that currently seems in short supply? Only you, our future generation, can answer that question.

So what is it going to take to foster spiritual vigor and to be successful in God's eyes? What must you know, and be, and do in order to make an impact for Christ and His Kingdom during the twenty-first century? Doubtlessly, a thousand things could be listed and, if they were, they would only serve the purposes of intimidation and discouragement. No one has all the necessary knowledge, the requisite gifts, and the essential graces that some think mandatory for effective ministry. It is worth reminding ourselves—and a powerful encouragement—that all of the biblical saints were seriously flawed; yet men like Moses and Samson and David are included in the roll call of the faithful (Heb. 11). We must not, however, use their defects as an excuse for our own. Let us covenant with God to be all that we can be, and do all we can by His grace and for His glory!

Trimming an extremely long list to the barest basics leads me to suggest that you focus your attention and concentrate your energies upon the following three principles.

First, ministry and piety must be inextricably yoked together. Any ministry without the legitimacy of personal holiness and prevailing prayer is high crime against God; for as Charles Spurgeon reminds us, "Of all causes which create infidelity, ungodly ministers must be ranked first." If you have been called to ministry, you have been called to holiness. Those most likely to receive spiritual power for significant deeds in God's kingdom are not usually those most gifted, most professional, or most educated, but those who take discipleship seriously, those who most consistently practice the spiritual disciplines, and those who "set an example for believers in speech, in life, in love, in faith, and in purity" (1 Tim. 4:12 NIV). Leadership is not so much what you do but what you are as a disciple.

Today's media document in excruciating detail the notorious escapades of embarrassed clergy. Many contemporary ministers practice leadership devoid of integrity, expertise detached from spiritual authenticity, and oratory severed from the anointing of the Holy Spirit. What is sadder than to witness the success of some who quickly become intoxicated with vanity? Their pride unveils their spiritual deficiency and precedes their fall. May such dishonor never be your experience! Only the most constant vigilance can protect you!

Many years ago, when I was a young pastor, I attended a "farewell" for a retiring colleague, a man who had served more that forty years in small town or rural churches in Nebraska and Minnesota. He made a little speech in which he said, "My brothers and sisters in the Lord, I have come now to the end of my pastoral ministry. I never served a large church, never received much recognition of crowds, and never wrote a book, but as I stand before you today my hands are clean before God." Of course, we all knew that he was not claiming perfection, but simply that he had been faithful, that he had done the best he could with his gifts, and that he had done nothing to bring disgrace upon the name of Christ or His church. Many times I have been reminded of Robert Murray McCheyne's words: "It is not great talents God blesses so much as great likeness to Jesus. A holy minister is an awful weapon in the hand of God." If this were truly believed in evangelicalism today, we might give a little less attention to polishing our technique and much more attention to those things that promote godliness in our leaders. "Since we have these promises, dear friends, let us purify ourselves from everything that contaminates body and spirit, perfecting holiness out of reverence for God" (2 Cor. 7:1 NIV).

Second, in spiritual leadership, theology matters. In our day, theology seems increasingly unimportant in the leadership exercised by many. Yielding to the pressures of our day has fostered a religion of style, not substance. Panache seems more important than substantive doctrine, and a wide range of temporal affairs and managerial sophistication seem to preempt biblical exposition and theological precision. Many ministers have shockingly weak or unbiblical convictions. Preaching has become increasingly anthropocentric rather than theocentric. But just as the true weapons of our warfare are spiritual, not fleshly, so the crucial questions of our day are theological, not methodological (despite enormous cultural coercion to believe otherwise).

It has taken many, many years for me to come to the settled conviction that theology truly matters and that nothing spiritually enfeebles our churches so much as the curious reality that theology has moved to the fringes of ministry in the practice of many church leaders. My counsel to every young Christian leader includes the forceful admonition to study theology, which of course necessitates serious exegesis of Scripture utilizing the original languages and the best tools of our trade. Ministry must be theology driven, not forged by catering to the fickle wants of the crowd. As someone has said, "Before you get the message out, you'd better get the message straight." Our job as spiritual leaders is not to accommodate the culture by adapting the message, but to confront the culture with the truth of the gospel. In order to do that, we must have both courage and theological clarity. Only a fanatic devotion to biblical truth is capable of making much difference in our world of sensualism and materialism. The most elegant methodology, devoid of theological exactness, cannot produce disciples; and producing disciples is at the heart of our mission.

Third, spiritual leadership necessitates personal compassion for all kinds of people. There are those who target the upwardly mobile, who covet the preeminence of leadership positions, and who relish the attention of crowds, but who care little for individuals; especially, it seems, the poor and the disenfranchised of our society. It is easy to slip into a modus operandi of catering to those who can substantially contribute to the institutional advancement of our ministry and thereby neglect the most needy people of our community. Entrepreneurial skills pale in importance compared to the tireless compassion for hurting people. The pastor's heart—if that is your direction—is not that of a CEO, but that of an empathetic shepherd.

Some years ago I was invited to preach in the Sunday services of an extremely large church in a distant part of the country. I arrived on Saturday morning and was entertained like royalty. Between the Sunday morning services, an elder gave me a tour of the eye-popping facilities, after which we visited together in the luxurious church parlor while waiting for the next service to begin. The elder reflected about his pastor who had been there for many, many years: "You know, Pastor _____ has accomplished a great deal here in our church. He has exceptional platform skills and is a dynamic personality, but [long pause] he's not a loving man. I hope he retires soon." I suspect the elder little realized the seriousness of his indictment. Without the stalwart compassion and sacrificial love of Jesus, the pastor is merely a resounding gong or a clanging cymbal; in reality, nothing (1 Cor. 13:13). The best preaching and the most fruitful ministry—always— flow from a pastor's heart, not from a leader's lips, a scholar's mind, or an orator's tongue.

My closest friend for more than thirty years has said: "We must do all the good we can to all the people we can whenever we can and for as long as we can." Not a bad philosophy of life! Such is impossible, however, without personal spiritual authenticity, theological soundness, and the compassionate love of Jesus. May God bless you in your diligent pursuit of these vital ingredients for a productive ministry.

Sincerely,
James Means

Questions for Reflection

1. "Of all causes which create infidelity, ungodly ministers must be ranked first." Reflect upon any examples of Spurgeon's assertion that you have observed. What safeguards are in place in your life to foster congruence between what you teach and how you live?

2. To what extent does theology matter in your ministry? What steps are you taking to ensure that you get the message straight before you get the message out?

3. To what extent might your compassion and ministry be motivated more by self-serving concerns than by the unconditional and universal love of God? Are the most needy in your community being touched by your ministry?

THIRTY-SIX

Learning About Building to Last

David Miller is president of Western Baptist College in Salem, Oregon. He has been a professor at that school for thirty-two years, chairing for most of that time the division of Biblical Studies. In addition to his responsibilities at Western, David has also organized and pastored a church for seventeen years. He speaks frequently at various conferences both in the United States and abroad.

Dear Friend,
Most of us have heard the short verse

> Only one life, 'twill soon be past;
> Only what's done for Christ will last.

Such a statement brings encouragement to our work and ministry since we often wonder if there is any lasting significance to what we are doing. Recently I came across a book that gave another perspective on activity that lasts.

In *Built to Last,* authors James Porrass and Jerry Collins examine twenty of America's premier companies that have endured from generation to generation. They are companies built to last. The authors conclude that although individuals come and go, yet companies, organizations, and institutions frequently last through generations.

As I reflected on this concept, I thought immediately of my father who pioneered and pastored a church in eastern Washington. At the church's fortieth anniversary, I was invited to represent my father who had passed away some twenty years earlier. There were not many people left who had even known Dad personally, but the church was still there, continuing to function, having outlasted him and subsequent pastors.

I thought also of presidents who have come and gone since my first connection with Western Baptist College where I serve. Yet the institution remains, making a difference in the lives of students through multiple generations.

Scripture speaks of "a time to be born and a time to die" (Eccl. 3:2 NIV). Yet the organized church which is a manifestation of the body of Christ continues on, generation after generation (Matt. 16:18), providing another example of people coming and going but an institution outlasting them all.

If it is true that individuals come and go while institutions last, should we not examine how we spend our lives? To be sure, none of the work we do for God will be lost (1 Cor. 3), but would not our work have a more lasting effect if we invested our lives and resources in institutions that bear fruit for years to come, even after we have gone home to be with the Lord? Would it not be wise for us to develop a philosophy of ministry in which we think institutionally rather than just individually?

In *Built to Last,* the authors contrast "time-telling" with "clock-building." In what follows, I will use the illustration of clock building to discuss the vision, the essence, and the strategy of being involved in activities with lasting impact.

The Vision of Clock-Building

A question for every leader to consider, therefore, is am I a "clock-builder" or a "time-teller"? But what is the difference? Clock-building is the construction of a valuable tool that will meet a long-term need. People can turn to a clock whenever they need to know the time. Time-telling, on the other hand, is performing a function that serves only an immediate need. It does not give guidance for the future. In terms of our subject, clock-building is the activity of a person who helps build an organization, institution, or company. Time-telling is doing a job merely for the paycheck or as a stepping stone to the next opportunity. Every organization has these two kinds of people within it.

As president of Western Baptist College, I have tried to be involved in clock-building activity. At the end of my first five years as president, I listed the activities I had thought about, worked on, and accomplished to evaluate how many were clock-building and how many were time-telling. I was pleased to identify many activities I would define as clock-building. One such activity was the developing of a vision for the college. A vision gives direction. It speaks of possibilities, of what enterprises can become. In *The Leadership Challenge,* Kouzes and Posner write, "To begin your own thinking about your

own vision, ask yourself this question: 'Am I in this job to do something, or am I in this job for something to do?'"

A clock-building activity is designed to do something. Other clock-
building activities I initiated include clarifying what we believe, rede-
signing our bylaws, adopting our basic philosophical underpinnings,
producing necessary policies and procedures, forming necessary
teams, maintaining our roots while broadening our base, initiating
an assessment culture, developing training programs, and introduc-
ing new, strategic opportunities.

If you are involved in a Christian church, college, or other
parachurch ministry, you can be involved in clock-building. You can
help build something bigger than yourself, namely an organization
that can live on for decades even after you have passed from the scene.

When I am confronted with a college employee thinking of moving on to another job in order to advance his or her career, I like to
share the concept of thinking "institutionally" rather than merely "individually." Ironically, putting the needs of an organization before
personal aspirations can result in personal benefits as well. To illustrate, let me share the following story that Zig Ziglar tells in *See You
at the Top:*

> Several years ago on an extremely warm day, a crew of men
> were working on a road bed of the railroad when they were
> interrupted by a slow-moving train. The train ground to a stop
> and a window in the last car (which incidentally was cus-
> tom-made and air-conditioned) was raised. A booming,
> friendly voice called out, "Dave, is that you?" Dave Ander-
> son, the crew chief, called back and said, "Sure is, Jim, and
> it's really good to see you." With that brief exchange Dave
> Anderson was invited to join Jim Murphy, the president of
> the railroad, for a visit. For over an hour the men exchanged
> pleasantries and then shook hands warmly as the train
> pulled out.
>
> Dave Anderson's crew immediately surrounded him and
> to a man expressed astonishment that he knew the president
> of the railroad as a personal friend. Dave then explained that
> over twenty years earlier he and Jim Murphy had started to
> work for the railroad on the same day. One of the men, half
> jokingly and half seriously asked why he was still working
> out in the hot sun while Jim Murphy had gone onto become
> president. Rather wistfully Dave explained, "Twenty-three
> years ago I went to work for $1.75 an hour, but Jim Murphy
> went to work for the railroad."

A good contrast, isn't it? One man's life was an example of clock-building while the other's life was an example of time-telling. While you may not always become president, there are usually personal benefits if you think institutionally rather than individually. But even if no benefits are apparent, building something bigger than yourself will always mean more than building only yourself.

The Essence of Clock-Building

But mere building isn't enough. As Paul stated in 1 Corinthians 3:10, a believer must "take heed how he builds" (NKJV). In *Built to Last,* the authors point out that the single most important concept in their book is "creating tangible mechanisms aligned to 'preserve the core and stimulate progress.'" They state that this represents the essence of clock-building. I would like to rephrase this and instead declare that the key to building the clock is in preserving the core and processing the culture.

Charles Swindoll talked about preserving the core and processing the culture when he became president of Dallas Theological Seminary: "To meet tomorrow's need, I must be willing to leave today's comfortable familiarities without disturbing yesterday's essential foundation."

In an insightful article entitled, "Evangelical Protestant Colleges and Secularization: An Analysis of Superficial Versus Core Value Change" (published in *Research on Christian Higher Education,* Vol. 2, 1995), Lisa Graham McMinn looks at several Christian colleges and shows how some resisted core value change while others changed those values. One college she studied had a statement of purpose indicating their Christian origins, a standard of conduct which spoke pointedly to issues of acceptable morality, a requirement that all faculty make a profession of faith, a requirement of ten units in religious studies, and a requirement of chapel attendance. But that was forty years ago; today, this same college does not have any of those characteristics. The core was changed as they gave in to the dominant culture of the day.

On the other hand, it is important to recognize that not everything is in the core. Recently a visitor came to our campus to spend a couple of days. The visitor had attended Western in the late 1940s. Upon leaving the campus, he came to speak to me. He said that he had observed that the music had changed as well as the dress (i.e., the culture). But he said that our commitment to the Scriptures was the same (i.e., the core). He said that he had purchased one of our sweatshirts and was going to wear it with pride.

The main job of any leader is preserving the core and processing the culture. This is the essence of clock-building.

The Strategy of Clock-Building

All of this works when the right leader is in place. But what happens to the institution after the individual is gone? Is the core still preserved while the culture is still being processed?

A strategy must exist for every Christian organization. I believe the strategy is to *hire from within.* Collins and Porass state that one of the myths of business today is that the only way to bring about change in an organization is to bring in the president or CEO from the outside. They point out that when the main leader is brought in from the outside, what usually takes place is a change of the core. On the other hand, organizations that hire from within do bring about change, but the core values remain intact because those leaders have been brought up with the core values of the organization and therefore understand them. Interestingly, in a study of America's premier companies, the authors conclude that "across seventeen hundred years of combined history in the visionary companies, we found only four individual cases of an outsider coming directly into the role of chief executive" (p. 173).

After spending twenty-five years in the classroom at Western, I was chosen to be that school's next president. Prior to joining the faculty, I had spent four years as a student being trained in the core before returning to pass it on to others. I understood Western's core values. I have also brought together the present administrative team from those who had served in other positions *within* the college. It is the desire of the trustees, the administrative team, and myself to carry on this strategy whenever possible in order to encourage those within the organization to recognize both that there are opportunities for advancement within our school and that we desire people who share the same proven core values.

In April of 1996, United States Commerce Secretary Ron Brown and thirty CEOs of American companies perished in a plane disaster. The Gannett News Service wrote, "Most companies are not prepared when the unthinkable happens: the sudden death of the CEO." One executive recruiter was quoted as saying, "Succession planning is weak throughout corporate America." The board of trustees at our college has included within their policy manual the responsibility of ensuring that a viable strategy for succession planning is honored as one of their most important obligations.

I believe this concept is even more important for Christian organizations because of the distinctive and defining nature of our core beliefs, which of course are based upon the absolute truth of God's inspired Word.

I had the privilege of being the founding pastor of a church where

I served for seventeen years alongside my role as a Western faculty member. When I accepted the position of college president I left my position as pastor of that church. My successor was hired from within that church. In fact, the transition was so gradual that the church had a hard time figuring out when I had left and when he had come! Three years later, at the twentieth anniversary of the church, I was asked to come back and speak at the special celebration. As part of the celebration they had a farewell party for me since they concluded that they had never really said good-bye.

While I realize that this transition was handled in a somewhat unusual way, I like what happened. The new pastor assumed his ministry and the church went on with the same core values they had always held. In addition—and to my amazement—the church continues on today with all but one of the core families remaining. This is in stark contrast to the church-hopping that is so prevalent today. I think that the reason why these families have stayed is their loyalty to the core beliefs upon which the church was begun and their conviction that these beliefs must live on through multiple generations. The church hired from within and has been successful in *preserving the core* while *processing the culture.*

Conclusion

Recently I stood before the pyramids in Egypt, observing that they were certainly built to last. The sight caused me to reflect on how important it is for our individual efforts to last as well. To be sure, as servants of God, we desire our life's activities to have eternal consequences. But we also want the consequences to be reproduced continually in the lives of others for generations to come. When we someday pass from the scene, will we have built a clock? I believe we will, if we have practiced thinking *institutionally* and not just *individually;* if we have remembered to *preserve the core* and *process the culture;* and if we have the wisdom to *hire from within.*

Sincerely,
David Miller

Questions for Reflection

1. Inventory your activities over the last few months. What percentage was devoted to clock-building and what percentage to time-telling? Do you need to make some changes to increase the former and decrease the latter?

2. "To meet tomorrow's need, I must be willing to leave today's comfortable familiarities without disturbing yesterday's essential foundation." What are the implications of "perserving the core" and "processing the culture" for your present responsibility? How might you distinguish between the "comforting familiarities" that might need to be left behind and the "essential foundation" that must be preserved?

3. How much thought has your ministry organization given to leadership succession? What would be the pros and cons of hiring your successor from within?

THIRTY-SEVEN

Learning to Be Vulnerable

Elisa Morgan is president of MOPS ("Mothers of Preschoolers") International, an organization that focuses on meeting the needs of mothers with children from infancy to kindergarten. She also hosts the syndicated daily radio ministry, *Mom Sense*. Among Elisa's publications are *Mom to Mom, The Mom's Devotional Bible, What Every Mom Needs,* and *What Every Child Needs.*

Dear Friend,

People are watching. Minute-to-minute, day-to-day, month-to-month those around you are constantly watching. They wonder, "What is her relationship with God really like?" "Is He more real to her than He is to me?" "Does she ever have doubts as to how to use the gifts God has given her?"

Let me encourage you to resist every temptation that tells you to "board up" the real you under a facade of "Christianese." What people need most from their leaders is honest and candid reality.

Vulnerability is believability. It's not the perfect person who never struggles with sin that we turn to in the middle of the night with our fears and disappointments. Instead, it's the person who transparently says to the world, "I haven't arrived at the point of perfection; I'm still learning and growing. But I know God is real and that He has the power to help me and to help you." It's this kind of person that we fall in beside. It's this person that we allow to teach us and mold us into God's image. It's this person that we choose to trust because he or she is so believable. He's real. She's genuine. We can relate.

Vulnerability is believability and Christianity is believable when it is lived out by vulnerable Christians.

Almost as a rule nowadays, I make it a practice to tell about my goofs, inadequacies, and "soul-holes" when I speak on any platform. Such honesty and transparency draws others close to me to see not just how I mess up, but how God enables me to start again and, therefore, how He can do the same for them. Interestingly, this vulnerability from the pedestal frees me to relate more authentically in private as well. I have no image to keep up, no persona to perform. So I can tell about how I holler as I clean up cat vomit on the carpet, how I weep as I discover new lackings in my walk with God, and how I shrug my shoulders as I uncover yet another blooper in a relationship with someone I love.

Jesus was vulnerable as He walked the face of the earth. God clarified Himself as He gave His Son as a human to live and walk and die. This made Christianity believable.

Vulnerability before others means living a resurrected life with scars of nail prints still visible in your hands. May God give you the grace to be vulnerable before others.

From my heart to yours,
Elisa Morgan

Questions for Reflection

1. How transparent and vulnerable are you in sharing your personal shortcomings and struggles with others? What factors keep you from the kind of honesty described by the author?

2. Sometimes Christian leaders feel that they must be examples of perfection as opposed to examples of ongoing growth. How might a focus on the latter enable a leader to still be a model worthy of emulation without having to pretend his or her Christian life is better than it really is?

3. Under what circumstances (if any) do you think that candid transparency from a Christian leader might be counterproductive to the spiritual growth of others?

THIRTY-EIGHT

Learning Balance
As a Pastor-Leader

John W. P. Oliver assumed the pastorate of Trinity Presbyterian Church in Montgomery, Alabama, in 1997. He previously pastored First Presbyterian Church in Augusta, Georgia for twenty-eight years after serving for five years in assistant pastor roles in Illinois and Alabama. John serves on multiple boards, including that of Columbia International University. He is also Ministerial Advisor for Reformed Theological Seminary (Charlotte, North Carolina).

Dear Friend,

I speak in my letter principally to those who follow the Lord's calling to serve as pastors and leaders in local congregations of Jesus Christ. My own calling to leadership has been for three decades as the pastor of a local congregation. Thus I say from the outset, you must develop a clear understanding as to what constitutes leadership for a local church.

The pastor-leader, as I shall hereafter refer to him, is neither a moderator nor a dictator. To lead, one must know where to lead, what steps are necessary to achieve these goals, and how to motivate the followers to move in the desired direction. The pastor-leader needs to have desirable and workable ideas to offer the people to be led. He cannot merely be the moderator, to hear all ideas with little comment in order to "see what the people want to do." As essential as it is to be receptive to the thinking and ideas of people in the congregation, it is even more essential to have ideas, goals, and strategies to offer. True leaders always have something to offer. Genuine openness to the thinking and the ideas of people without abdicating leadership will avoid the snare of becoming a virtual dictator. Followers are not just subjects who exist to carry out the directives—or worse, the demands—of a dictatorial leader. The positive ideas of an authentic leader are distinguishable from preferences. Preferences can be surrendered. Ideas that are good may be modified and improved, but are not to be set aside like a preference.

What are the overarching goals and attendant guidelines of leadership for a local congregation regardless of size, ecclesiastical connection, geographical location, or make-up of its constituency? Would such not emerge from an understanding of a passage such as the fourth chapter of Ephesians? Would not the good pastor-leader exercise leadership in moving the people to biblical information and spiritual formation so that all the areas of ministry are present in a balanced and fruitful work? I would commend to leaders the goal of balancing all the various emphases of Christ's biblical assignments and so lead the people that they are functioning harmoniously as a healthy body, equipped by its leadership and energized by the Holy Spirit, to do the total work of the ministry.

It is of first importance, then, for the leader to know the major ministry assignments from the Scriptures incumbent upon the congregation of our Lord Jesus Christ. Theology, Christian living, local evangelism, world missions, mercy ministries, teaching, corporate worship, small groups, and the like are all necessary ingredients of a full-orbed and balanced ministry. Thus, for example, doctrine is to be in tension with practice. Ministry to one another within the body of believers is to be balanced by ministry by the body of believers to those who are beyond the borders of the church. Mercy ministries to those in unfortunate conditions nearby must have global evangelism "pulling against" them. Prayer meetings must be in tension with dutiful service. The pastor-leader must know these things and provide leadership that steers a steady direction even though the course resulting from that leadership may be a zigzagged line rather than a straight one. Thus, a particular area of ministry needs to be stressed when its counterpart has been overstressed. Does it appear at this point that the pastor-leader needs to be clear in his own mind as to the major biblical components of a healthy, balanced productive congregation? Yes, indeed! And, beyond that, to be committed to them and their proper tension in the work he leads.

Thankfully, these things came to me early on in the role of pastor-leader. They became guidelines of a sort that helped to critique church programs as well as provide criteria for dealing with the enormous claims for the use of time and energies. The enormity of those claims is often seen in unreasonable expectations with which the pastor-leader and his people are saddled. How the balance of components for the church's ministry and what the balanced leader would be, came through my observation of pastor-leaders.

There were those who predominantly remained in the study and poured over the literature at hand in preparation for a sermon or two per week. Such pastor-leaders seemed to be heavily into conveying strong theological material not dissimilar to what might be given in the classroom of a theological institution. It seemed as though the primary—and perhaps even sole—aim was to produce followership that was theologically literate and precise in its grasp of his communication of biblical truth. Precise theological understanding and effective communication are admirable and desirable. A balanced body of believers, however, is more than a theological society; it is a caring, ministering fellowship as well.

By way of contrast, there were those who seemed ever active, even ubiquitous, participating in everything and with everyone, whose widespread involvement with people in the church and in the community was favorably labeled "being a good pastor." It did not take extensive analysis to conclude that in most such cases both substance and effectiveness in the pulpit and in the Bible class were lacking.

It is true, of course, that propensities and abilities vary widely among pastor-leaders; but it is also true that the pastor-leader must be able to teach and feed the flock as well as shepherd it and minister to it. Thus, knowing the major components in a biblically balanced ministry and what should be the resulting cardinal claims to time and energy is of highest consequence. The pastor-leader must be clear in his mind and in his ministry if he is to make clear to those whom he leads what is a proper balance in the life and work of the congregation they comprise.

An important benefit of such balanced leadership is, for example, having an established criterion for assessing the plethora of programs and materials that flood the desk of present-day clergymen. How does one glean benefit from all of these marketed programs and materials without enslavement to the latest products and programs, all of which are a "must" if the pastor-leader and his church are to be successful? Is not the use of the criterion of balance the answer?

Thus, if there is a vital, fruitful missions conference already in place in the local congregation, do the leader and his colleagues need to spend several days learning how to conduct a successful missions conference? Cross-fertilization of ideas and challenges to stale patterns notwithstanding, a critical leader will know how to evaluate and even withstand undue pressures to "sign up." Observation through the years has revealed pastor-leaders who participate in a multiplicity of programs but who apparently lead basically unproductive ministries despite much training received and many programs adopted. At the other extreme are those pastor-leaders who need both the challenge and critical thinking that such programs, products, and seminars can provide. But the assessment of need and/or participation and use is made by understanding the biblical principle of balance and effectiveness for the pastor-leader and for the ministry into which he leads his people.

Preaching, teaching, and the preparation for it, then, will be held in tension with the need of a flock to be tended by an undershepherd. A commendable concern for the poor, the disenfranchised, the imprisoned in one's own community will be balanced by a heart for the "regions beyond." Music and message, large assemblies and small groups, evangelism and education, Christian living and Christian service will all be present in proper proportions only as a result of wise leadership. The leader understandably must bear the lion's share of responsibility to lead in such a way as to provide the pattern so that the followers can become more and more what the Lord and King of the Church intended them to be.

May you become that kind of leader!

Sincerely,
John W. P. Oliver

Questions for Reflection

1. How well are you avoiding the extremes of being either a moderator or a dictator in your leadership? To which extreme are you most tempted, and what do you need to do to minimize your vulnerability to that temptation?

2. How balanced is your feeding and shepherding of your flock? Are you most attracted to the study or to personal interaction with those whom you serve?

3. What criteria do you use to determine whether or not a particular seminar or program might be useful to you and your ministry? How do you feel about the criteria suggested by the author?

THIRTY-NINE

Learning That Any Old Bush Will Do

Luis Palau is one of the most respected evangelists of our time. During the more than thirty years of full-time ministry, he has spoken to hundreds of millions through his radio and television broadcasts, and face-to-face with more than twelve million people in sixty-four countries. His many publications include *God is Relevant, The Only Hope for America,* and *Healthy Habits for Spiritual Growth.*

Dear Friend,

Whenever a great preacher came to our church in Argentina, some of my friends and I would try to get an interview with him. Our questions were always the same. "How can we get victory over temptation? How can we live holy lives?"

Usually the visiting preacher would ask, "Are you reading the Bible?"

"Yes, when we get up at five every morning before going to school or work. We read several chapters every day."

"Great! But are you testifying for Jesus?"

"Yes. We hand out tracts, teach children's classes, and even hold street meetings."

"That's terrific! But are you praying?" the preacher would ask. So we'd tell him about our all-night prayer meetings.

Our frustration must have been obvious. "What else do we need to do?" we'd ask.

"Well, pray some more, witness some more, read the Bible some more." So we did. And we just about killed ourselves, we were so eager to be holy.

I was on the verge of giving up, not because I saw a lack in God, but because I was weary of fighting and struggling and seeking on my own to persevere through sheer dedication.

I wondered when I'd ever catch on. Would I give up, after all that I'd been through? I wanted to please and love and serve God. I wanted people to be saved. I would sing, "Oh, Jesus, I have promised to serve Thee to the end," while I would think, even if it kills me.

One day I was invited to view a brief film of Billy Graham speaking to Christian leaders in India. Although he spoke before an unbelievable crowd of tens of thousands, he seemed to be staring right into my eyes as he quoted Ephesians 5:18: "Do not be drunk on wine, which leads to debauchery. Instead, be filled with the Spirit" (NIV). It was as if the crowd in India didn't exist. He was looking right at me and shouting, "Are you filled with the Spirit?"

I knew that was my problem; I wasn't filled with the Holy Spirit. That was the reason for my up-and-down Christianity. That was why I had zeal and commitment, but little fruit or victory. When would it end? When would I find the answer?

I finally found it in the United States after several frustrating months of Bible school.

I came to the States through the patient prodding of Ray Stedman, pastor of Peninsula Bible Church in Palo Alto, California. The first two months, I lived in his home. I was argumentative and wanted to discuss theology and doctrine for hours. I had come to learn, but maybe I wasn't yet ready to admit that I didn't have all the answers.

After those two months with the Stedmans, I went to Multnomah School of the Bible in Portland, Oregon. Multnomah was a demanding school, and I found the first semester particularly rough.

Our Spiritual Life class professor, Dr. George Kehoe, only added to my frustration when he began every class period by quoting Galatians 2:20: "I have been crucified with Christ, and I no longer live, but Christ lives in me. The life I live in the body, I live by faith in the Son of God, who loved me and gave himself for me" (NIV).

I was still frustrated in not being able to live the lifestyle I saw in men like Ray Stedman and several others both at Peninsula Bible Church and at Multnomah. Their lives exhibited a joy and freedom that I found attractive. But the more I sought it, the more elusive it seemed.

My spiritual journey seemed like a climb up a tall cliff. I clawed every inch of the way only to slip and slide back down. Although I had experienced times of blessing and victory, for the most part I felt the struggle was impossible. I couldn't go on that way, especially when no one else knew about it. It was my secret, private death.

I felt like a hypocrite. If I were to describe myself in those days, I would have to say that I was envious, jealous, too preoccupied and self-centered, and ambitious to a wrong degree. I was smug about other speakers, silently rating their illustrations or delivery against my own. That left me feeling mean and ugly and petty. No amount of wrestling with myself would rid me of those sins. And yet I tried. I felt despicable, and hated the idea that I was a hypocrite.

Maybe that's why I didn't like the constant reminder of Galatians 2:20 and was getting annoyed at Dr. Kehoe's quoting that verse every day. It can't be that Bible verse's fault that you get so upset, I told myself. It must be you. Rather than let that verse penetrate my pride, I conveniently decided that the verse was self-contradictory, hard to understand, and confusing (especially in English).

Shortly after Christmas break, Major Ian Thomas (founder and director of Torchbearers, the group that runs Capernwray Bible School in England) spoke at our chapel service. I usually sat in the back of the auditorium and dared the speaker to make me pay attention. If he was good, I'd honor him by listening. Otherwise I would just daydream or peek at my class notes.

Ian Thomas talked about Moses and how it took this great man forty years in the wilderness to learn that he was nothing. Then one day Moses was confronted with a burning bush (likely a dry bunch of ugly sticks that had hardly developed), yet Moses had to take off his shoes. Why? Because this was holy ground. Why was it holy ground? Because God was in the bush!

Here was Major Thomas' point: God was telling Moses, "I don't need a pretty bush or an educated bush or an eloquent bush. Any old bush will do as long as I am in the bush. If I am going to use you, I am going to use you. It will not be you doing something for Me, but Me doing something through you."

It suddenly hit me that I was that kind of bush: a worthless, useless bunch of dried-up sticks. I could do nothing for God. All my reading and studying, asking questions, and trying to model myself after others was worthless. Everything in my ministry was worthless, unless God was in the bush. Only He could make it happen.

Thomas told of many Christian workers who failed at first because they thought they had something to offer God. He himself had once imagined that because he was an aggressive, winsome, evangelistic sort, God would use him. But God didn't use him until he came to the end of himself. That's exactly my situation, I thought. I am at the end of myself.

Thomas closed his message by reading (you guessed it!) Galatians 2:20. And then it all came together for me. "I have been crucified with Christ and I no longer live, but Christ lives in me." My biggest spiritual struggle was finally over! I would let God be God and let Luis Palau be dependent upon Him.

I ran back to my room and in tears fell to my knees next to my bunk. "Lord, I now understand!" I prayed in my native Spanish. "The whole thing is 'not I, but Christ in me.' It's not what I'm going to do for You, but rather what You're going to do through me."

I stayed on my knees until lunchtime, an hour and a half later. I asked the Lord's forgiveness for my pride.

Well, God still had a lot of burning to do, but He was finally in control of this bush. He wanted me to be grateful for all the small things He had put in my life, but He didn't want me to place my confidence in those opportunities to make me a better minister or preacher. He wanted me to depend not on myself or on my breaks, but on Christ alone: the indwelling, resurrected almighty Lord Jesus.

That day marked the intellectual turning point in my spiritual life. The practical working out of that discovery would be lengthy and painful, but at last the essential realization had come. We have everything we need when we have Jesus Christ living in us. It's His power that controls our dispositions, enables us to serve, and corrects and directs us (Phil. 2:13). I could relax and rest in Him. He was going to do the work through me.

Over the years, I've learned many other lessons: about meeting with a small group of men regularly for accountability, about the value of working with a dedicated evangelistic team, about working with the whole body of Christ, about beautifying my wife, about raising tenderhearted children in a tough world, and about planting my family's roots deep into the local church, just to name a few. Yet, wherever I go, whenever I speak at a Christian conference, I feel that I haven't done my duty if I don't speak about the life-transforming power of "Christ in me."

I've had pastors and missionaries with decades of ministry experience—true veterans—weep as they've talked with me. "If only someone had told me this earlier," they tell me. "I've done all the right things, but I haven't had joy, I haven't had power, I haven't felt truly blessed by God until now."

Don't wait another day to begin experiencing Christ at work in and through you, bringing good for His glory, honor, and praise.

Resting in Him,
Luis Palau

Questions for Reflection

1. To what extent can you relate to the author's frustration of trying to be holy and effective in ministry? How might his discovery of dependence on the power of Christ similarly free you from that frustration?

2. What is the difference between the biblical dependence upon Christ described by the author and an unbiblical passivism? Meditate upon the biblical synergism suggested in Philippians 2:12–13.

3. Are there any biblical truths that you are trying to ignore but which will need to be embraced if you are going to learn an important spiritual lesson?

FORTY

Learning to Rethink Traditional Practice and Teaching

George Patterson is currently supported through Mission to the Americas to serve as a trainer, consultant, and coach for several mission agencies and churches in a wide variety of countries. George also serves as an adjunct faculty member at Western Seminary in Portland, Oregon. He has planted dozens of churches in rural Honduras during his more than twenty years of missionary service there. George also developed Theological Education and Evangelism by Extension (TEEE), also known as "Obedience Oriented Education." He is the author or coauthor of many church planning and leadership training materials, including *Church Multiplication Guide* and *Tiros en la Noche*.

Dear Friend,

Here are some key principles I have learned (through hard bumps) during my many years of church planting and pastoral training.

First, *obey the commands of Jesus Christ above and before all other rules and policies*. That's the Great Commission. The three thousand converts of the first church in Jerusalem, before the end of Acts chapter 2, are obeying all of His basic commands: repenting, being baptized, receiving the Word, breaking bread, praying, giving, and loving each other. This is foundational. Whenever I tried to build obedience on a doctrinal foundation alone, I failed. In Honduras I tried that and failed; we made scholars, not disciples. But when we built our doctrinal teaching on the foundations of obedience, we got both!

An example: like many missionaries, at first I used baptism as a graduation ceremony following a long beginner's doctrine course. This is not at all what the Bible teaches that baptism is, and our disobedience in delaying this confirmation of converts' repentance resulted in a paralyzing legalism. Also, at first we did not permit new churches to celebrate the Lord's Supper without an ordained pastor. But the rules for ordination were man-made and totally irrelevant to that culture; as a result, the churches felt disobedient and second-rate. We had to face this question squarely: do we let them obey Jesus with childlike, loving obedience, or do we enforce policies that keep us firmly in control? I now coach church-planting teams in many cultures and continue to discover the same truth: if they fail to teach basic, loving obedience to Jesus above all else, they soon have problems with authority (who is in control?), focus (what are we supposed to be doing?), and plans for ministry (how do you know God's will for the future?). When they begin with foundational obedience, most of these problems disappear.

Second, *relate and emphasize Jesus' resurrection as you witness.* Like most missionaries, I emphasized Jesus' sacrificial death when I witnessed, and did not consider His resurrection an important part of the gospel proclamation (as He said in Luke 24:46–48). But I learned that Jesus is not only the Savior in a legal sense (providing forgiveness legally by His death) but also in the sense that His resurrection body, like the ark, is the very vehicle that carries us to glory. He alone is the resurrection and the life. Faith is not correct belief; it is a correct relationship with the one Source of all life and forgiveness. We have eternal life only because we are one with Christ—in Christ, i.e., in a correct relationship with Him—so that we are raised in Him (Eph. 2:6). Even the unsaved dead are raised by Him to judgment (John 5:24–30).

The most accurate illustration in Scripture is probably the ark of Noah, which Peter used to illustrate salvation by the resurrection of Jesus (1 Peter 3:21, in context). Like the ark, Jesus' risen body is the very vehicle in which we escape death and are conveyed into the Father's presence in glory. To say that we have innate immortality is like saying we are omnipotent or omniscient. The emphasis in my argument here is on the word "innate." Only God has the innate attribute of immortality (1 Tim. 6:16). Our mortal bodies are clothed with God's immortality in the resurrection and transformation at Christ's appearing (1 Cor. 15:53–54). Calvin and others introduced Greek classical philosophical beliefs about the inherently immortal soul into evangelical Christianity and it is hard to root out—the first lie in Eden. When I started emphasizing Jesus' resurrection as the source of life and holiness (as well as His sacrificial death as the means of forgiveness), I found that the Holy Spirit brought far more converts to repentance. It was always the punch line of the apostles' witness in Acts. Try it, if you don't believe me; you'll see the difference!

Third, *train leaders by discipling (mentoring) them.* We must supplement classroom instruction with apprenticeship training for the best results. When we began training pastors by discipling them on the job in Honduras, churches started to multiply (provided we used methods and equipment that they could use immediately). Jesus never commanded His disciples to do anything they did not see Him model and could not imitate immediately. Like many Western missionaries, I relied too much at first on gadgets, electronics, "methods," and sophisticated knowledge. I learned that nothing is as powerful for training leaders as modeling for them in a way that they can model for others (the 2 Tim. 2:2 chain reaction). God works this way. The best way to mentor a leader, besides having him accompany you in the work, is to listen to him. Let him report what his people are doing. (We are talking about training leaders, and one is not a leader unless he has a flock; though at first it may be only his family.) Then, after listening, it is safe to help him plan his ministry for the next few days or weeks, and to assign reading in Scripture or books that support his plans. The traditional teacher reverses the order, teaching from a long syllabus only what he has prepared, without listening to the student's report. Then, he might assign some practical application. Jesus and His apostles did most of their teaching in response to people's questions, complaints, and reports. Most of the epistles were written in response to real situations in the lives of the people and churches. Again, try it and you will see a big difference!

Sincerely,
George Patterson

Questions for Reflection

1. To what extent is your strategy for making disciples built upon the foundation of doctrinal understanding more than practical obedience? Do you agree with the author that if you emphasize the latter, the former is more easy to secure as well?

2. Is the significance of Jesus' resurrection underemphasized in your evangelism? If so, how might you elevate it to its rightful place?

3. To what extent does your leadership training reflect the "responsive" dynamics described by the author? What are the advantages and challenges of the author's approach?

FORTY-ONE

Learning to Depend on the Sufficiency of Christ

Charles Price is principal of Capernwray Bible School in Lancashire, England (a one-year Bible school drawing students from around the world), and vice chairman of the world-renowned Keswick Convention. He is the author of commentaries on Joshua and Matthew as well as several devotional books (including *Christ for Real* and *Alive in Christ*). Charles travels extensively in both conference and convention ministry, making several visits each year to North America. He has also ministered widely in Australia, New Zealand, Asia, Africa, Europe, the Caribbean, and the Middle East.

Dear Friend,

I would like to begin by asking you what you now consider to be the essential qualifications for your ministry? You have your clear sense of calling from God, your education and training, your God-entrusted gifts, your personality that in some ways sets you apart as one others are willing to follow, and many other ingredients that make you who you are and cause people to recognize you as a leader of others. All of these are essential and good, and need careful and disciplined attention. Your most essential qualification, however, is none of these. Your most essential qualification is Jesus Christ!

This may sound very strange for me to say. I don't mean by this that Jesus Christ must be your Savior, though of course He must. I don't mean that Jesus Christ should be your Lord, though I am sure He is. I don't mean that the words of Jesus Christ must be the substance of your message, though we have no truth to declare that does not derive from Him. I don't mean that Jesus Christ must be your example and model for life and ministry, though of course He should. I mean something much more than any of that. I mean that Jesus

Christ is your life, and as such He must be your strength, your wisdom, and the ultimate resource from which you are to draw continuously, and upon whom you must continuously depend. When He gave you His Son, God endowed you with the one necessary source of everything else of significance in your life. Sometimes we regard Jesus Christ as the giver of life, but He is more than that. He is the life itself. He actually and literally lives within you, something you share in common with every other regenerate person; for He said, "I am . . . the life" (John 14:6 NKJV).

In the first years of my Christian life I tried hard to live for Christ. I tried hard to work for Christ. But He was effectively not much more than the patron of my Christianity, the one in whose name I tried to function and by whose teaching I tried to live. I loved Him deeply and wanted to think He smiled on my attempts, but deep down I knew it wasn't working, and in my realistic moments I knew it couldn't work. I hadn't understood what Jesus taught in John 15:5, "Without Me you can do nothing" (NKJV). It is possible to be extremely busy yet to accomplish nothing—as measured by God's criterion—unless it derives from complete dependency on Christ.

In trying to understand effective leadership it is important to ask how Jesus lived His life and performed His ministry. We can do no better than find out His qualifications for ministry and seek to make them our own. It may come as a surprise to discover that of all His works, His miracles, and His teaching, He Himself claimed to do nothing. When the Jews were accusing Him of making Himself equal with God, Jesus gave this response: "I tell you the truth, the Son can do nothing by himself; he can do only what he sees his Father doing, because whatever the Father does the Son also does" (John 5:19 NIV). He reiterated a few verses later, "By myself I can do nothing" (v. 30 NIV). On a later occasion, Jesus said, "When you have lifted up the Son of Man, then you will know that I am [the one I claim to be] and that I do nothing on my own but speak just what the Father has taught me" (John 8:28 NIV). Then what is the explanation for all the words, works, and wonders that emanated from Jesus? He explains: "Don't you believe that I am in the Father, and that the Father is in me? The words I say to you are not just my own. Rather, it is the Father, living in me, who is doing his work" (John 14:10 NIV). It is His union with the Father—"I am in the Father and the Father is in me"—that is the source of the work. Similarly, He explained to His disciples in the same discourse (which took place in the Upper Room on the night of His betrayal), that His relationship of dependency upon the Father must become their relationship of dependency on Him. "If a man remains in me and I in him, he will bear much fruit; apart from me you can do nothing" (John 15:5 NIV). As Christ did nothing outside of His dependency upon the Father, so we can do nothing apart from our dependency on Christ. This is not only crucial to our effectiveness, but when we grasp it, it liberates our whole life. In the words of Paul, "The one who calls you is faithful and he will do it" (1 Thess. 5:24 NIV). You know God has called you, but do you equally know that the One who calls you is the only One who can do what He has called you to be and do?

There isn't space in the span of this letter to show how fully and centrally this principle permeates the whole of Scripture, so permit me just a few examples. God called Abraham to be the father of a great nation when he and his wife were already beyond the normal age of parentage. Who gave them their son Isaac? God did, and He did it twenty-five years after He had made the promise. Abraham did try to work things out himself in the meantime and produced Ishmael. God called Moses to bring the Israelites out of their bondage in Egypt. Who sent the plagues against Egypt, opened the Red Sea for them to cross, fed them every day with manna, gave them water from the rock to quench their thirst, and eventually brought them through the Jordan into Canaan? God did! Who gave David victory over Goliath? God did! David explained to Goliath, "This day the LORD will hand you over to me . . . the whole world will know that there is a God in Israel" (1 Sam. 17:46 NIV). It may be the world knew there was a crack sling-shooter in Israel too, but the point is that David's dependency was not on the accuracy of his shot, but on God.

The most important thing in your life is where you place your dependency. You must study, you must have the necessary gifts for your ministry, you must widen your experience; but the center of gravity in all this must be your dependency on God. Don't depend on your scholastic abilities, don't depend on human abilities, and don't depend on natural resources. God said to Jeremiah, "Let not the wise man boast of his wisdom or the strong man boast of his strength or the rich man boast of his riches, but let him who boasts boast about this: that he understands and knows me, that I am the LORD" (Jer. 9:23–24 NIV). Strength, wisdom, and riches are all valid and valuable, but do not boast of them and do not place your dependency on them. It goes against most things we have been taught to realize that we can never be too simple for God, but we can be too clever for Him; we can never be too weak for God, but we can be too strong for Him; we can never be too poor for God, but we can be too rich for Him. When our wisdom, strength, and riches become the object of our dependency, we effectively write ourselves off from any lasting, eternal significance to what we do.

Please don't despise all the ingredients that make up your life. God is all the time building things in our experience that will be the means of His working more effectively through us, but the criteria for usefulness to God is very different to the criteria the world (and sadly, often the church) places on us.

Our natural strengths are actually our areas of vulnerability. When the devil attacked Jesus for forty days in the wilderness, he was interested only in His strengths. He tempted Him to do things that only He could do. I personally have never been tempted to turn stone to bread, to rule the world, or to jump off a high building and be caught by angels, yet Jesus was tempted in each of these areas! These things belong to the areas in which Christ was capable, and I am not. The tactic of the devil was to exploit His strengths so that He would perform by His own ability, out of the will of His Father. The Father had many things for Jesus to perform, but He did not call for performance outside of dependence. This was the key to His life and ministry as a man.

The measure to which we depend on any alternative to God, we are fatally weakened by that dependency. We can maintain the momentum of our programs, but at the end of the day they will be barren. Paul wrote, "I will boast all the more gladly about my weaknesses so that Christ's power may rest on me . . . For when I am weak, then I am strong" (2 Cor. 12:9–10 NIV). God does not simply give us strength— He is our strength! And the measure in which we obey His instructions and depend on His Spirit is the extent to which we will be effective. The writer to the Hebrews says, "Anyone who enters God's rest also rests from his own work" (Heb. 4:10 NIV).

This doesn't mean you adopt a stance of quietist passivity. That was not true of Jesus, or of Abraham, Moses, and David, whose examples I gave above, and will not be true of you. Jesus lived in union with His Father, allowing Him to direct His paths. Every opportunity the Father placed in His path He had the resources to take. Get on with all that God has given you to do, and as you live in union with Christ and are dependent on Him, you will discover the reserves and strength to do far more than you ever thought you would! Like Peter when the crippled man was healed at the temple gate, you will be amazed as anyone at how God works. Peter said to the crowd who gathered around the healed man, "Men of Israel, why does this surprise you? Why do you stare at us as if by our own power or godliness we had made this man walk?" (Acts 3:12 NIV). In other words, he says, "This is not something we have done for God! Don't call this an act of an apostle; don't congratulate me on a miracle, for this is something God has done."

What a way to live! Nothing God gives you to do will ever be too much. No problem will ever be too big, no anxiety will ever be too deep when you relate everything to Christ and not to yourself. Learn this, and most other principles of leadership will find their place. Fail to understand this and you will probably burn yourself out.

Your friend and brother in Christ,
Charles Price

Questions for Reflection

1. Read through Moses' encounter with God in Exodus 3–4. Note what God stated He would do and what God asked Moses to do. How do these two aspects relate to each other? You might want to rewrite the dialogue, placing you and your calling in the place of Moses and his calling.

2. In 1 Corinthians 1:26–28, list the criteria that are not what God called (e.g., "wise . . . influential") and then list the criteria that are what God called (e.g., "foolish . . . weak"). Which category best describes you? What does Paul say about that category? Then read verse 29. What is Christ to become for us? Does verse 31 truthfully reflect where you place your dependency?

3. "Our natural strengths are actually our areas of vulnerability." To what extent has this been true in your life? How can you better learn how to avoid the snare of self-sufficiency described by the author?

FORTY-TWO

Learning to Think Rightly About Leadership and Ministry

Earl D. Radmacher is president emeritus and distinguished professor of theology emeritus of Western Seminary. He served as president of that institution from 1965–1990 and as its chancellor from 1990–1995. Prior to coming to Western in 1962, Earl ministered in pastoral, chaplaincy, and academic settings. His preaching and teaching ministry continues to extend worldwide. Among his publications are *The Nature of the Church, You and Your Thoughts,* and *What to Expect from the Holy Spirit*. He is also the general editor for *The Nelson Study Bible* (NKJV).

Dear Friend,

I am honored to be asked, as one who has spent forty-six years in the ministry of God's Word and thirty-five years in leadership positions, to provide some reflections for you. I share them with deep gratitude to God for His gracious and merciful dealings with me.

First, I urge you to *know your gift*. Spiritual gifting was not a part of seminary training in the fifties. Before 1960 there was not one single listing in *Books in Print* on the doctrine of spiritual gifting. Can you imagine that? But God created us with an insatiable appetite to know, and our nature abhors a vacuum. That vacuum will be filled with something. Thus, in 1960 we were catapulted into the Charismatic Movement through an experience of an Episcopalian minister in Van Nuys, California. The movement spread like wildfire through just about every denomination on earth. Publishers grabbed the opportunity, and many books (many with little or no exegetical research) began flying off the presses on the subject. The vast majority of believers had no acquaintance with the subject and thus little or no awareness of their spiritual gifts. Out of that came a request to me from three major missions organizations to do a Spiritual Gifts Conference for pastors at Arrowhead Springs. I had no seminary notes to turn to and no books available, so it drove me to the Word of God. As I look back, I realize how gracious it was of God at that strategic time in my life, as a very young seminary leader, to confront me with the very important truth of spiritual gifting. From that time on, God enabled me to do over five hundred Spiritual Gift Conferences in this country and overseas to help people discover, develop, and deploy their gifts in and through their local churches. After ten years, we convened a group of faculty and graduate students to develop, over several years, a biblically grounded Spiritual Gifts Inventory to help people identify their gifts. More recently the conference has been made available on both audio and video cassettes. All of this and much more has come because God has pressed me to help fill a vacuum in evangelical leadership training. Whatever measure of success God has allowed me to experience as a leader of Western Seminary has been largely due to understanding this vital truth. When I became president in 1965, God graciously brought alongside me as Dean of Faculty W. Robert Cook, whose administrative gift of management beautifully complemented my gift of leadership for the seventeen years that he served with me in that relationship. Leadership is the ability to mobilize people for action. Management is the ability to organize so that the action is carried out effectively.

If I were to go back into pastoral leadership today, I would consider it a key responsibility—in the light of 1 Corinthians 4:1–2 and 1 Peter 4:10–11—to mobilize meaningfully the membership of the church through systematic mentoring of each one to discover and develop his/her spiritual gift(s) and to find an appropriate place of service. I would do this not just to obey personally God's mandate, but also to enable these believers to receive a good report when Jesus evaluates their stewardship of their gifts and determines their capacity of service to Christ's glory in His coming kingdom.

Second, *be a team person*. It is not the biblical pattern to develop in isolation, but in relation. Jesus provides a model for us at this point. He chose twelve that "they might be with Him." Out of the Twelve, He had a smaller group—Peter, James, and John—those with whom He shared even more intimately. I believe it is very significant that the first church, as well as every other New Testament church, had plurality of leadership. Much of church growth today, however, focuses upon a single, strong, natural leader. We would do well to hear again the words of Charles Jefferson in the Lyman Beecher Lectures at Yale in 1890: "A petty, parochial pope is a sorry caricature of a minister of Jesus Christ." The single-leader system caters to the ego and is not only hurtful to the individual but is even more destructive to the contribution of the other members of the body, all of whom are specially gifted by God. No individual leader has all of the gifts, so he needs the gifts of the total body. Furthermore, every leader has the need for checks on his own sin nature. There is a good reason why Scripture puts such strong emphasis on "one to another." I thank the Lord for the people He has surrounded me with who have contributed their gifts to me and allowed me to contribute my gift to them.

The first church in Jerusalem was able to deal with their problems of growth not only because they had a caring heart to hear the problems of the people but because they also recognized their own priorities of ministry; and of equal importance, they recognized the great potential of the gifted people they were leading (Acts 6:1–7). But this required a particular attitude—namely a servant attitude—which leads me to another area that I believe to be basic.

For you must also strive to *be a servant leader*. I have found this to be talked about far more than practiced. It is very easy for leaders to develop a *prima donna* kind of attitude and feel that others need to serve them. We see this vividly portrayed by the Twelve in the Upper Room. They had been so busy arguing about who was going to be greatest in the kingdom that they couldn't rise to the servant task of washing feet. Thus, Jesus showed them the way to true blessing (John 13:17) by giving them an example (v. 15) of servant leadership.

I have been so impressed with the powerful sculpture of Jesus washing Peter's feet by artist Max Greiner that I have a special window in my washroom at home made from the pencil drawing of it. And if I were to be in leadership again in seminary training, I would personally raise the money to put that sculpture in the entrance hall where faculty, staff, students, and administrators would all be reminded daily that we are in the business of training *servant* leaders. We have so many leadership seminars today that it makes me wonder if we wouldn't do more for true leadership training if we had a few more followership seminars. And perhaps this would be accomplished better if we really got serious about another biblical motivational principle, to which I now direct your attention.

That principle is this: *privilege begets responsibility*. There is probably no passage of Scripture that has impacted me more over the last thirty years than Hebrews 10:19–25. Notice the emphasis of its two parts: ". . . having . . . having . . . let us . . . let us . . . let us . . ." Privileges possessed beget responsibilities. And the greater the privileges, the greater the responsibilities. Certainly the greatest privilege the believer has is access to the throne of grace through the blood of Jesus Christ; thus the greatest responsibility is to use that privilege faithfully as spelled out in the faith, hope, and love exercises of verses 22 through 25: faith in the person of God (the upward response), hope in the promises of God (the forward response), and love for the people of God (the outward response). Notice the logic of this responsible action: a growing faith in the *person* of God will lead to a growing hope in the *promises* of the person of God which in turn will lead to a growing love for the *people* of the promises of the person of God. It all starts by accepting the Father's invitation to draw near to the throne of grace through the blood of Jesus.

My wife Ruth drove this principle of privilege home to me very forcefully during our period of dating in college days. I was a leader on campus and one of my very important responsibilities was delivering the notes from the men's dorms to the women's dorms and vice-versa. Because I delivered them, I had first access to them. I could usually find Ruth's note even in the dark because she wrote thick notes and they were scented with a particular perfume (called, of all things, "My Sin"). On one particular night, however, I had a hard time finding her note so I came alongside a lamp post, hoping that its light would provide some needed help. I finally found it: thin, and with no scent at all. Nervously I tore open the envelope and pulled out one measly sheet which began not with the normal greeting ("Dearest" or "My Darling" or something similar that I could read a great deal into and then fairly float back to the men's dorm) but with simply, "Dear Earl." And then, only two sentences: "I am tired of being taken for granted. You have had it. Ruth."

Now what was Ruth's problem? Well, everywhere big Earl, the campus leader, went he expected that little Ruthie would be following along. In the words of "My Fair Lady," I had grown accustomed to her face; but she had grown tired of being a tag-a-long-tu-lu. She thought, "If this is the way it is before we get married, what will it be like after we are married? I'd better break it off while I have a chance." And she did. I learned a great lesson that I have never forgotten, namely don't treat precious privileges tritely, lest you lose them.

Now I have never received a letter from God saying, "Dear Earl. Haven't seen much of you lately. You have had it. God." But God would have had even more cause to send it than Ruth ever had, but He won't. Why? Because He is faithful to His promise (Heb. 10:22). Now should His faithfulness cause me to be less faithful or more faithful? Surely the latter! The privilege of leadership begets greater responsibility and accountability. James, the brother of the Lord and first martyr of the church, put it succinctly: "My brethren, let not many of you become teachers, knowing that we shall receive a stricter judgment" (James 3:1 NKJV).

You will also want to *develop a biblical concept of reward*. This too was missing in my training and, for the most part, is still missing in evangelical preaching today. Yet it is the most frequently used motivation for endurance in the Word of God (being mentioned nearly one hundred times). In the earliest pages of the New Testament we find Jesus motivating His disciples with "great . . . reward" if they properly process the persecution that they receive for His sake (Matt. 5:10–12). Later, Jesus admonishes these same disciples to deny themselves and take up their cross and follow Him because "the Son of Man will come in the glory of His Father with His angels, and then He will reward each according to his works" (Matt. 16:27 NKJV). Still later, when Peter complains that he has left all to follow Christ, Jesus does not rebuke him for his insensitivity in the light of what He has left for them, but rather encourages him by announcing to him and the others the return that is going to come on their investment: "Assuredly I say to you, that in the regeneration, when the Son of Man sits on the throne of His glory, you who have followed Me will also sit on twelve thrones, judging the twelve tribes of Israel. And everyone who has left houses or brothers or sisters or father or mother or wife or children or lands, for My name's sake, shall receive a hundredfold and inherit eternal life" (Matt. 19:28–29 NKJV).

Think of it! One hundredfold! That's ten thousand percent. What is Jesus saying? Simply this: the remuneration will always far outweigh the renunciation. Or to put it in the immortal words of a famous missionary martyr, "He is no fool who gives what he cannot keep to gain what he cannot lose." This same understanding caused the apostle Paul, another missionary martyr, when speaking of this "prize" to say: "I discipline my body and bring it into subjection lest, when I have preached to others, I myself should become disqualified" (1 Cor. 9:27 NKJV). Paul had gotten a good view of the "far more exceeding and eternal weight of glory" (2 Cor. 4:17 NKJV).

There is not only the possibility of phenomenal eternal reward, however, but the tragic potential of the loss of that eternal reward. Thus, from heaven Jesus warned the church in Philadelphia: "Behold, I am coming quickly! Hold fast what you have, that no one may take your crown" (Rev. 3:11 NKJV). And the same one who recorded those words of Jesus, the apostle John, also writes: "Look to yourselves, that we do not lose those things we worked for, but that we may receive a full reward" (2 John 8 NKJV). Or again: "And now, little children, abide in Him, that when He appears, we may have confidence and not be ashamed before Him at His coming" (1 John 2:28 NKJV). What does it mean to experience loss at the judgment seat of Christ? To be ashamed? To be naked? The apostle Paul pictures it as a person being rescued from a burning building, dragged out naked through the ashes of all that he had worked in life to build (cf. 1 Cor. 3:8–15). This concept of loss at the time of evaluation is a very sobering teaching, and yet I cannot remember one hour of instruction in twelve years of college and seminary concerning the tragic implications of loss when Christ evaluates our works. Thus, I would urge you, as a leader of others, to keep the goal of the kingdom and the potential "weight of glory" in your vision. Hear the words of Jesus from heaven: "To him who overcomes I will grant to sit with Me on My throne, as I also overcame and sat down with My Father on His throne" (Rev. 3:21 NKJV). "And behold, I am coming quickly, and My reward is with Me, to give to every one according to his work" (Rev. 22:12 NKJV). In summary, you are becoming today by what you do (sanctification salvation) with what God gave you (justification salvation) what you will be in the life to come (glorification salvation). Today is a day of becoming; then is a day of being what you have become. Today is a day of change; then is a day of no change.

Finally, always remember to *keep your focus upon Jesus*. Right action is the result of right thinking, and right thinking comes from thinking rightly about God. "You will keep him in perfect peace," Isaiah states, "whose mind is stayed on You, because he trusts in You" (Isa. 26:3 NKJV). A century later God says through Jeremiah, "Let him who glories glory in this, that he understands and knows Me" (Jer. 9:24 NKJV).

Through many years there is no book, outside the Bible, that Ruth and I have benefited from more than A. W. Tozer's *The Knowledge of the Holy*. In that book Tozer writes:

> The gravest question before the Church is always God Himself, and the most portentous fact about any man is not what he at a given time may say or do, but what he in his deep heart conceives God to be like. . . . Without doubt, the mightiest thought the mind can entertain is the thought of God. . . . That our idea of God correspond as nearly as possible to the true being of God is of immense importance to us. . . . A right conception of God is basic not only to systematic theology but to practical Christian living as well. . . . I believe there is scarcely an error in doctrine or a failure in applying Christian ethics that cannot be traced finally to imperfect and ignoble thoughts about God.

Long before Tozer, Brother Lawrence captured a similar truth in his *The Practice of the Presence of God*: "Counting upon God as never being absent would be holiness complete." Or, to put it another way, if I never had a wrong thought about God, I would never sin. But is this kind of thinking possible? I have to conclude that it must be or the apostle John could not have said, "My little children, these things I write to you, so that you may not sin" (1 John 2:1 NKJV). The solution is in our focus. I come then to my life verse: "But we all, with unveiled face, beholding as in a mirror the glory of the Lord, are being transformed into the same image from glory to glory, just as by the Spirit of the Lord" (2 Cor. 3:18 NKJV). But what is this glory that we are to behold steadfastly? None other than Jesus, the member of the triune God who became flesh and dwelt among us so that we might behold the glory of God incarnate. And that revelation was not exhausted in a generation but was supernaturally inscripturated so that every generation of believers may look and focus upon it moment by moment. That is the key to living. I commend it to you even as did the writer of Hebrews. After giving the marvelous chapter of the victories of faith, he states the key to endurance: "Looking unto Jesus, the author and finisher of our faith, who for the joy that was set before Him endured the cross, despising the shame, and has sat down at the right hand of the throne of God" (12:2 NKJV).

From that exalted position at the throne of God where He ever lives to intercede continuously for us, He invites us to come trustingly to Him. The resources of heaven are available. Come!

Looking unto Jesus,
Earl Radmacher

Questions for Reflection

1. How faithfully are you helping those to whom you minister discover, develop, and deploy their gifting with a view toward them being faithful stewards of those abilities?

2. "Privileges possessed beget responsibilities. And the greater the privileges, the greater the responsibilities." As you reflect upon the most significant privileges God has given you (including access to Him in prayer), how faithfully are you living up to the accompanying responsibilities?

3. What role does the biblical doctrine of rewards play in your personal motivation to serve God and in your attempt to persuade others to serve Him?

FORTY-THREE

Learning to Avoid Some Significant Ministry Pitfalls

David Roper currently codirects, with his wife Carolyn, Idaho Mountain Ministries (a support ministry to pastor couples in Idaho and surrounding states). Prior to his current ministry, Dave was a YMCA director in Plano, Texas (1957–61), associate pastor at Peninsula Bible Church in Palo Alto, California (1961–78), and senior pastor of Cole Community Church in Boise, Idaho (1978–95). Among his publications are *A Man Like Us, A Man to Match the Mountain,* and *The 23rd Psalm: The Song of a Passionate Heart.*

Dear Friend,

You asked what I've learned in recent years about ministry that I wish I'd learned earlier. Good question, though one better suited for a book than a letter. Here, given the limits of brevity, are some of the thoughts that came to me.

First, *be realistic in your expectations.* Carolyn and I know so many pastors who were launched from seminary or Bible school with the tacit assurance that their congregations would listen to what they have to say and move toward intimacy with God. Then they discovered to their dismay that most people have little or no interest in spiritual things no matter what they do. It's then that they may begin to lose confidence in themselves, their call, and in God.

It's for discouraged workers like this that Jesus served up the parable of the sower and the seed. It was His way of helping all of us come to terms with apparent failure. It teaches us that most people are not interested in pursuing godliness (and may never be), and there's not much we can do about it. Their disinterest is due to factors beyond our control.

Our task is not to change people, but to sow; in other words, to scatter seed whenever and wherever we have opportunity, "publicly and from house to house," as Paul would say (Acts 20:20 NASB). There's life in the seed that, if received, will produce fruit. However, the response is dependent solely on the condition of the soil in which the seed is strewn. Hard hearts, divided hearts, and distracted hearts deflect the seed or deny it an opportunity to take root and grow. Even where the soil is soft there will be a varying yield: "a hundred, sixty or thirty times what was sown" (Matt. 13:8 NIV).

Is the condition of the soil permanent? Not necessarily. God rains His grace on every soil; He harnesses the plow of suffering and breaks up the hardest heart. (It's worth noting that our word "tribulation" comes from the Latin word for plow, *tribulum*.) God never gives up, nor should we. We must keep on loving, serving, praying, and proclaiming; but the hard truth is that many—if not most—of the people we serve will remain carnal, cold, and indifferent no matter what we do. They will refuse to hear. It's from these folk that most of our stresses come: the dysfunctional families, the marital infidelities, the immoralities, the addictions, the harsh or unjustified criticisms, and the other difficulties that make our work so tiresome.

So what's the answer? Work harder? Work longer? Work until we burn out or decimate our families? Worry ourselves sick and eventually out of the ministry? No. Just keep on sowing. Many will not receive the Word, but there are a few "good and noble hearts," as Luke would say, in which the seed will take root and begin to grow. These are the men and women who have prepared their hearts for God. This is the fertile soil. Which leads me to my next thought . . .

"Go to those who want you, and especially to those who want you the most." John Wesley said that, and it's pure wisdom. Preaching and teaching are the means by which we appeal to the many, but there's more: that quiet, hidden work of equipping the few. Richard Baxter, the Puritan vicar of Kidderminster, wrote, "I know that preaching the gospel publicly is the most excellent means, because we speak to so many at once, but it is far more effectual to speak it privately to a particular person. . . ."

It does no good to pursue people who have no interest in following the Lord. Lavish love on them, pray earnestly for them, teach them as long as they'll permit you to do so, but you should spend your premium time with those "particular people" who want to hear what God has to say through you. Look for those who want to grow in grace and prayerfully invest yourself in mentoring them. There may be only one or two at first, but these are the "faithful" souls whom Paul encourages us to instruct (2 Tim. 2:2).

Though a quiet ministry to a few may seem improvident (it will always seem more efficient to speak to the masses), it was the method Jesus chose to bring salvation to the world. He taught the crowds, but His primary work was done with the few and—here's the interesting thing—as Jesus drew near the end of His life on earth He spent more and more time with fewer and fewer people. That's just backward from our point of view. We expect to start small and grow very large, but there's always something to be said for doing things God's way.

"Small is beautiful," a friend of mine says. God has always done His best work through a tiny remnant.

Next, *befriend people and impart the truth to them.* Paul summarized his efforts in Ephesus this way: "I was with you the whole time, serving the Lord . . . (and) did not shrink from declaring to you anything that was profitable and teaching you publicly and from house to house" (Acts 20:18–20 NASB).

Paul's activities suggest two elements around which everything revolved. He was with people and he taught them. Those were his primary tasks: befriending others and imparting the truth. This was the essence and genius of Paul's ministry, the blend and balance of what he called "serving the Lord."

Paul was with people, spending time with them, getting to know them, entering into their lives—much like Jesus, who was "God with us." Jesus Himself spent a seemingly inordinate amount of time eating with people, fishing with them, strolling by the sea, going to parties, being neighborly. He had an infinite job to do and only three-and-a-half years to do it; and yet He took time to make friends.

Most of us are much too busy for that sort of thing. It's wasted time; or so we think. But time spent friend-making is never wasted. It's an essential part of serving the Lord, which means that you and I will have to deal with our much too busy lives, which in turn means that we will have to deal with our egos, for much of our self-worth is bound up in staying so busy that we have no time to make friends.

The other element in Paul's work was impartation, or proclamation: "I did not shrink from declaring . . . anything that was profitable and teaching . . . publicly and from house to house."

Befriending is more than mere togetherness and small talk; it means telling others what we've learned from God. As God teaches us we need to give that truth away. Like Jonathan, who went to David at Horesh and "helped him find strength in God" (1 Sam. 23:16 NIV), a real friend is one who leaves another with a word that strengthens his or her grip on God.

Befriending and imparting suggest a rare balance that many find hard to maintain. I know I do. I tend to be more solitary and reflective;

others are more social and outgoing. We're all naturally inclined one way or the other, but our natural tendencies can be curbed and disciplined by God. If we want balance and ask for it, He'll level out our lives.

Teach whatever God is teaching you. Jesus said we shouldn't worry too much about what to say or how to say it: "At that time you will be given what to say" (Matt. 10:19 NIV).

God's thoughts spring up naturally if we let them, but that's not to say that He fills our minds with thoughts we've never had before. Rather He draws from a deep reservoir of accumulated wisdom those things He wants us to say.

The Servant of the Lord had a good word on the matter: "The Sovereign LORD has given me an instructed tongue, to know the word that sustains the weary. He wakens me morning by morning, wakens my ear to listen like one being taught. The Sovereign LORD has opened my ears, and I have not been rebellious; I have not drawn back" (Isa. 50:4–5 NIV).

What an intriguing image! Every morning God drew near His Servant, calling Him by name, awakening Him, inviting Him to sit at His feet, giving Him His message for the day, preparing Him for its duties and demands. Every day our Lord listened "like one being taught."

That's what enabled Jesus to speak such gracious words to those so desperately in need. He knew the source of wisdom. He said of Himself, "I . . . speak just what the Father has taught me" (John 8:28 NIV); I am "a man who has told you the truth that I heard from God" (John 8:40 NIV); "These words you hear are not my own; they belong to the Father . . ." (John 14:24 NIV).

And so it is with us. Every morning our Lord invites us to sit at His feet, to listen like one being taught, to take what words we need for that day. That's how He gives us a wise, instructed tongue; that's how we "know the word that sustains the weary."

Some of the older translations render Isaiah 50:4, "The Lord GOD has given Me the tongue of the learned" (NKJV). The text actually speaks of "the tongue of a learner." In later Jewish literature the word came to mean "a disciple." We must be discipled before we can disciple others; we must be taught before we can teach; we must learn before we can ever be "learned."

The more we receive the more we have to give. It's through prayerful, thoughtful Bible reading and quiet meditation that our Lord speaks from His depths to ours. We must give ourselves to prayerful contemplation until His heart is revealed and our hearts are exposed. We must listen until we know what He feels, what He wants, what He loves, what He hates. Then we can give that word away. "What I tell you in the dark," Jesus said, "speak in the daylight; what is whispered in your ear, proclaim from the roofs" (Matt. 10:27 NIV).

If you have nothing to say there's just one cure: "Hide yourself in God," George MacDonald said, "and when you rise before men speak out of that secret place."

Be sure to speak this truth in love. Be forthright in your proclamation of the Word—never holding back through fear or favoritism—but never bully people. Though you may have to contend for the faith, don't be contentious, quarrelsome, argumentative, unpleasant, and in other people's faces. "He who wins by force hath won but half his foe," Emerson said.

As Bishop Kallistos Ware states in *The Orthodox Way,* "At some point [one] stands perplexed, above all at the sight of human sin, and . . . wonders whether to combat it by force or by humble love. Always decide: 'I will combat it by humble love.' If you resolve on that once for all, you can conquer the whole world. Loving humility is a terrible force: it is the strongest of all things, and there is nothing else like it."

The Puritans were right when they enunciated the principle of consent. Faith can never be foisted on another. We can't compel obedience. Railing at people, threats of punishment or harm, manipulation, domination are all contrary to the spirit of Christ. Consent must be gained by gentle persuasion and reason. "The act of faith still remains an act of choice which no one can force upon another" (W. H. Auden).

"The Lord's servant must not quarrel," Paul insists, "instead, he must be kind to everyone, able to teach, not resentful. Those who oppose him he must gently instruct, in the hope that God will grant them repentance leading them to a knowledge of the truth, and that they will come to their senses and escape from the trap of the devil, who has taken them captive to do his will" (2 Tim. 2:24–26 NIV).

We must be patient and courteous in our proclamation, nondefensive, humble, gentle, patiently instructing those who oppose the word in the hope that God "will grant repentance leading to a knowledge of the truth." Those who oppose are not the enemy; they're victims of the enemy, taken captive to do his will.

In our enthusiasm we must not resort to severity. Others' salvation depends upon it. Apparently, the Good News only sounds good when it's announced with good manners.

> Yet in my walks it seems to me,
> That the grace of God is in courtesy.
> —Belloc

I also urge you to *celebrate your incompetence*. God tends to surround Himself with a bunch of incompetents. The people He uses have rarely been great people, nor have great people been the people God uses. He looks for misfits. It's not that He has to make do with fools; He chooses us.

> You know Paul's words: "Brothers, think of what you were when you were called. Not many of you were wise by human standards; not many were influential; not many were of noble birth. But God chose the foolish things of the world to shame the wise; God chose the weak things of the world to shame the strong. He chose the lowly things of this world and the despised things—and the things that are not—to nullify the things that are, so that no one may boast before him. It is because of him that you are in Christ Jesus, who has become for us wisdom from God—that is, our righteousness, holiness and redemption. Therefore, as it is written: 'Let him who boasts boast in the Lord'" (1 Cor. 1:26–31 NIV).

Oh, to be sure some of God's children are rich and famous, but there aren't too many. (Lady Hamilton, a member of the British noble family, once quipped that she was saved by the letter "m," for, as she put it, "Paul said 'not many are called.' He did not say, 'Not any.'") Most of us are ordinary people, unimportant, insignificant, and unnecessary in the eyes of the world. Few of us have clout; we're neither superstars nor super-saints. Like St. Francis's "jesters," we're the joke that God is playing on the world.

But therein lies our strength. Paul, who was inclined toward paradoxes, put it this way: "When I am weak, then I am strong." He explains, "If I must boast, I will boast of the things that show my weakness. The God and Father of the Lord Jesus, who is to be praised forever, knows that I am not lying. In Damascus the governor under King Aretas had the city of the Damascenes guarded in order to arrest me. But I was lowered in a basket from a window in the wall and slipped through his hands" (2 Cor. 11:30–33 NIV).

Paul came to Damascus thinking he was God's gift to the world. He had reason to be confident: "circumcised on the eighth day, of the people of Israel, of the tribe of Benjamin, a Hebrew of Hebrews; in regard to the law, a Pharisee; as for zeal, persecuting the church; as for legalistic righteousness, faultless" (Phil. 3:4–6 NIV). He was an Israelite indeed; he was the little engine that could!

And so he tackled the thing that couldn't be done and he couldn't do it. Instead of a revival he precipitated a riot. The Christians in

Damascus put him in a fish basket, lowered him over the wall and sent him packing, pleading with him not to return lest he undo all that God had been doing.

What a bitter embarrassment! It was the worst day of Paul's life—and the best. That's the day that he learned that he was, as he later put it, a "nobody" (2 Cor. 12:11).

But not to worry! Paul became "somebody." He rounds out the picture this way: "But we have this treasure [deity] in jars of clay [humanity] to show that this all-surpassing power is from God and not from us" (2 Cor. 4:7 NIV). Deity in humanity—God in an earthen jar. Paul carried about in his own body the presence and essence of God.

And so it comes to this: nothing in us is a source of hope; nothing is worth defending; nothing is special and worth admiring. Every virtue, every endearing quality, every proclivity toward goodness comes from God. Without Him, we can do nothing. When we accept that fact we can rest in Him who alone is wisdom, righteousness, and power.

God has promised to meet every need we have, but He can't do it until we admit our need and cast ourselves on Him. When we've done this, we don't have to worry about whether He'll find us fit enough to do His work. In the words of the old hymn, "All the fitness He requireth is to feel our need of Him."

Next, be sure to *take heed to your soul.* As Richard Foster wrote, "God doesn't need more busy people . . . He needs more 'deep' people."

I'm told that Henri Nouwen sought out Mother Teresa on one occasion and asked her what he could do to become more effective as a pastor. She replied with characteristic simplicity, "Spend one hour a day in adoration of Jesus and you'll be all right." My mind goes back to that simple dictum again and again because it's the key to all we do.

Ministry flows out of worship. Without prayer, adoration, reflection, quiet times spent at Jesus' feet we have nothing to say. That's why "soul work," as the Quakers say, is so important. We've got to take time to cultivate spiritual depth in our souls.

Ministry inveighs against depth. We have sermons to prepare, letters to answer, meetings to organize, counsel to give, visits to make, phone calls to return—a dozen different and distracting activities. We live such busy lives we have no time to grow deeper. We remain shallow and superficial. We have no tranquillity and wisdom to bring out to others. We're easily dismissed, easily forgotten. That's the tragedy of being in this business but having no time for God.

David, in one of his poems, speaks of those who "live quietly" and deeply (Ps. 35:20). These are the men and women who live withdrawn from life's ambitions and frenzied pace, and who have entered into a life that's hidden in God. These are the "quiet people" who show poise under pressure, who are unshaken by life's alarms and who radiate God's peace and presence wherever they go. Those who live outside that quiet place necessarily live fretful, care-ridden lives and their ministries reflect that restlessness.

F. B. Meyer says that most of us are like folks living in a one-room house located too close to the street. There's no way to get away from the noise and commotion outside. But we can build a little sound-proof room within and make it our dwelling place—a secret chamber to pray and to ponder God's Word. "We fill our little space," Meyer says, "we get our daily bread and are content; we enjoy natural and simple pleasures; we do not strive, nor cry, nor cause our voice to be heard in the street; we pass through the world, with noiseless tread, dropping a blessing on all we meet."

Learn to be quiet. Make time for Jesus. Take your anxious worries and nervous energy to Him. When people disappoint you, confide in Him. When storms sweep over you, hide yourself in Him. When people jostle one another and jockey for position, when they compete for fame and fortune and their passions begin to infect you, go into that secret chamber and shut the door. It's there that you'll find that transcendent peace of which Jesus speaks; it's there that you'll be given bread and wine to bring out to others.

George MacDonald put it this way: "There is a chamber—a chamber in God Himself which none can enter but the one, the individual, the particular man. Out of which chamber that man has to bring revelation and strength for his brethren. This is that for which he was made—to reveal the secret things of the Father."

Let me conclude with a few more assorted thoughts.

"Seek obscurity," Francois Fenelon said. We must be willing to be unknown and unnoticed, to serve quietly in a hidden place where no one but God knows what we're doing. We must wait for advancement until God brings it to us. "Do you seek great things for yourself?" Jeremiah asks. "Seek them not." Personal ambition is a terrible trait. We've all got to deal with it.

We must keep growing toward personal holiness. "Let your progress be seen by all." Being is the essential thing. Peter says we must "make every effort to add to [our] faith goodness; and to goodness, knowledge; and to knowledge, self-control; and to self-control, perseverance; and to perseverance, godliness; and to godliness, brotherly kindness; and to brotherly kindness, love. For if you possess these qualities in increasing measure, they will keep you from being ineffective and unproductive." (2 Peter 1:5–8 NIV).

Ineffectiveness and unproductivity stem from what we are, not from what we do. George MacDonald said, "If you try too hard to make people good you will only make them worse. The only way to make people good is to be good—remember the beam and the mote. The time for speaking comes rarely, the time for being never departs."

Other thoughts rush into my mind, but for now I must leave this letter as it is: an interim effort forced out of me by your question and by my own need to "take heed to myself."

As for you, press on! "Faithful is He who calls you, and He also will bring it to pass" (1 Thess. 5:24 NASB).

Affectionately,
David Roper

Questions for Reflection

1. "Go to those who want you, and especially to those who want you the most." What implications does Wesley's exhortation have for your priorities in ministry?

2. To what extent do you combat human sin by humble love instead of by force? Why is the former much more effective than the latter?

3. Which of the other counsels shared by the author seems to be particularly timely at this point in your ministry?

FORTY-FOUR

Learning That There Is No Such Thing As a Comfortable Cross

Moishe Rosen is the founder of Jews for Jesus and served as its executive director from 1973–1996; he continues to serve on that organization's board. Prior to founding Jews for Jesus, Moishe ministered for seventeen years with the Beth Sar Shalom Hebrew-Christian Fellowship (American Mission Board to the Jews). He is the author of many pamphlets and articles; his book publications include *Sayings of Chairman Moishe, Share the New Life with a Jew,* and *Christ in the Passover.* Moishe currently continues his worldwide preaching ministry.

Dear Friend,

We are surrounded by truth tellers, yet we're not always willing to hear the truths they tell. From years of experience, I have concluded that people were telling me all along what I needed to hear, but I was not ready to receive it.

I came to Christ in 1953, and God called me to ministry in a unique way. He used Paul's testimony and personalized it to me through Acts 20:21: ". . . testifying to Jews, and also to Greeks, repentance toward God and faith toward our Lord Jesus Christ" (NKJV).

I never felt called only to the Jews. Nevertheless, I was discipled through the American Board of Missions to the Jews. They paid my way through Bible college, and there was no doubt that I would join their staff after I graduated.

During my first couple of years of missionary ministry in Los Angeles, I was groping, still sorting things out, and trying to figure out how to do what most other Christians knew to be impossible—mount an effective evangelistic campaign to Jews. Due to the help of my faithful wife and dear friends who came alongside, my work was seen as a success. Yet that "success" was more illusory than actual.

True, in the decade of 1957 to 1967, I personally baptized 245 Jewish people and led many more to make decisions for Christ. In a sense, those were easy victories because the Southern Californian Christians trusted me and helped me. They witnessed to their Jewish friends, and when they felt they couldn't go any further, they would bring me in on the matter. Likening my accomplishments to sales work, I was simply functioning as a closer where others had already made a good presentation.

My apparent success brought me to the mission's New York City headquarters, where I was acclaimed as the "fair-haired boy." The greater New York area was where I had graduated from Bible college in 1957 and had taken my basic missionary training. Though I was raised in Denver, in a sense I was more comfortable in New York City. Now I was charged with the duty of recruiting and training new missionaries, setting up systems and building a successful outreach in New York. I was supposed to duplicate the success of my work in Los Angeles.

However, the mission, founded by Leopold Cohn, had undergone a transition. The man who built the American Board of Missions to the Jews was Leopold's son, Joseph Hoffman Cohn. Joseph was a tough-minded pragmatist. Under his leadership, the mission grew and became successful in winning and discipling Jews because he held the missionaries accountable. After Joseph's death in 1953, the habit of being accountable gradually faded. I was brought in to try to sew a new patch on an old garment. It didn't take me long to find out that what I was brought to New York to accomplish was truly impossible. In New York City I never found Christians to help me as I had in Los Angeles.

Within a year, I knew I was failing. Yet as with so many of my other failures, no one seemed to notice. Perhaps it was because I had come to believe what others believed about my "success."

Three things happened in short order that jarred me into the realization of my failure.

First, a society of professional missionaries, of which I was a member, had their biannual meeting at Nyack Missionary College. They wanted someone from the Jewish community (not a Christian) to speak at the meeting about the image of missionaries to the Jews in the Jewish community. Dr. Sidney Lawrence, who was then the head of the Jewish Community Relations Council of Kansas City, graciously accepted the invitation.

Dr. Lawrence gave a very brief address on "The Image of the Missionary in the Jewish Community." He said, "You don't have an image. If you did, it would create a crisis." He explained that the way the Jewish community was organized, its concerns were voiced and directions were set at conferences. He said that in his forty years as an official of the Jewish community, he had attended several such conferences on a national and international basis, and had noted that no one had ever mentioned Christian missionaries. His statement, "You have no image," rang in my ears. My fifteen years of experience in Jewish missions told me that he was right.

When the rather large program committee met after the meeting, they attempted to devaluate Lawrence's statement. Some said things like, "He really knew how to discourage us." All seemed to agree. But I knew that he had told us the truth.

Shortly after that, the second incident occurred. InterVarsity Christian Fellowship in New York had a leadership training conference at Columbia University. It was attended by several hundred. Afterwards a Jewish man, who was somewhat younger than I, confronted me about a joke that I had told about hippies. He introduced himself as a believer and asked a question that forced me to admit that I had never met a hippie. Then he said, "Well, do you think that you should be making such jokes when you've never met these people? These are young people who are spiritually searching, and you need to reach out to them, not ridicule them." I knew he was right and I was wrong.

The third thing that showed me how much of a failure I was at evangelism happened during my mother's final illness. I flew to Denver to be with her and was in a moral dilemma. My father had disowned me when I had first become a believer. Then, after a year, he had sent our rabbi as an emissary to seek reconciliation, but it had to be on my father's terms. I was never to mention God or the Bible in his presence again. Intrinsically, I knew there was something wrong with that. I consulted with a deacon in my church who had watch care over me. He said, "Tell your father that you'll agree, provided that you have the right to discuss it if he asks," to which my father agreed.

But now decades had passed, Dad had never asked, and my mother was dying. I went to her hospital room directly from the airport and awkwardly tried to witness to her. Though she was weak, she reviled me in the harshest of terms.

I not only felt bad that I had broken the agreement with my father, I felt even worse that I had agreed not to attempt to tell my father and mother that their only hope was in Jesus. Eventually both of them went into a Christless eternity.

Those experiences left me with a sense of failure and inadequacy.

Success in evangelism wasn't just a matter of learning a new technique or finding a better way to relate. I just knew that I was a failure at reaching out and winning people. Not only that, I felt that the whole field—my field of Jewish missions—was a failure.

Then I tried to do something about it. I decided that though I was a mission executive and people usually saw me by appointment, I had to put myself where I was vulnerable. I took a stack of gospel tracts, went out on the street corner at West 72nd and Broadway in New York and tried to hand them out. A few people took them, but not many. One of the problems was that the tracts were over twenty years old. Their content and archaic approach was more appropriate for church people than for unbelievers.

I sat down and roughed out what I felt was a more contemporary message. It was much shorter and to the point. The tract was so different that I couldn't get my mission to print it, so I paid for the printing myself. Young people began responding to that kind of grassroots communication and gave their lives to Christ.

I wrote more tracts that used simple hand calligraphy and talked about the issues of the day. They were different from most gospel tracts because they weren't like sermons. Each one closed with a scripture verse, but they used humor and discussed current issues. Then some of those barely saved young Jews started helping me distribute them. "Jewish Jesus Freaks" they were called. But the press used our slogans and called us Jews *for* Jesus, and it stuck.

Next we tried street preaching, but only a few people would listen. Street preachers were perceived as frustrated pastors without a pulpit. So instead of preaching to gather a crowd, we began writing and singing gospel songs with Jewish melodies, which did get people's attention. When it came to personal witness, we didn't wait for people to come to us. Park benches, street corners, or campuses were where we did our teaching, preaching, and soul-winning. Thus, Jews for Jesus began. We left behind conventional methods and materials. But it wasn't just the creativity of our methods and materials that made us distinct, nor was it our enthusiasm and zeal. It was our principles.

Three important principles made us different. We had to make ourselves visible, vulnerable, and available—the way Jesus did. Visibility meant a public image. Vulnerability meant a willingness to be hurt by those who wanted to hurt us. Availability meant a willingness to be out in the open for others whether they wanted to hear us or hurt us. Perhaps the three can be summarized in one term: crossbearing!

It takes the spiritual stamina and willingness to bear pain and rejection of public cross bearing to accomplish successful evangelism.

That spiritual stamina only comes from abiding in Christ and His abiding in us. True cross bearing is not merely enduring the pain and unpleasantness. It is the way to enter into the resurrection joy that all believers can have, even while they are just enduring.

What is it that I wish someone had told me that I didn't know before? That there is no such thing as a comfortable cross (Matt. 10:34–38)!

Sincerely,
Moishe Rosen

Questions for Reflection

1. To what extent do your parents support your Christian faith and ministry? What difference has their support (or lack of it) made in your life?

2. The author found that he had to create a new evangelistic approach to reach Jews effectively. In what ways might God be calling you to likewise experiment with new methods in reaching the people group most on your heart?

3. To what extent are you willing to make yourself "visible, vulnerable, and available"? How might a failure to do so adversely impact the effectiveness of your ministry?

FORTY-FIVE

Learning the Value of Listening

Donald K. Smith is Distinguished Professor of Intercultural Communication and Missiology at Western Seminary in Portland, Oregon, and codirector of the Institute for International Christian Communication. He served as a missionary journalist and educator in Africa for thirty years, during which time he cofounded (with his wife Faye) Daystar University in Nairobi, Kenya. As a missions consultant he has advised over seventy different Christian groups in nearly fifty countries. Don also pastored Faith Baptist Church in Portland for nine years. Among his publications are *Make Haste Slowly* and *Creating Understanding*.

Dear Friend,

I wish somebody had told me the lesson that I want to share with you. In all honesty, they probably tried to, but I simply did not hear because I wasn't listening.

Among all the things I wish I had learned much earlier in life, the most important thing is the willingness and skill to listen—really listen. I don't mean nodding and smiling politely when someone was talking, while I formed my own words. Nor do I mean careful listening so I could rebut points and win arguments. I mean listening behind the words to understand desires and anxieties—listening deeply enough to visualize the dreams shaping that person's sentences.

Learning that I needed to listen was a blessed by-product of being a missionary. Hour after hour, day after day, I sat in church meetings not even sure whether they were having devotions or doing business because it all was taking place in a language then unknown to me. All I could tell for sure, while these new sounds and strange words deluged my ears, was that some carried deep conviction, others were enthusiastic, and some sought carefully for the way forward. And I listened. I listened trying to pick out single words, then tying those words to attitudes. Eventually a whole sentence clearly emerged from the cacophony!

Listening, I "heard" the gestures that emphasized the sounds of words. I saw the resentment or gratitude carried by posture or touch. Not understanding the grammar and vocabulary, I learned to listen for meaning. Then I discovered that this was also useful in English!

Of course I should have learned that earlier, much earlier. But I was so busy trying to be sure I was right that I did not bother to pay close attention to the other person. If I could be sure that I was right, then surely the correctness, the truth, of my position would be enough. If I could just get them to listen to me, they would agree with me and all would be well. Well, being right is important, but it is not enough.

If I have not listened to the other person, trying to understand that person's feelings and perspective, I will be unable to link what I know to what that person knows and feels. What good does it do then to be right, if the other person does not understand what I am trying to say?

It is not only a matter of learning by listening, but a matter of courtesy and respect. When I am focusing so strongly on what I think and know, I do not extend common courtesy. I show little respect for a person when I disregard his or her feelings, especially when I answer in a way that belittles his or her ideas.

And I learned late that leadership demands more, much more, than just having great ideas and persuasive speech. Why don't our training centers teach listening along with a mastery of Scripture and how to deliver a sermon? Listening must begin with learning to listen for the voice of God in daily living, and then proceeds to learning how to listen to those who are wandering, lost, broken. Should we not require training in listening before we train in exegesis and speech?

I wish I had been taught to listen, how to concentrate on the other person, how to ask probing questions so I could know that person deeply. But I am so thankful that God not only saw that serious deficiency, but put me where I had no choice but to listen.

Hopefully you can learn and practice this basic skill of communicating, without the perplexity and fatigue of listening in a totally strange language for months!

In His service, as a listener,
Don Smith

Questions for Reflection

1. Many interpersonal communication experts advise us to seek first to understand, and then to be understood. Do you agree? Why or why not?

2. Would other people consider you a good listener? Ask a half-dozen or so people for their evaluation of your listening skills, and prayerfully seek some practical ways in which your skills might be improved.

3. In your interactions with others, try to "listen" for the feelings and perspectives behind their words.

FORTY-SIX

Learning About Caring and Self-Sacrifice

Boone Sumantri is the codirector of Contextualized Urban Ministry Education/Northwest, an adjunct faculty member and director of Urban Ministry at Western Seminary, and founder/president of Servants, Incorporated, and Indonesia Missions Advance, Inc. (both headquartered in Portland, Oregon). He is also currently involved in leadership roles at the Asian American Bible College and Mission Portland. Boone is the author of *Your Life Story, The Job Hunt Manual,* and *The Isaiah House: A Manual for Establishing Transitional Homeless Shelters.*

Dear Friend,

My mother had a magnificent dream when she was carrying me in her womb. In her dream a huge, bright, full moon came down from heaven—and she had to swallow it! I can still picture her looking at me quizzically as she later recounted that dream. What was the future holding for her son? A powerful leader for our poor country of Indonesia, perhaps? One of our ancestors, the legendary Jaka Tingkir, King of Pajang, was such a powerful leader. The story is told that on one occasion King Jaka, while traveling with his retinue, needed to cross a river; but there was not a single boat or canoe around. No matter! King Jaka saw alligators basking in the sun on the bank of the river. He simply ordered them into the water, to line up side-by-side from one bank to the other, so that he could cross on their backs. Such was the power that King Jaka Tingkir commanded. When many think of leaders, they often think of similar power that demands respect and obedience.

But my mother taught me a different side of leadership. She was a small woman, but ever busy from dusk to dawn. She devoted her entire

life to serving her husband and eight children. I often saw her praying and meditating late at night, surely including prayers for the security and protection of her family. For these were trying times, the
period of Japanese occupation in the 1940s. She instructed the servant to buy food supplies with care so that we would have enough to
eat until my father's next paycheck. During the last week of the month,
however, the food would still be pretty meager: lots of boiled rice and
cheap vegetables, and maybe a small slice of dried fish. Mother scraped
clean the rice colander and pots, so that no food was wasted. She
would then carefully divide the food equally on our plates (including
the servant's, who ate with us). I noticed that her plate always had a
smaller portion than the rest. Even in our scarcity, Mother taught us
how to share. I remember one day when a beggar knocked on our
front door; without a moment's hesitation, she took one spoonful of
food from each of our plates (including hers, of course!) and gave
that food to the beggar.

On another occasion, my sister needed new eyeglasses but there
was just no money to buy them. Mother quietly took off her glasses
and said, "We will go to the eye doctor tomorrow and trade these
glasses in for a good pair for you."

This season of poverty stayed with us during the entire period of
Japanese occupation. But I learned some rich lessons from my mother
about genuine caring and self-sacrifice, two essential traits of servant-
leadership. I later saw these same traits exemplified as well in Bob
McLaughlin, my pastor at Calvary Baptist Church in State College,
Pennsylvania. Pastor Bob's life truly reflected the love of Christ lived
out in actions of personal caring and concern for all he encountered.

I learned another dimension of leadership from my uncle Subroto,
who studied under the famous Indian poet-philosopher Rabindranath
Tagore. Uncle was a small, wiry man full of energy and determination. His was a life of tough self-discipline and hard work. My brothers, sisters, and cousins were frightened by him, but I was intrigued
by his way of life. So I asked and obtained permission from my parents to live with him and his family.

Uncle Subroto was assistant principal of the vocational technical
school I was attending. I noticed how the students spoke of him with
great respect. The depth of that respect was graphically illustrated one
day just after the Indonesian war of independence concluded. War
veterans had returned home to complete their schooling. Many had
trouble readjusting to the routine of learning, and some resorted to
violent outbursts of frustration and anger. Some of these students vio-
lated school regulations by bringing their handguns to class. One day,
during a particularly heated outburst, several hundred students staged

a sit-down protest in a large assembly room. When my uncle heard about this, he immediately went into that room and confronted the angry, armed students. With eyes aflame he ordered them to return to their classes, while promising to help resolve the issues which prompted their protest. Quietly each student filed out of the room and obediently returned to class. I will never forget that illustration of the personal courage, borne out of firm moral convictions, that leaders must be willing to demonstrate.

I framed this letter in my mind while sitting on a hard bench in the chapel of the Portland Rescue Mission with two of our seminary students. Around us are the homeless poor in every human form imaginable: young, old, male, female, white, black, mentally ill, physically frail. These are the people who servants like Mother Teresa lived and died for. These are the "least of the brothers and sisters" who Jesus teaches us to love. These are the people who have taught me and shaped my life during these past thirty years as I have slowly gained an understanding of the possible significance of my mother's dream. The moon is a dead object, and its beauty depends on reflecting the powerful light rays of the sun. Similarly my life is meaningless, except for reflecting back the love of Christ in service to all people. I pray that your life will also faithfully reflect our Lord's love for "the least of these."

Your fellow servant,
Boone Sumantri

Questions for Reflection

1. How do you respond to unexpected opportunities to help the needy? Do you wait for such opportunities to present themselves, or do you actively seek out opportunities to demonstrate charity and benevolence?

2. How would you have responded to the volatile situation faced by the author's uncle? What moral convictions would have produced that response?

3. How faithfully are you reflecting the moral perfections of Jesus to those around you?

FORTY-SEVEN

Learning About the Privileges and Dynamics of Leadership

Lee W. Toms served for forty years as pastor of Arcade Baptist Church in Sacramento, California. He has also been a board member for Western Seminary and president of the Conservative Baptist Association of America. Lee currently devotes his time to a preaching, teaching, and writing ministry.

Dear Friend,

You are one of a select company upon whose frail shoulders the mantle of Christ's ministry has been cast. This stewardship from God is both incredibly awesome and humbly appreciated. When its full impact strikes us, we are sorely tempted to seek a less demanding pursuit; but confidence returns when we realize that "if any man ministers let him minister in the ability that God gives." A lesson so slowly learned is that the authority is in the Word and the ability is in the Spirit. It will dawn upon us in the course of ministry that this is an unalterable truth. If our efforts are little short of a "beating of the air," a futile shadow boxing, it will be because this fundamental reality has been ignored. No new technology or state of the art methodology will ever replace a person called of God, under the authority of the sovereign Word, and in the ability of the resident Spirit.

You must also live under a constant and growing sense of privilege. We are not His servants by "right" but by a bestowment of grace. Paul's "by the grace of God I am what I am" extends to the confession "I am His servant." Whether you have some human being to whom you are responsible is a matter of personal choice, but there is a responsibility beyond time and place to which we are ever mindful. I find Paul's charge to Timothy in 2 Timothy 4:1–2 to be compelling: "I solemnly charge you in the presence of God and of Christ Jesus, who is to judge the living and the dead, and by His appearing and

His kingdom—preach the word" (NASB). We conduct our ministries in the sight of God and of Christ Jesus and in the light of His appearing, the establishment of His kingdom, and the judgment of an unbelieving world. While being mindful of the needs of those seated before me, would to God that I had ever been more mindful of the "in sight of" and "in light of." Everything must be seen in the brilliant light of the eternal. When the battle is hot, the pressure unrelenting, this upward vision will cast a heavenly light upon every dark and distressing place.

The task will be considerably easier when you rightly conclude that you cannot do everything and that you cannot please everybody. Either accept that as true, or kill yourself attempting the impossible. Much ministerial "burnout" is, in Oswald Chambers' words, nothing more than "disenchanted egotism." Pride is at the root of most, if not all, of the ministerial problems that we make for ourselves. For me, it has not been easily but painfully learned. Develop a philosophy of ministry that is driven by biblical considerations, not the shifting winds in the world's changeful sky. Stay true to the heavenly vision sovereignly given no matter what pressures are brought to bear.

I feel indebted to "flesh and blood" people, living and dead, whose influence whether personal or in writing have enriched my life. They are too numerous to mention, but apart from the many long-ago predecessors, others like A. W. Tozer, Martyn Lloyd-Jones, J. Gresham Machen, P. T. Forsyth, Carl F. H. Henry, and J. I. Packer have contributed greatly.

The autumn of life has come, but the bulk of the persuasion of truth learned in the spring and summer of life with few exceptions has been confirmed. The convictions of the "last lap" are not the products of aging, but hopefully the result of maturing truths long held. Gratefully, there have been corrections, but the confirmations of the rightness of the course have prevailed. Amidst the shifting scenery in the human drama (including changes of style and form), some basic things remain uncompromised and nonnegotiable.

The training of my generation seems in retrospect to have been sound—to lead in love and to feed on truth, to preach the everlasting gospel in its full dimension, and to pastor with shepherdly gentleness the sheep of God's pasture. Paul said he was made a minister both of the gospel and of the church. Faithfulness to both ministries seems to me the essence of a pastor/teacher's calling.

God is a faithful teacher even with slow learners like me. Though I was far too often sluggish and slow of heart to believe, He did not chide me but gave needed wisdom through both sunshine and shadow. Like the poet said, "Some of the most rapturous minstrels among the

sons of light said of their sweetest music, 'I learned it in the night.'"
Through it all the reminder came, "Whom the Lord loves He chas-
tens." The plow ran deep, but in it all He purposed a crop.

True success will never be measured here or by us. One day the
hand that conferred the privilege will receive it back when my busy
hands are still. Then, and only then, can the words we tremblingly
hope for be heard: "Well done, good and faithful servant." We must
wait; but may our working and watching be worthy of those words.
The ashes of wood, hay, and stubble are small compensation for the
work of a lifetime. We must do God's work in God's way. We will
never regret doing so.

Sincerely yours in Him,
Lee Toms

Questions for Reflection

1. Are you keenly aware of what a God-given privilege it is to serve
   as a ministry leader? How might a fresh sense of the "in sight of"
   and "in light of" truths of 2 Timothy 4:1 positively impact your
   ministry?

2. What do you believe Chambers means by the "disenchanted
   egotism" that the author believes is the source of much ministerial
   burnout? To what extent does egotism affect your life and attitudes?

3. What are some of the most important lessons about life you have
   learned in the "shadow" (i.e., during times of disappointment or
   challenge)? Why do affliction and suffering often create teachable
   moments that do not exist when life is going more smoothly?

FORTY-EIGHT

Learning to Value Learning

Mary Wilder is Associate Professor of Intercultural Studies at Western Seminary in Portland, Oregon. She served as a medical missionary in Pakistan from 1968–1984. She was a member and secretary of the Indus Christian Fellowship's Executive Committee from 1972–1982. She has written two articles for *Decision* magazine.

Dear Friend,

This letter is a list of things I am in the process of learning. I think it would be helpful for you to learn them too.

The following thoughts are not arranged in order of importance. Rather, they are the random observations that have come to me over the years.

There is an overarching principle that spares us all sorts of self-seeking and pride: "It is wonderful what can be accomplished if it does not matter who gets the credit."

First, *remember that people are more important than programs*. Pour yourself into the lives of others. Be willing to sacrifice to make them successful. I think of two neurosurgeons who poured themselves into my life, to make me a surgeon. I watched and assisted them until they were sure I knew exactly how a particular surgical task was done. Then they watched and assisted me as I did my best to do it as I had seen them do it. They were right there lest I would make a mistake and harm a patient, but they let me struggle with the technique until I had mastered it. They were there for me, but I had to do it.

Their kind patience marked my life. I will always remember Drs. Davis and Dennis and their determined, demanding mentoring of me. I owe them a great debt, which I have tried to repay as now I relate to students in medicine and ministry.

It is always easier to do it yourself than to watch someone else struggle to do it. But it is necessary that you stand by to encourage, to help, as they perfect their skills. They are building their confidence and ability. Your success is measured by their success.

Second, *value learning.* Embrace every opportunity to learn, even if you don't want to or it is not convenient. As educational opportunities become available, take them! I have seen students refuse to attend weekend seminars that were on useful topics, taught by internationally known instructors, just because they did not want to give up a free Saturday to attend. Besides, the course was not required for their major. That was their loss!

The Lord prepares us for future opportunities that we don't know to prepare for. Dr. Paul Brand, the internationally known expert on leprosy, tells of learning the building trade, going to medical school, doing research, attending Bible school, being drafted into the Army, being forced into a medical specialty he didn't really seek, and going to India to work in a mission hospital. All of this was to prepare him for an unexpected career of research and innovations in the treatment and rehabilitation of leprosy patients. God did not waste any of his preparation, even though Paul did not know that He was preparing him for such a career.

The Lord blessed me with the opportunity of working with those two neurosurgeons for five years. I never did go into neurosurgery as a career, but the diagnostic and surgical techniques learned there were utilized every day in different situations in Pakistan. Neurosurgery is not a usual track for missionary medical preparation, but the Lord knew I would need those skills and the confidence they gave me.

Third, *remember that God gives the resources we need for the doing of His will.* I was blessed to be born into a Christian family where I was taught God's Word on a daily basis. My father was my first (and best!) Bible teacher. My mother was my role model for being a godly woman in ministry. They were my preparation for life.

Later, in college and medical school, I came under the ministry of Pastor Russell Shive. He continued my education in God's Word. He was always available to encourage, to give wise counsel, or to pray. It was his input into my life that enabled me to survive my very difficult time in medical school. He commissioned me to my missionary service. I tell him that it is his fault that I made it! He was God's provision for my spiritual needs.

God provided the money for college and medical school. I was able to graduate debt-free, which was quite a miracle even in those days! God provided health, mentors, opportunities, financial support, and spiritual resources. Philippians 4:9 became real in my experience, as I saw Him provide all I needed.

Fourth, *learn from the lives of those who have gone before us.* Seek out the old people whose lives God has blessed and listen to their story. Read biographies of the giants of the faith. See what can be applied to your life and ministry. See the pitfalls and mistakes. See how God used ordinary people to accomplish extraordinary things for His glory. Learn from the past.

When I first went to Pakistan, life was daily both discouraging and difficult. I experienced the rigors of language study and culture learning, and often felt both frustration and despair. I doubted I would ever be equal to the task.

A wise senior missionary gave me a couple of very significant books: *Our India Mission (1855–1885)* and *Dr. Ira* (Scudder). These books were simple chronicles of the early days of ministry in India (Pakistan). There were stories of great disappointments, great opportunities, stress, victories, defeats, prayer, human frailty, and lives changed by meeting Jesus. Through it all, the grace of God was depicted, a dogged perseverance that refused to quit the struggle, the glory of redemption, and the eventual growth of His church.

My subsequent service in a tiny mission hospital in Pakistan was greatly influenced by those two books (and others I read later). I came to see that perseverance and faithfulness are what God blesses. There are no sudden successes to carry us along. There are many crises and disappointments along the way. But it is the grace of God and the awareness of His presence that sustains us from day to day.

I guess that is why my most favorite course to teach at Western Seminary is "The History of Mission." It is a continuing joy and encouragement to look at the whole two thousand years of history since the birth of Christ and see how He is using people like us to build His church!

That assurance gives eternal significance to the ordinary events and opportunities of each day. You never know when that young person whom you now teach and work with so patiently will grow up to be the William Carey, Hudson Taylor, Jonathan Edwards, or Jim Elliot of his generation.

Fifth, *remember to follow Jesus*. We do all of this life and ministry activity because we belong to Jesus and in response to His command to be His witnesses. This is the unifying principle of life: Jesus is alive, carrying out His work, building His church. He tells us to cooperate with Him. We do all that we can for Him, for His glory, and for the expansion of His kingdom in joyful response to Him. He is the vine, we are the branches. We are complete in Him.

In Luke 24 Jesus told His disciples who He is, drawing from the Old Testament. He opened their understanding. Then He went on to say that He died and had risen from the dead according to the Scriptures, and that repentance and forgiveness of sins should be proclaimed in His name to all the nations (Luke 24:46–49). Furthermore, this great work of witnessing would be done by them, those very human disciples who knew Him. The strategy was that they should begin there in Jerusalem, just where they were, telling about Jesus.

This great ministry would be carried out in conscious dependence upon the power of the Holy Spirit. It is the Holy Spirit who takes the things of Christ and makes them real to the listeners. It is His ministry that assures the success of our witness. It is Christ's promise, "I will build my church," that gives us the confidence, hope, and perseverance we need for each difficult, disappointing situation.

I deplore the current tendency to evaluate our ministry opportunities and thus determine God's call to us by how much the salary is, how good the benefit package is, how congenial the team is that we will be working with, how good the local schools are, how available medical care is, and how good this will look on my résumé. Jesus calls us to deny ourselves, to take up our cross and follow Him . . . and He died!

Finally, *never give up being faithful*. It is always too soon to quit. Following Jesus is our lifelong task and joy. With Luther Wishard (the first youth worker with the YMCA) we can say that we will go anywhere, at any time, and do anything for Jesus.

I long that you would enjoy the carefree abandon and passion to follow Jesus that marked the lives of so many of those who have gone before us. To hear Him say, "Well done, good and faithful servant" will be worth it all!

Remember the reason—Jesus!
Mary Wilder

Questions for Reflection

1. What opportunities for further learning are available to you right now that you may want to redeem? Have you found that God has used your past learning in unexpected ways to accomplish His purposes?

2. Which Christian biographies or autobiographies have had the greatest impact on your life? If you find this question difficult to answer because you've read very few, you may want to ask someone you respect to recommend a volume or two.

3. What are biblically valid criteria to employ in determining which ministry position is right for you?

FORTY-NINE

Learning a Formula for Victory

Bill Yaeger is Director of Church Relationships and Ministries for Western Seminary in Northern California and Minister at Large for First Baptist Church of Modesto, California (where he served as senior pastor for 24 years and founded the Institute for Church Imperatives). Prior to coming to Modesto, Bill served for eleven years as the founding pastor of a church in Los Angeles, California. He is the author of *Who's Holding the Umbrella?*

Dear Friend,

Let me pass on to you some of the principles and methods that have helped me greatly in the ministry. While I do not have the space to write extensively on the subject, I want to tell you about the most important things that have helped me over the years.

I begin with the importance of prayer. When you step into the arena of faith as a pastor, missionary, or in any role as a spiritual leader, you draw counterfire from the enemy. Be sure to make prayer a major part of your life. Get with people who practice prayer and who know how to pray. We learn to pray while being alone with God in prayer, but we also "get into" prayer by being with others who pray. Today, in many places pastors are praying together in prayer summits and in regular weekly pastor's meetings. Make prayer a first priority. When you link up with your heavenly Father in prayer, you draw down the joy and the power of heaven. You need joy in the midst of tension and sorrow. You need God's power in order to be an overcomer, a "winner" in the spiritual war you must fight.

In Modesto, California, pastors from thirty-four churches meet for prayer every Wednesday morning. They don't indulge in sermonizing or other "preacher talk"; they immediately begin to pray. Those prayers are bringing spiritual power to the churches and enabling pastors to "end well." Through prayer, pastors are helped to withstand the temptations and entrapments of the enemy. They are helping themselves through prayer to endure to the end. If you want to end well, learn to pray.

You will also need to follow Paul in not being ashamed of the gospel of Christ (Rom. 1:16). By faith I have believed in the testimony of Scripture. I have taken the Word of God to be the testimony of the Holy Spirit. I think that the Book of Acts could have well been entitled, "The Acts of the Holy Spirit." In 2 Timothy 3:16–17 Paul says, "All Scripture is God-breathed and is useful for teaching, rebuking, correcting and training in righteousness, so that the man of God may be thoroughly equipped for every good work" (NIV).

So be careful to maintain a high view of Scripture. In these days of change (which is sometimes change for the sake of change), don't be caught up in a current fad that says the preaching of the Bible is not important anymore. Perhaps you wouldn't buy that, but let me encourage you not to buy into the idea that the "X Generation" (or any other younger generation) will not respond to the preaching and teaching of the Word of God. Faith still comes by hearing, and hearing still comes from the Word of God (Rom. 10:17).

God's servant must have his or her life and ministry anchored in God's Word. I determined at the beginning of the ministry that God laid out for me that I had to be a "Bible man." At age twenty-six I was a professing atheist and completely lost. Through the death of my twelve-day-old son, Timothy, I came to know the Lord. From that beginning, I knew that I had nothing to say from my own knowledge and experience that would be of help to anyone. When called to ministry one year after conversion, I threw myself on the mercy of God and determined to speak forth His Word.

Nothing will take the place of the gospel in the ministry of the church. Beware of fads and crazy ideas that have a sound of wisdom, but which are just another concoction of man to substitute his ignorance for God's wisdom. Christ speaks through His Word. Only the Holy Spirit can open the heart and mind of an unbeliever. We may shift our approach as the culture changes, but we must not shift away from proclaiming the gospel of Christ!

If I were to share a "formula for victory," it would be this. Walk in the light and live a moral life. Faithfully preach and teach the Word of God. Keep your wife and family close to you and the Lord. Keep the church staff together and in harmony, and keep the official board together in unity. Pray for wisdom and for divine power and protection for yourself, your family, and the church. If you can do these things you will be invincible in the spiritual battle before you. If you want to be an overcomer, a "Nike," this is a good formula to follow.

Beware of pride and immorality! Proverbs 11:2 says, "When pride comes, then comes disgrace, but with humility comes wisdom" (NIV). According to this proverb, pride and immorality go together. While there are other sins and temptations in the ministry, sexual immorality brings more of God's servants down to the pit of disgrace and shame than all of the other sins combined.

Be warned! A sure way to disarm your spiritual immune system and open the door of your life to the invader is to get caught up in pride! When we are overtaken by pride, we first become full of ourselves and then self-exalting. God's servant must not ignore the fact that "whoever exalts himself will be humbled and whoever humbles himself will be exalted" (Matt. 23:12 NIV).

Regarding pride, always remember that our Lord Jesus Christ is the Great Shepherd of His sheep. He is the Pastor of the church. We who lead on earth are under-shepherds. So don't take yourself too seriously, but take your work seriously! You are doing holy work as a preacher and teacher, the most important work of all mankind, but you are not doing it on your own. It is all by grace! Study hard to know the facts of grace and learn well the working of grace in your life. When you get into trouble and disconnect from your Father, go back to your roots and live by grace again. It is by grace that you are equipped for ministry and it is by grace that you are enabled to serve.

Remember the holiness of God. There is a trap connected with spiritual immorality that you should be aware of. The servant who is living in sin is often misdirected and shielded from the truth by the fact that when he preaches the Bible, God honors His Word. This person, thinking that all is well, continues on in his evil way, not realizing that while God honors His Word, He will never honor an unrepentant sinner. If such a preacher continues, his sin will find him out. In these days when so many solid Bible expositors have fallen in disgrace, apparently thinking that God was not watching as they continued in sin, it will profit you to walk carefully and keep before you the holiness of God.

Don't ever underestimate the importance of carefully selecting leaders. Many leaders get into trouble at this very important function of their leadership, selecting leaders to work with them. Here is a list of criteria which has served me well. I give you the four most important questions to examine:

1. *Spiritual stance and proven godliness.* In observing and interviewing potential leaders, begin first with an attempt to find out where

the person is in his or her spiritual life. This would include faith in Jesus Christ, view of Scripture, prayer life, care of spouse and family, stewardship, and history of moral living.

2. *Emotional maturity and stability.* The last thing you need in leadership is someone who is emotionally immature. Such a person will almost certainly create more problems than solutions. The person's history will help you here. Will you have to be overly careful not to offend this person? Is he vain and does he require constant praise? How does he handle criticism, authority, responsibility, and confidentiality? Here is an important rule to follow: Never give an emotionally immature person a leadership role to help them. In selecting leaders, you need to find people who can help you. Then go on to help the immature person become mature in the Lord before he is asked to lead others.

3. *Spiritual gifts and talents.* Notice that I did not begin with the candidate's spiritual gifts and talents. Oh, we have to be aware of what the person can do and where he or she is gifted, but that should not determine whether or not that person should be asked to lead in that area. Here is a principle to follow: Everyone is gifted spiritually and many have talents, but the first qualifications for leadership are to be found in the spiritual area and the maturity that should come from it.

4. *Philosophy of ministry.* Here is the question that is not often asked or answered: What is the candidate's philosophy of ministry? You need a close match here if you and the candidate are to walk together and work together. His or her philosophy of ministry should be compatible with yours.

Finally, I strongly encourage you to have a plan and to follow that plan. Here are the key components of a good plan: (1) Have a shared vision; (2) Develop a strategy; (3) Decide how to implement the strategy with tactics or daily operations; (4) Recruit and train workers, being careful to choose only those who are motivated and excited about the ministry or project; (5) Begin the work; and (6) Complete the work and celebrate the victory with praise to God.

May He bless your ministry for Him!

Sincerely yours,
Bill Yaeger

Questions for Reflection

1. Evaluate your current prayer life. Do you have an appropriate blend of private prayer and prayer with others? Do you sense God responding to your petitions and drawing near to you when you pray?

2. How confident are you in the power of God's Word (as used by the Holy Spirit) to change lives? Do you ever find yourself being ashamed of the gospel?

3. What criteria do you use in choosing leaders? How might the criteria suggested by the author be useful in helping you to make wiser selections in the future?

FIFTY

Learning to Lead Wisely in Both Secular and Christian Settings

Paul F. Yaggy has served with OC International since 1981 in various leadership roles including Interim President, Director of Research and Strategy, and Senior Advisor to the President. Prior to that, he was Associate Pastor at Calvary Baptist Church in Los Gatos, California, for seven years. Before entering vocational ministry, Paul served for thirty years in key leadership positions with both NASA and the United States military.

Dear Friend,

I have served in leadership roles over forty years, divided nearly equally between so-called *secular* and *Christian* leadership. During the secular period, I participated in leading lay-ministry as well as my primary profession. Except for specific goals (products) to be achieved, I have discovered little difference in the principles of leading and the required personal character traits for a leader who is a Christian (secular work) and a Christian leader (full-time ministry). In my opinion, Christian leadership should never be considered elitist or unique from leadership by Christians in other professions. I have found this to be a vital consideration when ministering to leaders in the secular fields. I consider my secular role to have been as much a calling of God as I do my call to Christian ministry.

There are skills and principles of leadership that I have learned only through experience. However, there are three skills of a basic nature about which I wish someone had told me earlier in my leadership roles; I instead had to learn them the hard way. Perhaps recording them may make it easier for you and others who are beginning or preparing to lead.

Fundamental to my success in leadership has been to understand fully that it is a trust. The first thought that comes to mind is the trust placed in the leader by those who appoint him or her to leadership. In the beginning, this was my greatest concern. However, I have come to realize a much greater concern is the resources entrusted to the leader. The first commitment of a leader should be to the proper stewardship of those resources. There are various types of resources—money, facilities, equipment—all of which must be expended and used with discretion and effectiveness. But the primary resource entrusted to the leader is the people he leads. They are a sacred trust, for they are created in God's own image. They are most important, for without them nothing can be achieved. But unlike other resources, they are to be led and not used. Even further, they are to be served—a phenomenon that can be appreciated only by a Christian.

By nature, I am a driver, intent on achieving goals with excellence above all else. My tendency is to dominate and demand from—rather than encourage and develop—this vital resource. I did not realize the cost of failing to serve my followers, of suppressing initiative, of creating dissent and resentment, or of demeaning others—all leading to the loss of the very effectiveness that I sought to achieve.

If someone had only told me—and also helped me to understand fully—the meaning of this trust, both those whom I led and I would have profited greatly. We would have achieved much more, and our personal lives would have been enriched. As I came to realize and treasure the value of my followers, paid or volunteer, I wrote a new objective for myself: my primary task is to develop to the maximum the potential represented in those entrusted to my leadership. We became a team committed to each other and to the goals that we held together. As I put into practice my commitment to serve them, we became much more effective in reaching our objectives. It also multiplied far beyond our immediate goals. Some went on to significant leadership roles exceeding my own. I found personal joy in their achievements. I discovered that Paul's words to the Romans, "in honor preferring one another," have very practical rewards and reflect a personal trait worthy to be cultivated by every Christian leader. I just wish someone had taught me that earlier.

Successful leadership involves making right choices. Someone has said learning to make right choices comes from making wrong ones; but learning that way is often very costly. Others say it is a matter of making wise choices; but how does one know what is wise? My training and experience in aerospace research taught me to gather the facts and analyze them to understand how and why things work. From such understanding, choices can be made which lead to successful designs of aerospace systems. But if the understanding is incomplete or flawed, disaster may follow. I reluctantly admit that I had a few of those. Thankfully they were minor, but they did sufficiently shake my confidence in human wisdom.

As I moved into the role of leadership, I became more and more aware of the need for genuine wisdom and of my inadequacies in discerning it. I came to a crisis point when the opportunity opened for a major leadership position. The opportunities were great, but the pitfalls were obvious. It was here that I learned the reality and consequences of seeking to make a right choice. I knew all the facts, but I also knew that understanding of how they would interact in the future was beyond me. It could be a great success or a colossal disaster. I remembered Solomon's choice and determined to seek the wisdom of God and make it the only factor in my decision. God did confirm that accepting the position was indeed wise, and with that confirmation I led the organization to significant achievements and awards for excellence.

As I moved on into full-time Christian leadership, I became more and more aware of the necessity for seeking and following the wisdom of God. My time in the pastorate soon confronted me with a significant difference from my work in aerospace science; unlike the somewhat predictable behavior of inanimate objects, people behaved in random fashion. Making choices became less certain. When I moved into missions, it all became global and even more confusing. But my commitment to wait on God for wisdom has never failed me. In His time is my pacing criterion.

As I reflect on what I have said, you may think me naive about this. I realize that everyone will respond that their first and foremost desire is to seek and follow the wisdom of God. But I have learned something else. Seeking the wisdom of God is no small task. As leaders, we desire to do great things for God. We become enthused about the opportunities presented to us. Everything seems so right, so it must be the will of God. Success seems assured as good things begin to happen. But unless we have real confirmation of His wisdom, we might even be doing the work of the devil (so James 3:15 would seem to say). To really know the wisdom of God requires being right with God and diligently seeking it. To have the wisdom of God means knowing when to say yes and when to say no; sometimes yes to the hard challenge and sometimes no to the one that seems most rewarding. It means being totally submissive to God and singularly responsive to what He says, yielding all my aspirations to His desire. I wish someone had convinced me of that much earlier in my leadership role. I am sure I could have been more effective for building the kingdom.

A common cliché is "It's lonely at the top." This may be true when the time comes for making significant decisions and bearing the consequences. But a leader who is alone, by design or default, has missed a fundamental criterion for success. In my early experience as a leader, I placed great value in my authority as a means for achieving desired goals. My concept of preserving and effectively using that authority was to establish an aura of prestige, isolating myself from those I led. I did not want to reveal my weaknesses. Reflecting on this, I came to realize that this decision was protective and motivated by insecurity. Further, it was relying on position rather than earning the respect vital to the exercise of authority. I have been amazed over time by the number of leaders I see, both in secular and in Christian leadership, who practice this.

I am not certain what convinced me that this was an ineffective means of leading. I suspect it was a combination of many things. I can think of some whom I respected and who modeled a different leadership style. But I attribute it mostly to my studies of Christ and His model. Though He was God incarnate, He became one with those whom He led, shared an intimate relationship with them, and (I say it with respect) made Himself vulnerable to them. It was in this role that He led them to become great in their accomplishments of the work for which He was preparing them. I became, and continue to be, deeply impressed by the Beatitudes that define both my own dependent state and the means of empowerment for leading (mercy, peacemaking, and a pure heart).

It was in my role of secular leadership that I learned this lesson. The results of my decision to develop a dependence upon my followers were so great that I deeply regretted the losses of failing to understand and begin it earlier. A most significant factor was that although my followers were not Christians, this decision motivated by my Christian convictions and models was fully effective. This and other experiences confirm my early statement that for a Christian in leadership, secular or Christian, the principles of effective leadership and the personal traits required are the same. It was only my security in Christ that gave me the courage to make myself vulnerable and dependent, even on those who were not Christian. Dependence on Him allows dependence on others.

It should not escape our attention that there is much more involved here that relates to Christian conviction. Things such as "In the mouths of many counselors is wisdom." Dependence on followers permits things such as this, all of which lead to greater success. I wish someone could have told me earlier, and if they did, I wish I had understood and listened!

Sincerely,
Paul Yaggy

Questions for Reflection

1. Do you agree that the same basic leadership principles can (and should) be used in both Christian and secular settings? Why or why not?

2. How faithfully are you fulfilling the various entrustments that accompany your leadership role?

3. What process do you follow for seeking the wisdom of God for your ministry and life? Have you seen that process bear the same kind of fruit as described by the author?

ALSO FROM KREGEL PUBLICATIONS

The Vanishing Ministry

by Woodrow Kroll

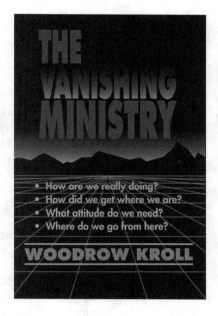

What can we look forward to in the twenty-first century? As general director of the *Back to the Bible* broadcast and a former Bible college president, Dr. Kroll has a front-row seat and is in a unique position to evaluate the panorama of Christian ministry today.

Kroll examines the decline in commitment to fulltime ministry and addresses primary attitudes which must be present in the thinking of men and women if they are to be sensitive to the call of God on their lives. He also looks at the lives of several Bible characters who influenced believers to be committed to ministry.

Kroll writes out of a deep concern for full-time Christian ministry. *The Vanishing Ministry* challenges the reader to examine his or her own personal commitment to service and then to influence others to pursue Christian ministry.

> "Kroll shows us how far we have gone, why we have gone that far, and the way back to where we ought to be in serving God."
>
> —*Baptist Examiner*

0-8254-3057-7 • 166 pages

ALSO FROM KREGEL PUBLICATIONS

How to Survive in the Ministry
by Leslie B. Flynn

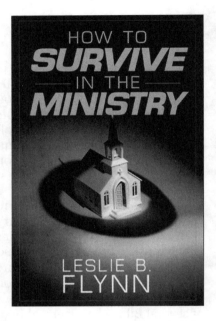

How does a pastor survive the stresses of pastoring a church today when the pastorate is probably tougher than it has ever been? Dr. Les Flynn recounts his methods of ministry and the personal experiences that have contributed to staying at the same church for forty years.

The themes discussed include making sure of one's call, delegation, celebration of lay achievements, handling difficult situations, and relaxation. Bernice Flynn, pastor's wife and mother of seven girls as well as an excellent writer, has an engaging chapter on family life.

> "Flynn's insights are so valuable that having read it, I almost wish I were at the beginning rather than near the end of my ministry years. What a treasure trove for those starting their ministry today. . . . The chapter on long-range sermon planning is especially helpful. That chapter alone is worth the price of the book. Extremely valuable for pastors and seminarians and fun to read."
> —*Bibliotheca Sacra*

0-8254-2637-5 • 160 pages

ALSO FROM KREGEL PUBLICATIONS

Ministry Nuts and Bolts
What They Don't Teach Pastors in Seminary
by Aubrey Malphurs

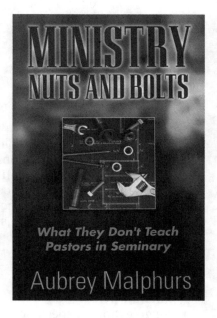

Many seminary graduates envision ministry as 95 percent preaching and 5 percent for everything else: weddings, funerals, visitation, and board meetings. The pastor's preaching and teaching ministry is often viewed as the primary vehicle for discipleship and outreach. Most pastors, however, do not and cannot devote extensive time to preparation for preaching or teaching and find their enthusiasm for ministry is sapped by a sense of confusion and frustration.

Ministry Nuts and Bolts provides the pastor or parachurch leader with a step-by-step guide for developing the basics needed to lead a ministry into the twenty-first century by examining the four themes that drive effective ministry—values, mission, vision, and strategy. As the author observes, "The evangelical churches that God is blessing in North America have carefully thought through [these strategies]. Thus, it behooves the rest of the churches to learn from their examples and pursue the same."

0-8254-3190-5 • 192 pages

ALSO FROM KREGEL PUBLICATIONS

Pastor to Pastor
Tackling the Problems of Ministry
revised and expanded
by Erwin Lutzer

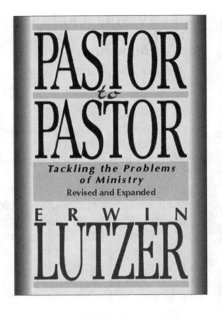

The role of the pastor as both leader and teacher is often complicated by many difficult situations and problematic issues. Well-known pastor and conference speaker Erwin Lutzer offers practical advice on how to handle issues such as:

- church splits
- burnout
- worship styles
- congregational expectations
- pastoral priorities
- politics
- church boards
- counseling

This revised edition provides encouragement and solutions to help pastors better serve God and their churches. In working through difficult situations of ministry, pastors and congregations can both grow spiritually.

> "Don't speed read this book. Pause, ponder, pray—and grow!"
>
> —Warren W. Wiersbe

0-8254-3164-6 • 128 pages